Other books authored or co-authored by Al Siebert:

The Survivor Personality
The Adult Student's Guide to Survival and Success: Time for College
Student Success: How to Succeed in College and Still Have Time for Your Friends
Student Success Strategies

Peaking Out

*How My Mind Broke Free From the
Delusions in Psychiatry*

by Al Siebert, Ph.D.

as told to Sam Kimball, Ph.D.

Practical Psychology Press • Portland, Oregon

Practical Psychology Press
P.O. Box 535
Portland, OR 97207

Cover design: Robert Steven Pawlak
Book design and prepress: Kristin Pintarich

Printed using soy based ink by Thomson-Shore, Inc.
Printed in the United States of America.

10 9 8 7 6 5 4 3 2 1

Publisher's Cataloging in Publication
(prepared by Quality Books, Inc.)

Siebert, Lawrence A., 1934-
    Peaking out: how my mind broke free from the delusions
in psychiatry / by Al Siebert as told to Sam Kimball.
    p. 308   23 cm.
    Includes index.
    Preassigned LCCN: 95-068297
    ISBN: 0-944227-10-4

1. Siebert, Al.   2. Clinical psychology—Biography.   I. Title.

BF109.S54 1995   150.92
                                  QBI95-20115

Preface

Peaking Out is an account of a series of events that took place between March 10th and September 30th, 1965. Immediately following the events I used my skills as a professionally trained clinician to record all conversations and interactions. I also made certain to preserve all documentation related to the events.

For reasons that will become evident, I have changed the names of my ex-wife and a few others. While I have recounted my experience as accurately as possible, the accounts and recollections of other people involved in this matter can be expected to be different.

Being over 60 and semi-retired, I am speaking out on behalf of psychiatric survivors to illustrate that a mental patient's perception of his or her so-called mental illness is much different from what psychiatrists typically report. For too many decades psychiatrists have been allowed to present their view of a patient and the patient's side as well. This situation is equivalent to allowing a plaintiff's attorney to present the defendant's case while barring the defendant from the court-room.

I hope that by publishing my story other psychiatric survivors will feel encouraged to tell their stories. Information about the Kenneth Donaldson Archives can be found at the end of the book.

Al Siebert, Ph.D.
March, 1995

Contents

Chapter One

An Unobstructed View

"What a spectacular view, Al! The Columbia River right outside your living room windows."

"It is impressive, Sam. I'm glad you could finally visit to enjoy it with me."

"It has such a magnificent, powerful feel."

"I like its energy, especially on a beautiful spring day like this. Why don't we sit out on the deck and you can tell me what's on your mind?"

"Great."

"I'll bring some juice out…"

"All right, Sam, what's up?"

"In the time that we've known each other, Al. I've had many opportunities to observe how you interact with the world. What I've seen intrigues me. You are successful in an unusual way. It's subtle, but you don't do things the way other people do. It is more than having good professional skills. Something else is going on. Somehow you live in a way that seems to *invite* success. It seems almost magical. I'd like to understand how you do it."

"What do you mean?"

"You have a knack for skillfully handling what I consider to be very difficult and challenging circumstances. And you do so in a relaxed and happy and buoyant manner, as if you *know* things will turn out well. Take the way the problem with building your new home turned out. You keep saying you are thankful your building contractor tried to force you to pay him thousands of dollars more than what your contract called for."

"That's true, Sam. I really am glad I had to take over as general contractor. I was totally inexperienced, but the place turned out much better than it would have otherwise."

"That's just it, Al. What could have been a personal night-mare with expensive lawsuits was for you a relatively stress-free stroke of good luck. You are clearly doing something right to have such consistently good outcomes. Life seems so easy for you. At least that's been my impression. Is it accurate?"

"Yes, I'd say so."

"Like I said, it's almost magical to me. How do you do it?"

"Life works well for me, Sam, because my mind is free."

"You say that so calmly, Al, but this is a startling statement to hear. It's also provocative. What do you mean?"

"Thirty years ago my mind broke free from the hidden controls that handicap the minds of most people."

"You've hinted at this in the past. Please, tell me more."

"It happened when I went through a peak experience in 1965."

"The kind of experience Abraham Maslow described?"

"Yes, although I didn't know what it was at the time."

"I've read Maslow's description of peak experiences. They are extraordinarily powerful. If yours was anything like what he reported…"

"It was, big time. It lasted for many weeks."

"I've never had anyone tell me about such an experience. What was yours like?"

"For me, it was like curtains parting to reveal a different world, one I had been in all my life but never saw before. I felt amazed. My mind was flooded with answers to questions I had asked. Connections suddenly appeared between diverse experiences and events. My mind rapidly comprehended how things are and how things work. I felt wave after wave of insights far beyond what any teacher had tried to teach me. I felt mental climaxes. Pleasant sensations rippled through my body. I felt thrilled, elated, joyous…ecstatic. That's a good word for it, ecstatic about my new knowing and being."

"Do you want to elaborate on that?"

"My peak experience transformed me, Sam. The old world and my way of functioning in it were gone. That was over. I knew I would never be the same again. My new awareness included knowing that I had been transformed and that I had moved beyond old habits and less effective ways of doing things into a new, better, more effective orientation to the world. It literally blew my mind. And that's okay because I was free; I had new abilities. Just like the young ducks out here in the river in the spring, now I could fly."

"Explain the image of the fledgling ducks."

"Imagine that all your life you struggled to follow after your mother, paddling your feet or waddling around. You flap these things at your side, but you don't know why. Then one day, in your effort to go faster you find yourself flying. The first time a young duck flies it quacks in frightened protest. It doesn't know how to get down! It eventually finds a way to crash land. Afterward, it is never the same again."

"That's what you mean by 'peaking out'—you did the equivalent of learning to soar on new wings?"

"Yes."

"What about the duckling's 'frightened protest' and 'crash landing.' Were you frightened? Was it hard 'to land?'"

"I felt scared at moments because of the circumstances and where I landed."

"Could you be more specific?"

Al takes a deep breath, turns, and stares across the river.

"I detect some reluctance, Al. If it's something you don't want to talk about…"

"It's not that. In the past when I've tried to talk about what I went through, very few people have been able to handle it. My experience has been similar to what Vietnam combat veterans ran into when asked about their war experiences. The average person could last only several minutes before having to escape from what they were hearing. It's discouraging."

"Aren't veterans being heard more and more?"

"Now they are. And I know you are an excellent interviewer."

"Did you know that the initials of my name are ASK?"

Al laughs. "That's right. I forget that your first name is Arthur. How much time do you have?"

"I don't have anything else planned for today or this evening. I really would like to hear what you went through. Why are you hesitant?"

"Remember what I said about controls that most people have in their minds?"

"Yes. Can you give a concrete example?"

"One control occurs when a person hears a negative label about someone. That label automatically controls the person's perception of the one who is labelled."

"But what's the connection with your peak experience?"

"My experience included being labeled a 'paranoid schizophrenic' by psychiatrists at the Menninger Foundation in Topeka, Kansas."

"Oh, no!"

"As labels go it is one of the worst, isn't it?"

"What can I say, Al? It's very damning. But I don't understand how you could be labeled that way. How could this have happened to you?"

"The basic facts are these. In the spring of 1965, I was completing my doctoral program in clinical psychology at the University of Michigan. At that time the Menninger Foundation awarded me a two-year post-doctoral fellowship. I finished my dissertation and in August moved to Topeka, Kansas, to start the program. Less than two weeks after arriving, however, I was declared severely mentally ill and locked up in the back ward of the VA hospital."

"The back ward! This is incredible. How did you react?"

"I was pleased."

"Hold on, Al. It's hard for me to imagine not being completely overwhelmed and feeling enraged and demoralized."

"I felt many feelings, Sam. But my basic feeling was to feel thrilled and delighted."

"But wasn't being locked up on the back ward frightening?"

"No. Keep in mind, my mind was soaring. Maybe a better analogy would be that I felt like a surfer who happened to find himself on a tidal wave. It was a dangerous and thrilling ride. I felt thrilled to be learning things about psychiatry I had never been taught in seven years of graduate school. My mind was churning with a flood of valuable insights. And this occurred in a dangerous setting. The people I had come to learn from were trying to knock me off my wave. They wanted to save me from something I was eager to have happening."

"But you didn't cooperate with their effort."

"Not at all. In fact, I've been signed out Against Medical Advice for thirty years."

"What?"

"Their discharge summary stated that my prognosis was poor without hospitalization and treatment."

"This is bizarre, Al. This is completely at odds with my image of people diagnosed as schizophrenic."

"In what way?"

"The public knows that some very successful individuals live private lives much different from their public personas. There are any number of people, for example, who give a public appearance of being outstanding members of society, but who are secretly violent to their spouses or children. Americans have had ample opportunity to reflect on such discrepancies between the public and the private person."

"Like O.J. Simpson, Jimmy Swaggart, J. Edgar Hoover..."

"Exactly. But the image of 'schizophrenics' is different. With the emptying out of psychiatric hospitals, many people once in treatment for schizophrenia are now among the homeless. They live impoverished if not frightening lives, especially those who talk and act in psychotic ways. It can be alarming to walk down the street and pass by a disheveled person with a contorted face—'a paranoid schizophrenic'—ranting and raving at no one in particular. They move out of kilter. They seem out of control, unpredictable in a dangerous way.

"To learn that a person who has accomplished what you have—being president and a board member of different professional groups, being elected to the school board and becoming chairman, being interviewed on television hundreds of times, and so on—was once diagnosed as paranoid schizophrenic . . . well, it flies in the face of how 'schizophrenics' have been represented by the mental health profession and the media. The public discourse on 'paranoid schizophrenia' does not elicit in my mind the image of an economically successful community leader, let alone someone who is a highly regarded keynote speaker, and in every other way a solid, well-integrated person. The incongruity is extreme."

"I agree. It is incongruous to know me and to learn that according to psychiatrists at the Menninger Foundation I am a paranoid schizophrenic signed out Against Medical Advice."

"If you signed yourself out that means you weren't involuntarily committed?"

"That is correct. But if I hadn't gone in voluntarily they would have tried to commit me. My best course of action at the time was to play along with them."

"You were actually willing to let them lock you up?"

"Yes. I want to emphasize I was playing with these developments. I was not a victim of the Menningers. I wanted events to happen as they did…"

"Wait, wait, wait, Al. You *wanted* events to turn out this way?"

"Yes. What occurred was the best thing that could ever have happened to me, Sam, and I knew it at the time."

"This I want to hear."

"Okay, let's start at the beginning…"

Chapter Two

Telephone Calls to the Sub-Basement

"My adventure began when my telephone rang on Wednesday morning, March 10th, 1965. I was sitting at my desk in my small sub-basement office at the university hospital writing a report on a patient I'd tested."

My office was standard institutional. Cement walls painted beige, brown speckled tile floor coated with layers of old wax, two dinged up metallic gray book cases, a gray metal desk with a matching swivel chair, and two armless gray chairs

"Dr. Giora on line two, Al."

"Thanks, Katy." I punched the second button on my phone wondering what my supervisor wanted. "Siebert here," I said.

"Al, this is Dr. Giora. Can you come over to my office at two o'clock?"

"Sure."

"Good, I'll see you then," he said, and hung up.

I was puzzled.

I tilted my chair back and looked up at the small segment of sky visible through the grating at the top of the window well.

I wonder what this is about?

Why can't he wait until our weekly meeting on Thursday?

I've dictated all my test reports so that can't be the reason. I attend staff meetings and conferences regularly. Hmm...

I mentally shrugged, turned my attention back to my work, and put the matter out of my mind for the rest of the morning.

Working half-time as a psychologist at the university hospital's neuropsychiatric institute was a perfect job for me. It gave me clinical experience in a teaching setting while allowing me to take a full load of graduate courses and teach part-time.

I liked being down in the sub-basement away from the staff on the floors above. Mine was the only office down there. I could enter and leave the hospital through the sub-corridors without being seen. No one paid attention to me, so I spent more time at the university than anyone knew. I just made sure that whenever I was supposed to be present I would come up from the sub-basement on the elevator.

At 1:55 p.m. I put on my long white coat that said "Psychologist" on the pocket. I walked down the corridor past the electroencephalograph laboratory and the other equipment rooms. At the end of the hallway I pushed through a heavy metal door and headed for the one-story brick building across the road. It was quite chilly, so I pulled the lapels of my coat up around my neck and broke into a jog.

Dr. Giora had been hired to fill the Senior Psychologist position at NPI about three months earlier. He and I were just getting to know each other. He was a small, slender man who loved to play tennis. He was an excellent clinician and was taking hold of his job quite well.

When I arrived at his office he smiled, shook my hand, and gestured for me to sit down on the wooden chair next to his desk. Giora had a large corner office with polished wooden furniture.

"Al," he said, "you've passed your written examinations for your doctorate and will complete your dissertation by summer. Have you considered applying for a post-doctoral fellowship?"

"No."

"I just learned that the Menninger Foundation is still accepting applications for their two year post-doctoral program in clinical psychology. They want a recent graduate in clinical psychology skilled in diagnosis and research but not interested in private practice as a psychotherapist. You're exactly what they're looking for. Would you like to apply?"

Surprise!

It sure is.

"No."

Maybe Giora thought I fit their bill, but I was startled. I had not thought of going on to do post-doctoral work. I was amazed to have made it all the way through graduate school.

"Of all the clinical psychology students here at Michigan," Giora said, "you're the only one I believe is qualified to apply for the Menninger post-doctoral program."

"I don't know," I said. "That's big league stuff. I'm just trying to be a good minor league player."

"You have the ability to succeed there."

"Maybe. But I'm happy here. I enjoy my clinical job, my teaching, and doing research."

"This is an opportunity you shouldn't pass up," he insisted. "With Menninger training you'll have your choice of jobs. You'll have it made for the rest of your career."

I wasn't impressed. "You may be right, but I'm getting tired of going to school."

Giora became more insistent. "Their program is the best in the country. You won't have to do any outside work. They'll give you a National Institute of Mental Health Fellowship paying seven thousand dollars the first year and eight thousand the second."

"That sounds good, but I'd hate to give up my sports. I'm on every psychology department team—volleyball, football, softball, bowling..."

"They will have plenty of recreational opportunities. Dr. Martin Mayman is the Director of Psychological Training there. Here is his address. Contact him immediately. We are slightly past their deadline. Write to him to request the application forms. Take a look at their program before you say no to it." He paused, then added, "You can always turn them down if they do offer you the fellowship."

That made sense. I chuckled and said, "Okay."

"Why did you chuckle, Al?"

"Partly because Giora wasn't going to take no for an answer. And partly because the idea was so unexpected."

"In what way? In singling you out, wasn't he acknowledging your qualifications?"

"That's just it, Sam. His acknowledgment was wonderful, and that's why I was laughing to myself. This development was totally unexpected. Let me give you some background. I graduated from Willamette University with barely over a 3.0 grade point average. I did reasonably well on the Graduate Record Exam but not outstanding. When I showed up at Michigan, I probably had the lowest college GPA and the lowest GRE score of all the entering graduate students in psychology. The other students had high grade point averages and long lists of accomplishments. They came from places like UCLA, Brandeis, Harvard, Tufts, and Antioch."

"But Al, if your qualifications were so low, how did you get accepted in the first place?"

"I wondered about that myself, so I asked Bill McKeachie. He was head of the admissions committee in 1958. He said he persuaded the committee to admit me because I came from a small West Coast college and was an army veteran. He told them I added balance to the class. He said he also wanted me at Michigan because he saw on my application that I had been named outstanding intramural athlete at Willamette. He said he had a private theory that natural athletes make excellent professionals."

"I never heard that theory before."

"McKeachie was an excellent athlete himself. He played on the psychology department softball and volleyball teams. The truth of the matter is that he had a personal motive for wanting me there. Michigan has a big intramural program for the faculty and graduate students. The Psychology and Mathematics departments were always among the top two contenders for the all-school intramural championship. McKeachie wanted to beat Math for the championship, so when he saw that I was an outstanding intramural athlete..."

"You mean you got an athletic scholarship to graduate school?"

"Close to it! That's partly why I was chuckling about Giora seeing me as the most qualified graduate student for this national honor. When I started grad school I struggled in the courses. I thought they'd made a mistake letting me in. Keep in mind I came from a working class family. My father was a truck driver. He died when he was in his thirties. My mother went to work as a hospital clerk to raise and support two children on her own. I was not an intellectual. I wondered how long it would take the people at Michigan to discover they made a mistake and tell me to leave. I would have said, 'Fine. I had a good time.' At the end my first year I was placed on academic probation because of low grades."

"How did you survive?"

"I decided I would have to work harder than the others just to get passing grades. Plus McKeachie had me sign up for three hours of special projects that he supervised. He gave me an A+, which brought my GPA up to just over the required 3.0."

"It sounds like McKeachie was a mentor."

"He was. Both he and Jim McConnell. McConnell was my advisor. He constantly challenged my thinking. McKeachie challenged me to take on jobs I didn't know I could do. I worked hard not to let him down. As time went by I did better and better. My fourth and fifth years in grad school I got top grades."

"You got marginal grades in beginning courses and top grades in the most advanced courses?"

"I know. It seems peculiar, but it is often that way for me. I flounder at first and then finish strong. I'm a very late bloomer."

"So all this is context for your reactions to Giora."

"Right. After years of feeling like a misfit in school, of being an outsider in clinical psychology. "

"An outsider as well?"

"Yes. I always wanted to be a teacher, but you can't major in teaching psychology. You have to have a 'field' or specialty area. I chose clinical psychology because I figured that learning about the deepest functions of the human mind would give me knowledge I could transfer to my teaching. As a result, I went through the clinical program as an outsider. I did not have the same desire as the other grad students to become a therapist or a clinician. I took the minimum required clinical courses and worked instead at getting a solid, broad education that would be useful to me in teaching all areas of psychology."

"I see. When Giora told you that you were a perfect candidate for the Menninger Foundation post-doctoral program in clinical psychology..."

"It startled me and cracked me up. It still tickles me to think about it."

"So you started grad school in 1958 naive and non-intellectual. You believed they made a mistake letting you in. By the spring of 1965, however, you are ending strong—getting top grades, teaching, completing your Ph.D. But the prospect of a postgraduate fellowship—no way."

"Exactly. I felt a combination of disbelief and excitement about Giora's assessment of my skills. The honor of being asked to apply was thrilling, but I knew there was no chance of being accepted. It just wasn't in my self-concept."

I walked back to my office thinking:
Incredible. There is no way this is going to happen.
Right?
Right.
So why bother to apply?
Giora wants me to.
Fine. I'll apply.

When I returned to my office I roughed out a short letter to Dr. Mayman. Because Katy and the other secretaries in the department were overworked, I decided to go home early to have my wife, Kathleen, type it.

I put some department stationary in my scuffed plastic brief case and walked down a corridor past the huge boilers. The corridor was always hot from the huge, overhead steam pipes, so I waited until I was at the upstairs exit at the front of the hospital before putting on my heavy brown corduroy coat. It was worn at the elbows from three winters' use but still plenty warm. I bought it at a J.C. Penney's spring sale and felt good about getting my money's worth.

As a married graduate student whose wife didn't work, I had to watch expenses carefully. I was very pleased, for example, when I found a defective meter in one of the big parking lots near the hospital. When I put a nickel in the meter, I got 25 cents worth of parking time. Since I often came to the hospital early in the morning to attend staff rounds, the space was usually empty and waiting for me.

My car was a seven year old, metallic blue Rambler Ambassador I had purchased used. It was rusty from the salt spread on the roads in the winter, but it ran well. The drive home took ten minutes.

When I opened the door to our small basement apartment, Kathleen was sitting on the maroon hide-a-bed couch in the living room embroidering a pillowcase for one of her nieces. She had her usual cup of hot tea nearby on the round maple table we had found at a thrift shop and had refinished. The table lamp was her great pride. It was brass with two hurricane lamps. She and her mother had pooled their books of green stamps to get it.

She looked up, surprised. "What are you doing home early?"

"Something very interesting has developed. Dr. Giora wants me to apply for a post-doctoral fellowship at the Menninger Foundation."

"What is the Menninger Foundation?"

"Sort of like the Mayo Clinic of psychiatry," I said, as I set down my brief case and took off my coat. I told her about my conversation with Giora.

I opened my briefcase and took out my letter to Dr. Mayman. "Here's the letter Dr. Giora asked me to send. Will you please type it right away so I can take it to the post office before it closes?"

"I'll be glad to." Kathleen took her tea with her and went over to the typewriter on the desk I'd set up in our living room. The desk was a small birch door I had finished and placed on top of two gray, two-drawer filing cabinets. One end was anchored in place by a tall bookcase I'd made of tan bricks and fir boards. I had designed it to hold my books, favorite objects, and stereo equipment.

Kathleen had agreed to type papers for me if she had a Standard Royal typewriter. A used one was all right, but it had to be a Royal. I watched her sit down and put the stationary in the typewriter. I liked watching Kathleen. I liked the way she sat with good posture. I liked the way she walked and the way she moved. She was a lovely, slender woman with a narrow waist and legs like a model. Her black hair and soft ivory skin reflected her pure Irish blood. She was raised by her mother to be a homemaker, and she excelled at it.

She made our apartment feel warm and cozy. Colorful pictures decorated the walls. Blooming flowers sat in small pots under the big front window. A red and white checkered table cloth with matching napkins brightened the kitchen. The orange, red, and yellow Afghan she'd knitted looked nice on the couch.

"Was she Catholic?" Sam asked.

"Yes, she never ate meat on Friday. She went to confession every week and Mass on Sunday. I never went with her, but it wasn't an issue."

"How did you meet her?"

"In 1960 I went to work as a psychologist at the juvenile court in Cleveland, Ohio. My job was to do psychological testing of juvenile delinquents. Kathleen had worked there for many years as a secretary-typist. That's where we met."

"Why were you in Cleveland?"

"After my first marriage broke up I went there for clinical experience instead of staying in Ann Arbor. My first wife had entered the Michigan graduate program in psychology at the same time I did. We had a romance and were married in the spring. The marriage didn't work out, however. After our second year in grad school we filed for a divorce and I left town to avoid being in the same classes with her."

"Wait a minute. You said Kathleen was strongly Catholic. The church wouldn't let her marry a divorced man and remain in the church."

"You're right. I didn't know about that law at first. The explanation is fascinating."

"What explanation? A church law is a church law."

"Yes, but they have another law that created an unusual exception. Our story goes like this. Kathleen and I were attracted to each other from the time we first met. I could feel her respond when I spoke to her or was near her. But when I asked her to go out with me she would blush, lower her eyes, and say 'no' in a way that indicated an inner struggle.

"I joined the Court bowling league and was pleased to learn she was on one of the other teams. Sometimes we would talk between games, but she usually avoided me. A few months later, at a bowling league party at someone's apartment, I cornered her and got her to talk to me. When she told me about being Catholic, I mentioned that my first wife was Catholic and that we were married by a justice of the peace. Kathleen stared at me and asked for more details. As I told her she broke into a warm smile. She put her hand on my arm and asked if I wanted to dance. Did I ever! We clung together like magnets. After a few dances I took her down the hall to an empty room. We started kissing passionately."

"What caused the change?" Sam asked.

"I didn't understand it myself. When I paused to breathe I asked her what had changed.

"Her explanation went something like this: 'As a Catholic,' she said, 'I cannot marry a divorced man. The Church does not recognize divorces. But because your ex-wife was a Catholic married in a civil ceremony, her marriage is not recognized by the Church. She was living in sin with you. In the eyes of the Church, you were never married because you married a Catholic in a ceremony outside any church. If she wasn't a Catholic, you would be a divorced man. Or if you'd married her in your church, you would be divorced now and I couldn't let myself be involved with you.' Then we started kissing again.

"Being a Methodist from Oregon, I didn't understand her explanation, but I sure liked the effect on her. We started dating. I'd go to her home every Sunday for dinner. I asked her to marry me when I moved back to Ann Arbor to continue grad school."

"What do you mean, being from Oregon?" Sam asked.

"Like many kids growing up in Oregon, I had the impression that a Methodist in Portland was about the same as a Catholic in Boston, a Jew in New York, or a Baptist in Alabama. Children raised in the Pacific Northwest seldom understand how deeply or extensively a religion can control what a person thinks, feels, and does."

"When did you and Kathleen get married?"

"December, 1962. I returned to graduate school in September and then went back to Cleveland during Christmas vacation to marry Kathleen. It was a church wedding. She was a beautiful bride. I loved her dearly. We were very compatible. I felt blessed to have her become my wife."

"You'd been married just over two years when Giora told you to apply to the Menninger Foundation."

"That's right."

"Did they respond quickly?"

"Yes. I got the application forms and a description of the program returned by airmail right away."

"I take it you liked the way the program sounded?"

"I did. They sent me an outline. The program offered many seminars and courses on psychological testing, clinical practice, and diagnosis and treatment."

"What was most appealing about the program?"

"They said the program allowed Fellows a two-year 'moratorium' in which they were free to reexamine and reintegrate their theoretical, clinical, and professional skills. I liked that. The application forms were lengthy, but I completed them by the next day and Kathleen typed them that night."

"Was there anything difficult about the application?"

"Yes. They asked me to describe myself in 500 words or less. That was a real challenge. I'd never written a self-description before."

"If I were on an admissions committee," Sam said, "I would want to know what the applicants think about themselves. A self-description could be very informative. Do you remember what you said?"

"Better than that. I have a complete file on what happened back then. I'll go get it and show you. Do you want more juice or anything while I'm inside?"

"No. I'll just sit and enjoy the view."

Al returns with a large file folder. He sits down and leafs through it. "Here. Here is my application with my one page self-description. Go ahead and look at it."

"Do you mind reading it to me?"

"I'll read a few key statements. I wrote, 'I am a person not used to describing himself to others. I prefer to let people observe what I do and how I do it and let each person perceive me as he will.

"'I've never liked having to memorize theories and I don't like to spend time arguing about abstract points or hypothetical situations.'

"I wrote, 'I've learned a lot about life. The world has been very good to me and I will not be happy in my old age unless I feel that somehow world is a little better off for my having been here. I am confident that I will add something to the world, because I set my goals at a level appropriate to my abilities, fully commit myself, work as hard as I can for as long as is necessary—and almost always succeed.

"'As for what bothers me, I feel irritated by "change agents" who try to impose a new set of attitudes or behaviors on me without first inquiring to find out what I have already thought through. I get along with people quite well and am open to change, but I expect my educators to be willing to talk things over with me if conflicts arise.

"'In general I enjoy life. Even though I have a highly developed sense of social responsibility there are times when I don't take life as seriously as some people do. I have a subtle sense of humor and amuse myself very much.

"At the end I wrote, 'In trying to verbalize what I believe I am, I have been intrigued by the fact that I feel internally consistent and yet see a number of paradoxes in myself. I am sensitive yet never overwhelmed, I am discontent yet satisfied, I am easygoing yet intense. Altogether I guess I see myself as quite a complex person.'"

"Hmmm, curious. I like your statement, Al, that you are open to change but expect your educators to be willing to talk things over with you if conflicts arise. Did you encounter conflicts with your professors at Michigan?"

"The psychology department professors were great about talking over disagreements, but not the psychiatric instructors at the hospital. There were several times when I had more up-to-date knowledge than they did, but they didn't want to hear it."

"Any serious conflicts?"

"Oh no. Minor incidents. I'd try to speak up during a staff conference on a patient and get squelched by a senior psychiatrist. Several would act superior and mildly ridicule new terms or perspectives they hadn't heard about."

"Much different than at the university."

"Very much so. McKeachie, for example, would come down to the sixth floor, collect three or four teaching fellows who happened to be in their offices, take us to the coffee room at the end of the hall, buy us whatever we wanted to drink, and then interview us about new developments in teaching."

"He interviewed *you*? He's the author of *Teaching Tips,* one of the best books available for beginning college instructors. He's a master at teaching how to learn to teach."

"That's why, Sam. He'd tell us he was going to speak at a conference on teaching and wanted to know the most recent publications and developments. He knew his graduate students were on the leading edge."

"I can see why he is so well respected."

"And became president of the American Psychology Association. The next morning I took the application to the post office and sent it air mail. Then I went around to the professors who had agreed to write letters of reference and gave each one the form Mayman had sent in the application package. Then I put the matter out of my mind."

"So you finished the application and submitted it even though you thought your chances were nil?"

"Yes. I applied because Giora insisted. He was my boss. I knew I wasn't going to be accepted."

"Then you went back to your normal routine."

"Yes. I tested several patients at the hospital, played several volleyball games, attended seminars and lectures, and taught my classes at the University."

"What classes were you teaching?"

"One was Introduction to College Teaching, a brown-bag seminar required for all psychology graduate students who wanted to become teaching fellows. We met during the lunch hour once a week and went through every conceivable challenge that could come up in teaching introductory psychology.

McKeachie had me take over the course when he became department chairman."

"He had you teach it even though you were still just a graduate student yourself."

"Yes. He said I could do it, so I did. When there was a teaching need someplace, McKeachie called on me. For example, this particular semester the department had more psychology majors needing a required course in personality theory than the regular professor was willing to take. There were over 80. McKeachie asked me to teach a class of about 40 of them."

"Had you ever taught an upper division course to psych majors before?"

"No. I was reluctant at first, but Bill convinced me I could do it. I was his utility instructor."

"What do you mean by that?"

"Oh, he had me teach his Psychology of Religion class when he was out of town. One time he picked me to teach an experimental course where all the students in the class had the same psych instructor and the same English instructor."

"You were like a utility player in baseball, an athlete who can play any position?"

"Like that," Al says, nodding.

A week after I sent in the application forms, the phone on my desk rang.

"Long distance for you on line three, Al."

"Thanks, Katy."

"Mr. Siebert?"

"Yes."

"This is Mrs. Falley, Dr. Mayman's secretary. Just a moment please. Dr. Mayman would like to speak to you."

(Pause)

"Al, this is Marty Mayman. We have received your application forms and would like to arrange for an interview. Can you come to the Menninger Foundation next week?"

I was startled. "You want me to come there?"

"Yes. Can you arrange it?"

"I suppose so."

"We'd like you here all day Tuesday and Wednesday for interviews with the staff. My secretary will make reservations for you at the hotel."

"Who is going to pay for the plane ticket and hotel room?"

"We will reimburse your travel and meals. Will you come?"

"I know I can get out of my classes and other work. Let's see." I glanced at my calendar. "I guess I could get back in time for my volleyball game Wednesday evening. It's a nine o'clock game. Yes. I can come."

"Fine. Please be at my office at ten o'clock Tuesday morning."

"All right."

I hung up, feeling like a kid.

This is exciting! It's like graduating from high school and winning a free trip to Washington, D.C.!

The Menninger Foundation! Wow!

All through graduate school I've read their books and papers.

Now I'm going to meet them! Incredible! Wait until Kathleen hears about this. And Dr. Giora.

I picked up the phone and called home. "Kathleen! Guess what!"

Chapter Three

A Capitol Visit

"What a way to cap your graduate career!"

"Yes, Sam, I felt excited. Honored."

"Did you feel nervous at all?"

"Not then. What I believed was a total impossibility had only shifted to a highly unlikely probability. I did spend much of the weekend in the university library though."

"Why?"

"The Menninger Foundation published a *Bulletin*. It contained information about Foundation and staff activities, lists of publications by Foundation members, book reviews, and articles written by their psychologists, psychiatrists, psychoanalysts, and other staff. I wanted to get as much from my trip as I could, so I looked through all the back issues of the *Bulletin* I read the articles that interested me. Then I looked through the books and chapters of books the Menninger staff had written."

"Very smart. What did you learn about them?"

"I learned that two psychiatrists, Dr. Charles Menninger and his son, Dr. Karl, founded the Menninger Clinic in 1920. They were both followers of Freud and wanted to create a center for specialists in the new fields of psychiatry and psychoanalysis. Karl's brother, Dr. William, also a psychiatrist, joined their clinic in 1926. In 1941 they established the Menninger Foundation. It became the leading psychiatric center in the U.S. The Menningers were also instrumental in founding a major psychiatric hospital for veterans in Topeka.

"In 1965 the Menninger Foundation was at the forefront of psychiatric research with an emphasis on the theories of Freud and the clinical application of his ideas. Several of the psychoanalytic articles were quite a stretch for me, however."

"What would be an example, Al?

"One was about phallic narcissism. It was about men's cars and neckties. According to the psychoanalyst who wrote the article, driving a big shiny car or wearing a necktie is a symbolic way of showing off your penis."

"What was surprising about that?"

"Thirty years ago such thinking seemed strange, even to psychology graduate students."

"Did you do anything else to prepare for the trip? Did you ask anyone for advice about interviewing for the Menninger fellowship?"

"I talked to Giora, McConnell, and several of my professors about what to expect."

"Were they helpful?"

"McConnell said that faculty interviews usually included an informal social gathering or dinner someplace. They mainly said I'd do fine."

"What did Kathleen think about your trip?"

"She wanted to know where Topeka was, so we got out a map and looked at it. We talked about what going there for the fellowship would be like."

"How was your trip? What happened in the interviews?"

When the day came to leave, Monday, March 29, I packed my things into an old canvas suitcase I'd had since my army days. Kathleen drove me to the Detroit airport early in the evening.

She was proud of me and excited for me. "I know they'll like you," she said. "You look nice and your crew cut is grown out just right."

I still wore my hair in the same crew cut I had as a paratrooper. She went with me to the departure gate and gave me a warm hug and kiss.

I had a window seat toward the rear. I leaned back, closed my eyes, and thought about what was happening.

I felt myself getting nervous.

You're nervous. Why?

What if they do select me?

Is it really possible they might?

This is unreal! Getting into graduate school was a fluke. Now here you are on your way to the Menninger Foundation to interview for a prestigious post-doctoral fellowship.

It doesn't make sense that this is happening to you.
So? Who says it has to make sense?
But a paying fellowship! Incredible!
Well, do the same as before. Let them find out their mistake for themselves. Don't make the decision for them. Just sit back and enjoy your visit.

"I had never thought of that before, not making the decision for them."

"Many people, Sam, assume others will think or decide a certain way, and act as though the decision is made. They don't ever find out. My attitude was that for me to *not* get the fellowship, the evaluation committee would have to make that decision."

"In other words you were open to being interviewed for the fellowship even when you didn't believe you would be chosen. That runs contrary to many books about the importance of positive visualization."

"Yes, but I wasn't imagining being turned down either. Remember, you started by asking me about magic. Maybe this is a clue. I was letting myself interact with whatever way the situation happened to evolve. Whatever the outcome, I had a great future ahead. Keep in mind also that I was managing my mind and emotions. Once I accepted I'd be turned down, I felt myself relax."

"That's amazing. A paradoxical approach to success."

"In sports, trying too hard can tighten you up. I needed to hang loose and have fun, to not have the interview be too important."

After I checked into the hotel I called Kathleen to let her know I had arrived safely. I ate a light snack and went to bed. I tried to sleep but couldn't. I felt anxious.

Relax. Take deep breaths Assume you are not going to get the fellowship. Treat this like a paid vacation.
Okay.
Look at it from their point of view. They must constantly recruit good people in order to keep their Foundation going. They need you more than you need them.

Right!
Remember that. They need you more than you need them.
Okay.
Keep repeating to yourself, THEY NEED YOU MORE THAN YOU NEED THEM!

It took about five minutes to fully relax and really accept that they needed me more than I needed them. It worked. I fell asleep.

Tuesday morning was clear and sunny. I put on the khaki pants and pale yellow shirt Kathleen had washed and ironed. I put on a brown blazer tie and my dark brown sport coat with large black plaids. I looked in the mirror. I felt good and looked good.

After breakfast in the hotel coffee shop, I walked outside and took a deep breath. The air smelled clean. The city felt peaceful.

The taxi driver knew where to take me. In recent weeks he had taken other fares to Mayman's office.

At 9:50 a.m. the driver stopped in front of a brown, freshly painted wood building that looked like an old army barracks. Flat, weedless green lawns covered the large open areas between buildings. Rows of recently pruned shrubs stood in perfectly straight lines along the walkways.

I wonder if mental patients do the gardening here like they do at state hospitals?

I paid the fare, got a receipt, and thanked the driver. I strode to the front door and walked in.

Two men and a woman in business attire sat in a small waiting room to the left. Classical music drifted out of an old radio on an end table next to a neat stack of magazines. The receptionist smiled as I walked up to her.

"Good morning. I'm Al Siebert. I'm here to see Dr. Mayman for a fellowship interview."

"Good morning!" She said. "I'll let them know you're here."

Before long a smiling, brown haired woman in a tan wool sweater and matching skirt came down the stairs. "Good morning, Mr. Siebert," she said, shaking hands with me. "I'm Karen Falley, the training program secretary. I'm afraid Dr.

Mayman was called to an emergency meeting this morning. He asked me to apologize for him and give you a copy of your interview schedule."

She handed me a sheet of paper.

"Here it is, Sam. The 'Interview Schedule' for 'Lawrence A. Siebert' dated 'March 30-31, 1965.'"

Sam takes the schedule from Al and glances at it. "They were well prepared for you."

"Yes. They had everything well organized. Even better than that sheet indicates."

Mrs. Falley stood by while I read through the schedule. It listed the times, names, and locations of my interviews and activities.

About ten interviews.

I attend a seminar this evening. Interesting. Another one tomorrow.

When do I leave?

The last interview tomorrow will end about 5:00. That will cut it close for catching my flight back in time for the game.

"Do you have any questions?" Mrs. Falley asked.

"Not right now," I said.

"I'll be in my office if you need any help. Please wait out here in the waiting room until Dr. Lerner comes over for you." With that she turned and walked back upstairs.

I went into the waiting room and sat in an old armchair with sagging cushions. The three others sat staring at magazines.

They seem uncomfortable.

Probably waiting to see their therapists.

I watched a man wearing a wrinkled, light brown suit walk over from a parking lot. He walked into the lobby and spoke to the receptionist.

About my size and age. Not in good physical shape.

Hair is oily. Needs combing.

The receptionist made a phone call. Mrs. Falley soon reappeared. She spoke to the man, gave him a page like mine, and left. He walked into the waiting room and sat down several chairs away from me.

I leaned toward him. "Are you here for the fellowship interviews?"

He peered at me. "Yes, that's right."

"I am too." I moved to the chair next to his and extended my hand. "I'm Al Siebert."

"I'm Jim Sears."

We shook hands.

"What's your schedule like?" I asked.

"I was supposed to meet with a Dr. Rosen," he said, "but he's in an emergency meeting."

I looked at his schedule and showed him mine.

I said, "we'll attend the psychology staff meeting and go to two seminars together."

They've paired two candidates together.

Interesting.

Yeah. Didn't expect that.

I leaned back in my chair. "Why did you apply for the fellowship?" I asked.

"My wife and I would like to live in the area," he said, "to be near her parents. How about you?"

"My advisor had me apply. It was a last minute thing. We had to rush the application and letters of recommendation."

"Do you have your Ph.D. yet?" he asked.

"No, my thesis committee just approved my topic, but I should have it done by June. How about you?"

"I'm writing my dissertation now."

"What's your topic?"

As Jim and I talked, we both seemed to know he probably would not get a fellowship. His heart wasn't in it. He was applying for the sake of his wife being near her folks, not out of enthusiasm for the program.

At 10:25 a thin, pale man in a dark suit walked in. He wore a white shirt with a dark bow tie. His dark hair was neatly trimmed.

About 28. Not athletic.

The receptionist pointed Jim and me out to him.

"I'm Dr. Lerner," he said, walking toward us. "Which one of you is Mr. Siebert?"

I stood up. "I am," I said, extending my hand.

As we shook hands, he said, "I'm in my first year on the same fellowship you are applying for." He looked at Jim and said, "Dr. Lependorf will be here for you soon. He is the other first year Fellow."

Lerner and I left Jim and walked outside.

"I'm supposed to escort you to a staff conference at the hospital," he said. "It starts at 10:30."

"Who will be there?" I asked.

"Anyone on the Foundation staff who wants to attend. One of the staff psychiatrists will be presenting a research report."

He seems frail...and edgy.

"The sun feels nice," I said.

"I heard you had a bad winter in the Great Lakes area."

"Tell me about it. We had many days below zero. It seems like the weather gets more extreme each year."

10:30 a.m. Staff Conference with Dr. Lerner

We went to a large conference room in an old building. About 60 people sat scattered around in a room that could hold many more. The psychiatrist talked about living with a tribe of natives in South America to test them for extrasensory perception. He claimed his results were significant. The audience listened and paid polite attention but didn't seem impressed. I wasn't either.

Outside, as Lerner led me toward the hospital, he asked, "What do you think about the report we just listened to?"

"I'm not sure," I said, "I was distracted by my concerns for the natives having to put up with the research party in their village."

"What do you think about ESP?"

"About three years ago, when I was working in Cleveland, I attended a lecture by J.B. Rhine, the famous parapsychologist. When he asked for questions I said to him, 'Perception results when meaning is attributed to a stimulus. Since electromagnetic wave lengths stimulate visual perception, chemical molecules stimulate olfactory perception, and air pressure waves stimulate auditory perception, what guesses do you have about the energy form that stimulates extrasensory perceptions?'

"Rhine looked at me thoughtfully and said, 'You'd think there would be an energy, wouldn't you?'

"I said, 'Yes. That's why I'm asking.'

"He was silent for a moment. Then he peered at me and said, 'Someday you are going to be very interested in ESP research.' Then he took another question. He evaded a question he should have knowledge about. He sure lost credibility with me."

Lerner smiled and nodded.

12:00 p.m. Lunch, Hospital Cafeteria with Dr. Lerner and Dr. Lependorf

The Menninger hospital was a new and large red brick building, a sharp contrast to the old wood buildings nearby. Modern but conservative, it was built to last a long time. The other buildings, the original Menninger Clinic, were probably built in the '20s and '30s.

When Lerner and I walked into the hospital cafeteria I paused, puzzled.

What's different here?

Patients are eating here too!

That's it. Not like at NPI back at Michigan.

I asked Lerner, "The hospital patients and the staff eat in the same dining room?

"Yes," he said, "the open ward patients eat here. Their philosophy is that the food must be good enough for both patients and staff."

I was impressed.

Fascinating! What an enlightened attitude.

Jim and the other first-year fellow walked up to us. Lerner introduced me. Lependorf was dressed like Lerner with a dark suit, white shirt, and bow tie.

He's taller, in good shape. Basketball player. Maybe tennis.

Jim and I went through the line ahead of Lerner and Lependorf. I took a small salad, sirloin tips with gravy on noodles, beans, a piece of chocolate cake, and milk. As I got out my wallet to pay, the cashier told Jim and me, "Your lunches will be paid for by the Psychology department." Jim and I looked at each other and smiled. We were pleased to save the money. We understood each other.

Interesting. The cashier knew in advance who we were.

Mayman really has this organized!

The four of us sat together and talked about our graduate school experiences and the Menninger Foundation. The chocolate cake didn't taste very good.

Not compared to Kathleen's.

1:00 p.m. Dr. Lerner—Annex

Outside, the warm sun felt really good. Lerner led me to the Annex building, in through a side door, and down a stairway. "They put me in a basement office," he said. "First-year fellows are low in the pecking order."

"I know, my office at the hospital is in the sub-basement."

Lerner's windowless office looked like a monk's cell. He had nothing in it but a gray metal desk, waste basket, chair, and bookcase. No photos or posters on the walls, no color, no hints of his personal life.

"I see that you are married," he said, looking at a copy of my application.

"Yes. I have a wonderful wife. She types all my papers, makes my lunch, takes care of the apartment. She spoils me."

"Does she work?"

"Part-time as a secretary when she can, but good paying jobs for student wives are hard to find in a university town. Are you married?"

"No, but I'm dating a woman who works as a bank manager."

He questioned me about the University of Michigan psychology department, my doctoral program, my background, and my experiences testing patients at Ypsilanti State Hospital.

He listened without comment. Suddenly he asked, "How do you feel about schizophrenics?"

They're OK, but I wouldn't want my sister to marry one.

"I get along with all kinds of patients," I said.

He sat looking at the top of his desk without speaking.

"Tell me about your seminars," I said, "and how you feel about the supervision you receive."

"Well, I like Dr. Rosen's seminars. Dr. Mayman is sharp on diagnostic testing. Dr. Shevrin is an expert on schizophrenia, but he's hard to understand sometimes." He filled in some details about the seminars. It all sounded good.

Here's an opportunity to find out what the official description of the program doesn't tell me. I want an insider's view. Lerner has it.

"What do you like least about the program here?" I asked.

His eyelids fluttered, he clenched his jaw, and his fingers tightened on his leg. "I keep asking for permission to conduct group therapy," he said. "But they won't approve it. They tell me it isn't one of the program goals. "

Notice the negative feelings he has.

I've touched on a sore subject.

He looked away from me, lost in thought.

He's uncomfortable. I'm uncomfortable. Change the subject.

"I read in the *Bulletin* that some staff members have an amateur acting company. Have you gone to any productions?"

"No, I haven't."

"What about sports here? Any Menninger teams?"

"The patients have a bowling team."

"Oh."

We looked at each other. We had nothing more to say.

I looked at my watch. "I have to leave for my appointment with Dr. Mayman."

We both stood up.

"I can find my way back to Mayman's office," I said. "Thanks for answering my questions." We shook hands and I left.

Lerner and I didn't connect. He was too self-conscious. I felt no warmth from him. He was a cordial professional until my question kicked him into a new mood. Then he became preoccupied.

2:00 p.m. Dr. Mayman—East Building

I walked back over to Mayman's office building. The receptionist told me how to find his office, the last one on the left, upstairs.

Mayman's door was open, but he was absorbed in the paper work on his desk. I knocked lightly on the door.

He looked up. "Hello, Al." He stood up and extended his hand. "I'm sorry about not being here to meet you this morning," he said. "I was called to an emergency meeting. Would you like a cup of coffee?"

"I don't drink coffee, but I will have some tea if there is any."

"There's a coffee lounge downstairs that serves tea," he said. He led the way out of his office and down the hall.

Mayman was about four inches shorter than I, making it easy to see the balding spot in his short dark hair. He wore an old blue blazer, old, but well-polished oxford shoes, and a maroon bow tie.

Stocky, somewhat overweight, but strong. About 45.

We walked down the back stairs to a lounge in the basement, served ourselves, and sat down. "The post-doctoral program," he said, "gives our fellows two years to question assumptions about mental disorders, study the therapeutic process, and examine assessment issues. We want fellows," he said, leaning toward me to add emphasis to his statement, "interested in research and teaching. We don't want someone to go through our program and then take advantage of the Menninger name by going into private practice."

"That's what Giora said."

"Do you have any questions about the interviews?"

"No, but I was disappointed when I saw that Steve Appelbaum wasn't on my schedule. I hoped to meet him."

"Why?"

"He is doing research on sensitivity training and I wanted to find out what he's doing. Results in this field are not easy to measure."

"Why are you interested in sensitivity training?"

"One summer Bill McKeachie took me to the National Training Lab in Bethel, Maine, to get Training Group skills. He said the skills would help me in running the teaching fellows seminar."

"I know Bill. I was in his office once. He has an impressive array of trophies."

"Yes, with all those softballs from the no-run, no-hit games he pitched."

"McKeachie thinks highly of you. Why did he make you a coauthor of the instructor's manual for his textbook?"

"I provided summaries and recommendations of psychology films to show with the material in each chapter."

"What qualified you to do that?"

"When I became a teaching fellow I felt frustrated trying to select good films to show to my psychology class. My second year I had an honors student help me review every psychology film in the university's audio-visual library. Then I reserved an empty auditorium and offered a 'Psychology Movie Hour' every week showing the better films. From that I created a lengthy annotated film guide for the other teaching fellows. McKeachie had me adapt my film guide for his instructor's manual."

"Tell me about the papers you published on the IQ scores of juvenile delinquents," he said, glancing at the clock. "How did you get over 50,000 test scores to analyze?"

"During my psychology internship at the juvenile court in Cleveland I found some filing cabinets that contained every IQ test administered to children brought to the detention center since 1929. The total number of test records was 51,808."

"That is an amazing N."

"It was. When Nate Caplan, the senior psychologist, and I analyzed the testing results, we discovered that the average IQ score for children tested at the detention center jumped from 80 to 91.3 during the 1930's. The court psychologist had switched to the new Stanford Binet IQ test. The new version had different norms."

"The norms are crucial." He understood immediately.

Good, alert intelligence.

Mayman questioned me about my experience in clinical psychology. He asked, "What is your dissertation research topic?"

"Superego sex differences," I said.

"What is the superego?" he asked.

His question startled me.

In all the time I've been asked to present my dissertation proposal, no one has asked me to answer that question.

Here I was about to start research on the differences between the superego in males and in females. I had taken classes on the structure of the personality and studied how the super-ego worked but had never been asked *what* it was. He seemed amused as I stumbled through a quickly created answer. I felt embarrassed about not answering his question well.

At 2:55 Mayman brought our conversation to a close and walked me back to the lobby. I liked him. I felt a good rapport with him. It was fun to talk with him. He had a good mind and felt emotionally solid.

3:00 p.m. Free Time

Jim walked down from the second floor as I stood looking at my schedule. He also had a free hour. After that we were both scheduled to sit in on a seminar led by Dr. Rosen at four. Since Jim had a car, we decided to drive out to see the Menninger museum and library at their West Campus. I ran up the stairs, two at a time, to Mrs. Falley's office and told her where we were going.

Three old rectangular brick buildings stood on the crest of a low hill. Fields of tall grass stretched out in all directions. To reach the buildings we had to drive up a long, winding drive-way past a big circular fountain that hissed out a fine spray. The center building housed the library and museum.

The head librarian, a small, librarian-looking woman wearing wire spectacles, was waiting for us. In a hushed voice she said she would be pleased to show us around the museum and the library.

Mrs. Falley must have called.

She took us into the museum first and introduced us to the curator. He led us to a room with cages, chains, leather straps, straight jackets, and other devices used years ago to restrain mental patients. He told us about the history of the Menninger family and the Foundation.

One room contained letters and mementos from Sigmund Freud. The curator proudly showed us his display of large glossy photographs of Anna Freud's visit to the Foundation in 1962.

As we left the museum area, the librarian said the works of art in the hallways were done by patients.

She led us around the library explaining how the works were organized. She said, "We believe this is the best psychiatric library in the world."

She stopped in front of a lighted bookcase with locked glass doors. "This contains all books written by the professional staff at the Foundation," she said, "and all books containing their writings."

I glanced at the books. "No it doesn't," I said gently.

"What?" She gave me a sharp look.

"Leonard Horwitz has a chapter in *Theories in Contemporary Psychology* edited by Melvin Marx."

She frowned. "Thank you. I'll look into that," she said. Then she hurried away.

I chuckled to myself.

That was fun.

Jim and I browsed around on our own. The library was impressive.

Air conditioning makes it very comfortable.

Yeah. But something is wrong here.

It was well lighted. There were comfortable alcoves for quiet reading. We saw rows and rows of book shelves. It looked as if they had every psychiatric book and journal ever printed. I noticed that the volumes of the journals containing my articles on the I.Q.s of delinquents were gone from the shelves.

Someone must have checked them out. Probably Mayman.

Something's wrong.

What?

Scan...

It's empty!

That's it. It's empty. Here is perhaps the finest psychiatric library in the world and no one is using it.

Except for several librarians working at the front desk, the library was completely empty. I'd never seen an empty library before.

Weird.

4:00 p.m. Dr. Rosen's Seminar on Psychotherapy—East Building

The seminar was held in a small, comfortable conference room. Jim and I sat at the large rectangular table with Lerner, Lependorf, and three second-year Fellows.

Dr. Rosen arrived at exactly 4 o'clock. He wore a neat gray suit with a white shirt and black bow tie. He looked more physically fit than most of the staff members I'd seen.

Jim and I listened while the five fellows discussed an article on therapy from a psychoanalytic yearbook. Dr. Rosen asked good questions and generated lively discussion. He was attentive and alert. I enjoyed the session.

When it was over I asked him about a large graph on the wall.

"That's Dr. Hall's," he said. "It shows the number of hours of psychoanalysis done here each year."

I thanked him and followed Jim out to the parking lot.

We had two hours on our hands. Nothing was scheduled for Jim or me until a second seminar with Dr. Rosen at his home at 7:00 p.m. Jim and I went to a steak house for dinner. We swapped stories about our army experiences, our graduate schools, and our in-laws. We drank more beer than we should have and were half high by the time we left. I enjoyed talking with Jim. I was pleased to have him there with his car. Evidently the interview plan included leaving us to our own devices for getting around.

7:00 - 9:00 p.m. Seminar on Test Inferences—Dr. Rosen's home

We arrived at Rosen's place about five minutes early. The two first-year Fellows, Lerner and Lependorf, and three psychology interns were present. Rosen's home was nicely furnished and felt comfortable. In the living room two couches and several chairs were arranged in a semicircle. It appeared that he regularly held seminars in his home. Hot coffee and hot water for tea were available on the kitchen counter. I made a cup of tea for myself.

I bet he gets a tax write-off for holding the seminar here.

We started exactly at seven. In this session the students compared the results of psychological tests administered to a patient before he started into psychoanalysis at the Foundation with the results of tests administered to him after several years of analysis. The students were very thorough. I was impressed with them.

While they talked I became interested in a painting on the wall above the fireplace. It was a portrait of a man in fancy medieval dress.

It resembles Rosen. Is Rosen part of the amateur acting company? Some of the hospital patients are good artists.

Is this a portrait of him from a play he's been in?

At exactly 9:00 p.m. Rosen stood up, indicating we were done. The seminar abruptly ended. The students put away their papers, shook my hand and Jim's, and said they had enjoyed meeting us. Then we all left.

No one stayed to socialize. Jim drove me to my hotel and said he'd pick me up in the morning about nine o'clock.

Some drunk, loud talking men in the hallway made it hard to fall asleep.

What an experience! This is great fun.

Would I like to come here?

It would be a fantastic learning opportunity. But something is going on with Lerner. Inquire more about that.

The next morning, after an early breakfast in the coffee shop, I walked around town. The stores weren't yet open. I walked through the grounds of the state capitol and then returned to the hotel. The walk was pleasant. I liked Topeka.

"What were you thinking?" Sam asked.

"I wasn't thinking. I was just observing, experiencing."

"You weren't thinking about the first day?"

"No. Like after a movie that has affected me. When I walk out and someone asks me what I think about it or whether or not it was a good movie, I have to tell them I'm not thinking about it. Maybe I'll want to talk about it later."

"You were just enjoying your trip, soaking it all up."

"That's right. I was just absorbing my experiences. My mind was silent. I was just feeling the weather, the sun, the spirit of the town, absorbing the look and feel of the Foundation and all the people I was meeting."

"So when Jim came to pick you up, you didn't talk about the Menninger program with him?"

"No. We said hello to each other, compared schedules for the day, and tentatively agreed to meet in the hospital cafeteria at 12:30. When we got to the Foundation offices, Jim dropped me off at the East Building and left for his appointment."

I went inside and asked the receptionist if I could leave my bag with her. She said I could. It looked out of place next to the filing cabinet behind her desk. She seemed amused.

9:30 a.m. Dr. Hall—Northwest Office

I enjoyed the morning sun and fresh breeze as I strolled over to the building where Dr. Hall's office was located. His secretary ushered me into his office at exactly 9:30. It was a large dimly lit corner office with a good carpet.

He must be important.

Hall was my height and thin. He wore an expensive, crisply pressed dark suit with a dark bow tie. He shook my hand when I greeted him, but gave me an unsmiling, penetrating look.

Not very strong, but probably plays golf.

I saw a leather couch against one wall and a large leather chair nearby.

Looks like Freud's couch and chair.

He gestured for me to sit on the chair by his desk. "How was your trip?" he asked.

"Not bad."

"How are your accommodations?"

"Clean but noisy. There was some noisy partying on my floor last night. It was hard to get to sleep."

He frowned and seemed to make a mental note to himself. Then he said, "You stated in your application that one of your outside interests is the stock market."

"Yes. I'm trying to educate myself with small investments."

"What stocks?"

"First Chrysler, then Comsat."

He gave a slight nod of approval. Still unsmiling and not looking at me, he asked in a stern voice, "What do you think the most difficult part of my job is?"

"I'm sorry, but I don't know what you do."

Damn it! I should have looked up the positions of the people on my schedule.

Damn! I sure slipped up on this one.

Yes. But just relax. Remember, they need you more than you need them.

Hall peered at me and raised his eyebrows, "I am the Director of Outpatient Services."

I tried to guess at his difficulties as director. He shook his head, then explained what they were. Then he asked, "Which staff member has impressed you the most so far?"

"I'd say Dr. Mayman."

"Why?"

"He asked me a question I couldn't answer well."

"Do you have any questions about the training program?"

"Well, there is one thing. Your program philosophy states that each fellow is free to explore and develop his clinical skills, but Dr. Lerner says he can't get permission to experiment with group therapy."

"There isn't anything wrong with the program," Hall snapped. "Dr. Lerner has some things to work out in his analysis." He scowled, clenched his jaw, and looked away once again as though making a mental note to himself.

Something is going on here.

Change the subject. Try to salvage something out of this.

"I noticed a chart in the seminar room. Something about the total hours of psychoanalysis done here?"

He looked toward me. His face brightened. "I got the idea from the airlines," he said. "They require a copilot to log a certain number of hours before he can qualify as a Captain. I believe a psychoanalyst should do over four thousand hours of supervised analysis before he solos. The chart is a record of the total number of hours done by outpatient analysts."

Good. He's finally smiling.

"There were a lot of hours there," I said. "How do you find enough people to analyze in this small city?"

"We receive applications from all over the country. We accept them into analysis only if they agree to move here and promise to stay for a number of years."

I checked my watch and saw that it was time to go to my next appointment. I stood up and thanked him for his time. We shook hands and I left.

Whew, what a cold person.

No eye contact with me. A very clinical person who looked me over intellectually, analyzing me.

Made no effort to be friendly, just asked me his diagnostic questions. I was on his schedule. No rapport.

I went outside to the taxi the receptionist had waiting for me.

10:30 a.m. Dr. Smith—Neiswanger Building, West Campus

Smith wore an old light gray suit and an old, poorly tied bow tie.

Average height and weight.

Not in good physical condition.

Smith was warm and friendly. I felt an immediate rapport with him. We chatted about my courses at Michigan. Then he asked, "What is the topic of your doctoral research?"

"Superego sex differences," I told him, hoping he wouldn't ask me to explain what the superego is.

"What is your hypothesis and how are you testing it?"

That I could handle. "My hypothesis," I said, "is that the male superego is an ego-alien, coercive force and that the female superego is an ego-syntonic, tolerant force. I'm testing this using a combination of semantic differential ratings, a metaphor check list, an authoritarian personality measure, and some of Hoffman's moral development story completion items."

"Excellent," he kept saying as I explained the details.

He was impressed. I was impressed with his quick understanding. We got along very well. Smith understood exactly what I was doing.

"Al, before you continue, explain what you mean by 'ego-syntonic,' would you?"

"It means to be in harmony with the ego. The general finding has been that women experience their conscience as a friendly voice inside themselves that gives them guidance they can trust."

"And 'ego-alien?'"

"Men tend to experience their conscience as an alien watchman that criticizes them and makes them feel guilty. A woman's conscience tends to caution her before she gets into something but enables her to feel okay with whatever she does afterwards. A man's superego tends to be less active before he gets into something that's questionable but afterwards tends to be hard on him for what he did."

11:30 a.m. Psychology Staff Meeting, Hospital

Since Dr. Smith was going to the meeting, I rode back to the hospital with him. As we pulled into the staff parking lot near the hospital, I noticed that most of the cars were old, dirty, and unpolished.

Why aren't there any new cars here? Why are their cars so cruddy?

The article—remember?

Yeah! On "phallic narcissism."

And that would explain why they wear bow ties!

Right! An ordinary tie would be a phallic symbol.

That must be it.

But they are so obvious! It draws attention to what they are trying to prove they aren't doing.

Smith and I walked downstairs to a basement conference room without windows. The psychologists quietly took their places around four tables shoved together to form a large rectangle. There were about fifteen of them. I sat with Smith and Mayman. Jim came in and sat next to us. One psychologist was a very old man.

Mayman noticed where I was looking and whispered, "That's Gardner Murphy."

Wow! It is really him.

The meeting gave Jim and me a chance to see the psychologists in a group and to get a sense of their part of the Menninger Program. Mayman introduced us to the group. The meeting was conducted efficiently and with good humor. They discussed a new research grant for a psychotherapy project. A committee reported on next year's fall program. They discussed their strategy for next summer's A.P.A. national conference. A volunteer was chosen to write a book review for the *Bulletin*. It felt good to be with them.

When the meeting was over, I watched as they quietly left the room.

Everything about the Foundation is quiet.

It sure is. The neighborhood, the buildings, the staff.

No one speaks or laughs too loudly. It's like a monastery.

As I walked into the hallway, Dr. Mayman called me over. "This is Dr. Appelbaum," he said. "He has arranged his schedule so that you can have lunch with him now in the cafeteria."

"Great," I said.

He's in better shape. Over six feet tall.

Could be a basketball player. Probably a forward.

Appelbaum had the same neat haircut, dark suit, and bow tie as the others. We went through the cafeteria line together. Knowing my lunch was free, I took an extra salad and two glasses of milk. They had the same chocolate cake out, so I took custard pudding instead.

After we sat down, Jim walked over to join us.

"Jim," I said, "Dr. Appelbaum and I want to have a talk."

Jim apologized, unnecessarily so, and left quickly. He sat down by himself a few tables away.

Appelbaum asked, "What is your interest in sensitivity training?"

"I went to Bethel, Maine, for T-Group training last summer. Then I took a practicum Ron Lippitt held in his home during the winter. I want to pursue it more."

"Why?"

"It made me realize I was beginning to make assumptions about people's feelings and actions. It is fascinating to see that when you question a person about how they feel and find out what their perceptions are, then everything makes sense to them from their point of view. Have you found that?"

"Similar to that."

"What excites me is seeing how, if you draw out the feelings and assumptions people in a group have about each other, a tremendous amount of conflict can be resolved. That's why I was very pleased to learn you are doing something with it here. I've already found that it helps me be a better teacher."

"You are quite interested in teaching, aren't you? I saw on your application that you just published a paper on teaching. What is it about?"

"The title is 'Personality Development and Classroom Techniques.' It covers how we've learned to apply principles of psychology in the way we teach at Michigan."

"Why are you more interested in teaching than private practice?"

"I figure I can accomplish more with thirty people in one hour of teaching than I can with one person in one hour of therapy."

He nodded. "It's a matter of values."

"Yes, I guess so. Please tell me how you became interested in sensitivity training and how you are connecting it to treatment."

We talked with intensity. He suddenly asked, "Don't you have an appointment at one o'clock?"

"Oh! Yes." I looked at my watch. It was two minutes to 1:00. I was so involved in our conversation I had lost track of the time.

1:00 p.m. Dr. Rosen—West Building.

I ran over to Rosen's office and arrived several minutes late. We shook hands and I sat down. I liked him as a person. I liked the way he had run the two seminars Jim and I had attended.

"What is your impression of the program?" he asked.

"I'm impressed with the depth of your seminars," I said. "I can see why the fellowship is so good."

"It's hard work. Do you know how much the fellowship pays?"

"Yes."

"Why would you want to come here for two years on the low pay it offers when you could immediately get a high paying job?"

I sat waiting for an answer to come. My mind remained silent. Finally I said, "I guess it never occurred to me to do that. I want to be as good as I can be and just naturally respond to an opportunity to make myself better."

"Why would you come here rather than stay at the University of Michigan?"

"Well, for one thing, I'm beginning to run out of people who can answer my questions."

Hey. That was a surprising answer. You've never realized that before, have you?

No. But it's true.

"How does your wife feel about coming here?"

"We've talked it over and she's for it."

"What is her education level?"

"High school."

He raised his eyebrows. "That's quite a discrepancy isn't it?"

"I know. I had some reservations at first, but I could see from her skill at crossword puzzles that she's very bright. And we came from the same kind of working class background."

"Do you have a picture of her?"

"I do," I said. I took out my wallet and showed him.

"She's lovely," he said. "You've been married how long?"

"A little over two years."

"But with no children?"

"Not yet. We've been trying, but no success so far."

"I understand you were married before. What broke up that marriage?

"It just didn't work out."

"What do you mean by that?"

"We were in the same entering class in the psychology department and got married the next spring. After about a year and a half we just couldn't make it work. I found a clinical placement in Cleveland and left school."

"Wasn't that avoiding a..."

"I don't run away from problems," I asserted firmly.

Rosen looked at me, startled. "Excuse me," he said. He was surprised at my sharp answer. He grew silent. I sat waiting for him to say something. I picked several pieces of lint off my slacks. He observed this and smiled slightly as though he had caught me doing something.

Damn it. Don't pick lint off your slacks. You know what he'll probably be putting in his report now. "Shows compulsive tendencies under pressure." Relax.

Right.

Remember. These people need you more than you need them.

He said, "You listed as outside reading the James Bond books and a book by Bob Hope. Have you read any other non-psychology books in the last year?"

"No."

"You should read classics to broaden your perspectives," he admonished.

"I know. I will eventually. But I haven't had time. I've been concentrating entirely on my graduate work. When I get a chance to read, I like it to be light and entertaining." He nodded his head. He knew what I meant.

As our interview came to an end, I noticed a small photograph of the painting I had seen over his fireplace in his home. I blurted out, "Is this a painting of you?"

His eyes popped open and his head jerked forward. He couldn't seem to believe what he had heard. "No, it's a man who pioneered psychiatric treatment. What makes you think it looks like me?"

"Oh, a resemblance in the eyes perhaps." He looked puzzled as I walked away.

Damn it. Be more careful about your questions.

Right. I should have asked, "Who is this a picture of?" Damn.

Sure. But forget it. Assume you are not going to get the fellowship.

Right.

Good. Believe it. Feel it.

Okay.

Good. Now relax and enjoy yourself.

2:00 Free Time
3:00 Dr. Mayman—East Building

I had an hour until my appointment with Mayman. I sauntered back to his building. I went upstairs to Mrs. Falley and asked where I could find a pop machine. She said it was on the landing at the back stairs. As I walked down the hallway, I glanced in an open door and saw a psychologist at his desk. I recognized him from the staff meeting the day before. He was dressed like the others. His office was plain and bare except for a five volume set of Freud's books on the end of his desk. His desk had nothing else on it. No pens, no pictures, no folders—nothing. He sat with a smile on his face looking at one of the open volumes. It was like the smile on a department store dummy.

He's weird.

I shuddered slightly.

I bought a soft drink, went downstairs, and pushed open the back door. I took off my sport coat, loosened my tie, and sat on the steps in the sun.

This is fantastic! Here I am, me, sitting at this famous place. I've met the staff, seen them at work.

You like this place.

Yup. And the interviews have gone well. They seem to like me.

Yes, I can tell. It's like going through fraternity rush at college.

You know, you could be offered the fellowship. If they do, what will you say?

God, I don't know. I came here because Giora insisted. I'm having a great time at the university. There are friends, constant learning, my sports activities.

Staying at Michigan would be comfortable, enjoyable, predictable.

But this is an incredible opportunity. Coming to Menninger's would be fantastic! The psychologists here, the ways they think excite me.

This is so unexpected. It's as if a door leading into a mysterious world has swung open for me.

What if I'm asked to step through?

I stood up and pulled on the door knob. The door had locked when it shut. I walked around the outside of the building and back inside. As I walked toward Mayman's office I saw the psychologist still sitting at his desk staring at the book by Freud.

He hasn't moved! That is spooky.

Mayman squinted at me carrying my sport coat and pushed up his glasses. "Are you feeling warm?"

"It is warm compared to our weather," I said.

"I suppose it is."

"Dr. Mayman, the only flight out this evening leaves at 5:15. Would it be okay to end my interview with Dr. Shevrin early so I can make that flight?"

"Probably. Ask him when you see him. How have your interviews gone so far?"

"I've enjoyed myself very much and want to thank you for this opportunity."

"What are some of your impressions?"

"Well, you certainly have an excellent program. The psychology instructors are outstanding. They are highly competent professionals—very thorough. I've been impressed with how friendly and interested everyone is. The fellows in the program speak highly of it. I observed them closely and they are responding well. I did run across one thing that concerns me, though."

"What's that?"

"Your statement of program philosophy says you encourage fellows to develop clinical skills, but Dr. Lerner says he can't get permission to try group therapy."

"He has some personal problems. What other reactions do you have?"

There it is again. An instructor bad-mouthing a student to an outsider.

"Just some general things. I was surprised that there wasn't a dinner or cocktail party planned for me." Smiling, I added, "When I went outside to drink a soda, I learned that the back door automatically locks."

"Are you aware of the oral theme in your remarks?" he asked.

I was startled. "No." I felt anxious for a moment.

"No, of course you wouldn't," he said, more to himself than to me. Then he asked, "Is there anything else?"

"Well, I was surprised that no one asked me about my childhood or anything."

He perked up, "Why?"

"I assumed that with the emphasis on psychoanalysis here, you would want to know all about that."

"Oh." He was silent for a moment. Then he led our conversation back to the purpose of the program and the importance of diagnostic testing skills. He talked about his own research and life in Topeka. As the hour drew to a close, he said, "We will discuss your application at the psychology staff meeting next week and I will inform you about the decision immediately."

"Thank you."

As we stood up he looked me squarely in the eye and asked, "If you are offered the fellowship, will you accept it?"

I looked him in the eye.

Choice point.

I said, "Yes."

"Good," he said and smiled.

"I'm impressed," I said, "with how quickly you handled this. It is refreshing to deal with an organization that can move so fast."

"We appreciate your promptness. We were past the deadline for applications."

We shook hands and smiled at each other.

Very good rapport.

4:00 p.m. Dr. Shevrin—Research Building, West Campus

I picked up my suitcase at the receptionist's desk, thanked her, and strode out to the taxi waiting for me. Shevrin's receptionist let me put my bag behind her desk. Then she guided me to his office.

Shevrin was about five-eleven, pale, overweight, and out of shape. He wore thick glasses, a rumpled dark blue suit, and a frayed, clip-on bow tie.

After he and I shook hands, I said, "I'm booked to catch the 5:15 flight. Would you mind if I left early?"

"I live on that side of town," he said. "We can leave about 4:30 and I'll drive you to the airport."

"Great! Thank You."

He cleared a stack of papers off the chair by his desk and I sat down.

With a hint of playfulness I asked, "What sort of research do you do here in the research building, Dr. Shevrin?"

"I'm assessing the cognitive processes of schizophrenics," he said. "In one test I show them a picture of a pen and then a picture of a knee. Then I ask them...Why do you smile?"

I laughed. "You want to see if they remember 'penny'."

"That's right!" He got excited. "Do you know that you are the first person who's understood it without an explanation?! The psychologists here..." He carried on for quite awhile about the difficulty he had getting his colleagues to understand what he was trying to do. He was more impressed with my observation than I was, however.

"Why was that, Al?"

"Because he *said* the words to me instead of showing me the pictures. It was easy to connect the sounds, Sam. Besides, many of the graduate students at Michigan were experienced with Sarnoff Mednick's test of creativity."

"What is that?"

"Mednick's Remote Associations Test gives you three words and you have to come up with another word that connects with all of them. For example, if I say 'wall,' 'precious,' and 'key,' what one word would go with all of them?"

"Stone?"

"Right. 'stone wall,' 'precious stone' and 'keystone.' We graduate students made dozens of such combinations to try to stump each other."

"That enabled you to pick up on Shevrin's test right off."

"I believe so. In any case, we both appreciated the value of a creative approach to research."

At 4:30 we left his office to drive to the airport. Shevrin's car was easy to spot in the parking lot. It was old and dirty, with heavily oxidized dark blue paint.

As we drove along Shevrin asked, "Have you considered going through psychoanalysis?"

"Not really. But they say people going into clinical psychology and psychiatry should, so I probably will."

He said abruptly, "Tell me about your childhood."

Hmmm. Mayman must have...

I'll play with him.

"Do you know you are the first person who's asked me about my childhood?" I said. "Everybody else stayed strictly to statements I made in my application. No one so far has asked. I was surprised. I expected that at a place with such a strong interest in psychoanalysis..."

"All right, all right," he said curtly, "Tell me about your childhood."

I told him a few facts. He listened as he drove but didn't seem interested. He was fulfilling his assignment. The trip to the airport was short, so I had time enough only to briefly describe my childhood.

He stopped in front of the entrance and got out of the car. As I leaned over to get my bag out of the back seat, some papers and my airplane tickets fell out of my coat pocket and started blowing around the parking lot. He helped me chase them down, but he didn't like it.

Siebert, that was a clumsy finish.

It sure was.

Chapter Four

Debriefing

"Al, what did you make of the experience on the flight home?"

"I felt quietly excited, Sam. I realized the fellowship offer could happen. I allowed the impact to seep into me. I felt 'Wow!' Then I started thinking ahead to the volleyball game and how close I'd timed getting back."

"Speaking of sports, just about every time you mention someone, you talk about their athletic fitness. Why do you do that? This intrigues me."

"It's a habit I developed in the paratroopers and continued in college and graduate school. In the paratroopers, when you're going on a jump and must make a 20 mile forced march carrying all your gear, you learn to size everybody up. You learn to quickly assess who can make it. You've got to. Your survival may depend upon being able to know at a glance who will keep up and who will fold."

"That would be true in many emergency situations," Sam said.

"Yes. It becomes a habit to size people up that way."

"And whether they'd be good at basketball or softball?"

"Right. Part of my payback to McKeachie was to organize the psychology department's intramural sports teams. I was always on the lookout for players. I was committed to having us win the all-school championship. I didn't want to load the teams with just anybody. I was always looking for grad students with good athletic skills."

"Did you make it back on time?"

"I did."

Kathleen stood at the arrival gate with a slight flush in her cheeks. She wore black high heel shoes, a black Cashmere sweater, black wool skirt, and the string of pearls I'd given her as a wedding present. I kissed her and gave her a strong, one-armed hug as we headed toward the exit gate.

She put her arm around my waist and matched my stride. "How did the interviews go?"

"Better than I expected. I'm afraid they may offer the fellowship to me!" I stretched my lower jaw like a child displaying mock horror.

"Don't you want it?"

"I'll accept it if they offer it, but the whole idea is so fantastic. You know how I've felt like a misfit in the clinical program."

"Did you like the people you met? What were they like?"

"I'd rather tell you later. I want to think things through first."

Kathleen tightened her lips.

Damn it, talk to her more. She needs to know.

"I'll tell you about Topeka and the Foundation in the car. Did you bring my athletic bag?"

"Yes, like you said. It's in the back seat."

"That's good. Please drive," I said, "so I can change into my gym clothes on the way."

"I washed them for you," she said "They were smelly."

"Thanks. I hope my old sweat shirt lasts until the end of the season." My faded, yellow Michigan sweatshirt with the arms cut off at the elbows was my trademark. I wore it to every game in every sport.

We arrived at the Field House about ten minutes before game time. It's a huge place. There were about eight volleyball courts set up for this evening.

Dick Schmuck yelled, "Al, we're happy to see you! I hoped you'd get back in time. How was the interview?"

"It went really well."

"Do you think you'll get it?"

"It could happen. We'll have to wait and see."

I stretched, jogged around the courts, and hit some warm up shots. John Lohman, Dick Pew and I were the spikers. Dick Schmuck and the others were setters. We'd been together for three years. Pew stood about 6' 4'' and was left handed. He hit devastating spikes from the right front corner. We won the match.

Kathleen drove in the back way through the apartment complex and parked in our usual space. As we walked up the sidewalk to our apartment I sensed extra excitement in her.

She's up to something.

She unlocked the door but instead of walking in stood aside for me to enter first.

I peered in.

When I looked at the kitchen table I saw a chocolate cake oozing with dark frosting. "All right! My favorite cake!" I gave her a warm kiss. The cake was delicious. I ate a fourth of it with a large glass of milk. Then we went to bed.

At 7:25 a.m. the next morning I walked into the small conference room at NPI to attend the morning staff meeting of the adult inpatient service.

I nodded and smiled at Lois Jackson, one of the social workers, and sat next to her. She was about 38 years old, average height, heavy set. Well suited for her work.

It's nice to work with someone who doesn't need words when I greet them.

Lois introduced me to a black haired young woman sitting on her other side. "Al, this is Noreen. She's a high school student visiting here for career day. She's interested in a social work career."

Noreen smiled at me.

Good eyes.

"How was Menninger's?" Lois asked.

"The interviews went well."

"Do you think you'll get the fellowship?"

"It might happen," I said, widening my eyes.

"I'll keep my fingers crossed for you," she said, crossing two fingers.

"Thanks."

About 20 people drifted in with cups of coffee or tea. They sat down with the usual yawns, groans, and "morning talk" at three large tables shoved together to form a "T." The three senior psychiatrists sat at the top. The head nurses from each of our two wards sat at the end of the head table. The rest us—psychologists, social workers, the psychiatric residents, and occupational and recreational therapists—sat along the other tables or on chairs along the walls.

Laura Stevens, the head nurse on the locked ward, gave her report first. Her ward on the sixth floor held newly admitted and more disturbed patients. The open ward on the fourth floor held the less disturbed, more responsible patients.

The psychiatrists all respected Laura. Every organization has one or two people you hope will take charge if a serious problem comes up. Laura was that kind of person. Her professional competence, perceptiveness, friendly eyes, quick wit, and playful sense of humor made her well liked and very effective with patients, their families, aides, other nurses, the ward doctors, other staff, and the administrators.

Her warm spirit set the tone for her staff. Her ward was more pleasant than one expects a locked psychiatric ward to be. A slender, attractive, divorced, 27 year old blonde woman, she handled the psychiatric residents the way first sergeants handle new second lieutenants.

"We have 15 patients on the men's side" Laura said, "and 14 on the women's. We had one A.M.A. discharge yesterday."

Noreen leaned toward Mrs. Jackson. "What is A-M-A.?" she whispered.

"It means Against Medical Advice," Lois whispered back. "It's a form patients have to sign when they leave the hospital against a doctor's advice."

The resident on duty the previous night told us about two new admissions. The open ward nurse, gave her report next. She was new but seemed capable. "Charles Shaw," she said, "eloped during the evening. We contacted his family. We have 12 patients on the woman's side and 15 on the men's."

"The patient who eloped," Noreen whispered. "He ran away to get married?"

"No," Lois whispered. "He escaped. Psychiatrists don't like to say that a patient escaped from treatment, so they call it eloping."

Dr. Bostian, the senior closed-ward psychiatrist, asked Dr. Frank Moran, a second-year psychiatric resident, about progress with a patient.

"He's a schizophrenic," Frank said. "After two weeks, he's still unresponsive and withdrawn. I can't get him to verbalize."

Bostian asked Laura, "How do you respond to this patient?"

"I don't feel much warmth for him," she said. "I've watched the aides and nurses. They walk by him like he's a piece of furniture. They've stopped trying with him. We've knocked, but there's no one home."

Bostian glanced around the room. "Has anyone felt any emotional contact with this patient?"

No one replied.

"That's a bad sign when a patient draws little warmth or response from the nurses and other staff." Turning to Frank, he said, "Start the paperwork to commit him to Ypsilanti State Hospital. He needs long-term care. This is a teaching facility. We can't keep anyone here who isn't a good teaching case."

When we finished at 8:00. Dr. Holmes, the senior open ward psychiatrist announced, "The admissions conference on Maureen Taylor scheduled for next Monday will be postponed until Thursday."

"Al," Lois said, "I have to make an emergency phone call. Will you please take Noreen up to the social work office?"

"Glad to."

I took Noreen out into the hallway and waited for the elevator to come back down. "Noreen, do you have any questions?"

She wrinkled her nose. "What is an admissions conference? Is that like confessions?"

"No. The admissions conference is a staff meeting held after a patient has been here three or four weeks. We tell each other what we've learned about the patient and turn in our written reports. Then the resident in charge of the patient develops a therapy plan."

"A resident is a doctor who lives here in the hospital?"

"No, a psychiatric resident is a medical doctor taking advanced training to be a psychiatrist. They don't live here. They work here. It is called a residency program."

"You are a psychiatrist?"

"No. I'm a clinical psychologist."

"What is the difference?"

"Psychiatrists have an M.D. They went to medical school to become doctors. Then they worked in psychiatric facilities as psychiatric residents to learn how to treat mental disorders. Clinical psychologists have a Ph.D. They went through a graduate program in psychology at a university and wrote a doctoral dissertation. A person with a Ph.D. is also called a doctor, but their training emphasizes research and diagnostic testing."

"You are Doctor Siebert?"

The elevator door opened.

"Not yet. I'll complete my Ph.D. program at the university in a few months. I'm an 'almost doctor.'"

Noreen giggled.

"You can tell each person's status from their clothing," I said, guiding her into the elevator ahead of me. "People with M.D.s and Ph.D.s wear long white coats with their names and degrees above the left breast pocket. Because I have a Master's degree, my coat says 'psychologist' here above the pocket. Social workers like Mrs. Jackson, medical students, laboratory technicians, occupational therapists and others wear short coats."

"I'll pay attention to the coats."

"Noreen, I'm curious. How did you become interested in social work?"

She told me about a social worker in her neighborhood as we rode up to the fifth floor. I took her down the hall and left her at the social work office. Then I returned to the main office to get my mail. I had one assignment for psychological testing, the daily hospital bulletin, and file copies of two of my testing reports. As I turned I bumped into Laura reaching past me to get her mail.

Nice perfume.

"I want to hear all about Menninger's," she said. "Did you enjoy your trip?"

"I did, immensely. They asked good questions, they have quick minds."

"How close are you to getting your degree?"

"I'll submit my request for subjects and start testing soon."

"Where do you get subjects?"

"From the psychology department. About 2000 students take intro psych each year. They're required to serve as research subjects for up to four hours."

"That is a lot of bodies," she said, with twinkling eyes. "Can you do *anything* you want with them?"

"Not *anything*. There's a research approval committee."

"Too bad! It sounded like it had possibilities."

I turned to walk away.

She touched my arm to stop me. "Al, I have a request of you."

I felt a surge of adrenaline.

"What is it?"

"I arrange an in-service session for my nursing staff every month. Will you meet with us some evening to explain psychological testing?"

"Sure, glad to."

Laura went up the stairway to her floor, and I got into the elevator.

I called Giora's office to make sure he was free and then walked over to give him my report.

"How did the interviews go?" he asked.

"Quite well," I said. "I was very impressed with the people I talked to. Seeing them in action gave me a lot to think about." I gave him a rundown on the two days so he would know what to tell future applicants to expect. Then I said, "One thing puzzles me, though."

"What's that?"

"They were tense. I expected them to be the most relaxed, self-confident, well-adjusted people in the world. They aren't. It's a subtle thing, but they're tense."

Giora laughed. I didn't ask him why, but I sensed that some useful information had registered with me.

At noon I took my sack lunch and went over to see Jim McConnell at his office in the Mental Health Research Institute just across the street from the university hospital.

"Well, well. No athletic events this noon?" he asked when I walked through his door.

"No, that was last year. Who's the lunch speaker today?"

"Our noble director, the eminent James G. Miller, will review the institute's research on system input overload. He is starting to work on a book on living systems."

"Great. I'd like to read the manuscript when it is ready."

"That can be arranged. Did you enjoy your trip to the capitol?"

"Very much. It was exciting to see the place. All the famous people, the way they work. They put an excellent schedule together for me."

"Do you think you'll get the fellowship?"

"It's possible."

"When will you know?"

"Next week. They'll make their final choices Thursday."

Jim tilted back in his chair and opened the door to a small refrigerator behind him. He took out a can of Coke for himself and handed one to me. He kept a large supply on hand. He took one with him when he lectured and when he drove home. We left his office and walked toward the room with vending machines. "How's the term looking?" he said.

"I'm working my butt off!"

He looked at my backside. "You don't have much to lose."

"I'll rephrase that. The personality course is more work than I expected."

He fed some coins into a machine and pulled a knob to get a cheese sandwich. "I assume you've come up with a creative teaching twist."

"I have, actually. I told the students that less is known about mental health than about physical health. Their term paper is to describe a psychologically healthy person."

"A challenging subject, indeed."

We walked down the hall toward the conference room.

"I'll be emphasizing," I said, "that mentally healthy people are receptive to new ideas. I've been amazed by the scientific community's irrational rejection of your memory transfer research findings."

"Experts don't like to have their cherished beliefs upset." He grinned. "But such is the lot of genius."

I laughed.

"How is NPI these days?" he asked.

"We had a funny incident," I said.

"And that was?"

"A student nurse assigned to our unit asked the head nurse how she could get inoculated against catching mental illnesses."

"Ha!"

"People are laughing at her and kidding her."

"Is she embarrassed?"

"She's taking it okay. She says she heard a public service announcement from the American Psychiatric Association stating that mental illnesses are diseases like any others."

"So psychiatrists claim."

"I know, but think about it. Have you ever heard of a case of a mental health worker catching a mental illness from a patient?"

"No, I haven't. There's 'folie a deux,' of course, where a sane person takes on the delusional thinking of a delusional person, but that's not an illness. I heard a panel discussion at an A.P.A. conference about cult members taking on the delusions of their leader, but that doesn't mean they have become psychotic."

"Right. So the question is, why say mental illnesses are diseases if they don't act like diseases?"

We sat in chairs lined up along the wall. Jim grinned. "That sounds like a question worth pursuing," he said. "Let me know what you find."

Typical James V. Always prodding students to ask questions and search for answers.

"Al, am I right in remembering that it was McConnell who conducted some unusual experiments concerning memory transfer..."

"Yes, Sam, in a primitive worm called planaria..."

"And didn't McConnell have trouble getting his research published?"

"Yes, in the 1960s and 1970s biological psychologists and others could not accept that learned behaviors can be recorded in a creature's chromosomes. Using planaria, however,

McConnell and his former graduate students proved over and over that memory can be genetically transferred."

"They proved that the genetic blueprint in chromosomes is not fixed for life."

"Yes they did, but McConnell couldn't get his research findings published in professional journals."

"Were his experiments well designed? Did he follow accepted experimental procedures?"

"Yes, he did. His solution was to start his own journal. At first he called it the *Worm Runner's Digest*, but librarians wouldn't order it, so he turned it over and named the back side *The Journal of Biological Psychology*."

"It must have been very frustrating for him."

"Somewhat, but he had a great sense of humor. He was more amused by the reactions to his work than upset. What bothered him the most were letters from high school students saying they had replicated his experiments and gotten the same results, but had received poor grades because the science project judges knew it was impossible for memory to be genetically recorded and transferred "

I walked over to my office at the psychology department. The 22 psychology teaching fellows were assigned three or four to an office. As TFs with most seniority, John Robinson and I took the office closest to the elevators and coffee lounge. Each TF had an indestructible dark gray metal desk, a gray metal bookcase, a gray chair with arms, and one gray chair without arms next to the desk. Each office had one large brown metal wastebasket.

The walls were probably cream colored. They hadn't been painted in recent years. We each added posters, signs, and various items to our desk areas. John and I lined up our intramural trophies on the top shelves of our bookcases. The other TFs in our office put up colorful posters.

John looked up when I walked in. "Agile Al!" he said. "How did the Menninger trip go?"

"It was exciting to see a big league operation."

"What were the psychologists like?"

"Quiet, neat—they all wear bow ties—well organized, thorough."

"So what do you think? Will you win the fellowship?"

"I might. Fate gave me a boost."

"In what way?"

"You know how we teach that perception is a function of contrasts."

"Yeh."

"Another candidate shows up on the same day who made me look real good. He's a nice guy, don't get me wrong, but definitely third string."

"What is it like to be interviewed?"

"It was fun. I had appointments with faculty members, went to seminars, attended a psychology staff meeting, saw most of the Menninger facilities, their library. One thing I learned, be sure to find out as much as you can about the individuals on your interview schedule. I almost dropped the ball in an interview with an important psychiatrist." I opened my desk drawer and lifted out several tattered folders. "But that's over now. It's time to move ahead with my dissertation research."

"Have you started testing your subjects yet?" he asked.

"No. I'll do the final version of my testing instrument this weekend. It will be several weeks before I start."

John looked at his watch and stood up to leave. "Time for class," he said, picking up his brief case.

I held up my hand to stop him for a moment. "Can you bowl next Tuesday evening? I'm one player short."

"What time?"

"The match starts at 5:00. Ann Arbor Lanes, like before."

He nodded. "I'll be there."

"Good."

As John walked across the hall to the elevators I yelled, "And our first softball practice is Thursday at five."

He waved.

Monday afternoon I took my research testing form to the head secretary at the psychology department office. I asked her to duplicate about 220 copies...

"Before you go on, Al, how did you get interested in superego sex differences anyway? What was interesting to you about that topic?"

"Do you want the truth?"

"Of course!"

"This is off the record, you understand."

"Certainly."

"I selected my topic after carefully thinking about the situation. I knew I didn't want to wind up like Marty Gold, a graduate student at Michigan who had been working on his dissertation for over five years. I made a list of four criteria for my dissertation. I wanted a topic that could be researched quickly, could use psychology students in the subject pool, could have the data collected using a paper and pencil test given to research subjects in groups, and could have the testing results processed through the university's big IBM main frame computer."

"You didn't start with a topic that interested you?"

"Not at all, Sam. After listing my four criteria, I played with a number of possibilities that were legitimate for the clinical area. Superego sex differences turned out to fit the criteria best. I could conduct my research using 100 male and 100 female students from the subject pool."

"A very practical approach to getting a doctorate!"

"I thought so."

"You had two hundred subjects. How did you contact them?"

"The psych department secretaries mailed postcards notifying them of the dates and times they were to participate. I had already reserved empty classrooms at various times to give the students a choice of times."

Kathleen asked if we could go visit her folks on the upcoming weekend. When I agreed she became excited. Moving to Ann Arbor was the first time she'd ever been away from her family. She missed her parents and the families of her brothers and sister.

Kathleen agreed to drive so I could read during the trip to her parents' home. I worked hard to make certain the students in my personality theory class received as good a course as the students in the other class. I finished reading the materials I'd brought and stared out the window.

"What are you reading?" she asked.

"It's a booklet by Melanie Klein, a psychoanalyst. I'm covering psychoanalytic personality theory with my class. Klein's view of how our adult thinking is rooted in our experiences as infants is fascinating."

I opened the booklet and read. "She says a mother 'represents to the child the whole of the external world; therefore good and bad come in his mind from her, and this leads to a twofold attitude toward the mother under the best possible conditions.'"

Kathleen gave me a blank look.

"Klein says that an infant cannot understand that his mother is both the good person and the bad person he experiences at different times. His brain deals with this by experiencing his mother as two different people, one good and one bad."

Kathleen wrinkled her nose.

Her 'that idea stinks' indicator.

I read from the booklet again. "Klein says, 'the young infant's self-preservation depends on his trust in a good mother. By splitting the two aspects and clinging to the good one he preserves his belief in a good object and his capacity to love it; and this is an essential condition for keeping alive.' The infant experiences the bad person as someone else."

"Psychoanalysts believe that babies think their mothers are objects?"

"When analysts talk about 'object relations' they're just using abstract concepts. What fascinates me is that Klein is describing an infant's personality theory. Its theory is that there are good people and bad people in the world. The infant's perception is controlled by his emotional reaction to his mother, but he doesn't know that."

Kathleen scowled. "Babies can't talk. How can they have theories," she said, not really asking.

"It's an emotionally controlled perception. The implications are stunning. If she is right, and I think she is, the belief that a person is either good or bad is an infant's personality theory."

"It is not. There *are* good people and bad people. Are you saying Hitler was not a bad man?"

"No. It's just that I'm trying to learn how childhood experiences influence our thoughts and actions as adults. I'll have to do that at Menningers."

Tell her about work, she likes that.

"Let me tell you about an interesting case I tested at the hospital yesterday," I said. "He is a 58 year old man, unemployed, and never married. He was transferred to our service from the intensive care unit. Early one morning last week he swallowed poison while sitting on a bench in front of the main entrance to the hospital."

Kathleen made face. "That's awful. Why did he do that?"

"A note in his pocket explained that he wanted to donate his body to the medical school. His plans were thwarted, however, because his effort to make it convenient for the school to obtain his body put him close to excellent emergency room treatment.

"Will he be all right?"

"Physically, yes. He told me he lived at home with his mother. When I inquired about his feelings he told me he used a machine in his basement to find out what he feels."

"Can a machine do that?"

"Yes, it's the basis for lie detectors. He holds two metal tabs, asks himself a question, and watches the dial. He told me he decided to end his life because, after careful analysis, he saw that he was taking up space on the planet without doing anything to justify his existence."

Kathleen made a face. "How awful."

"The testing took almost three hours. He was bright and talkative. He got an IQ score of 142. In fact, I learned something from him. Do you know what a spot on a playing card is called?"

"It's a pip."

"That's right! I didn't know that."

"It's the name for the spot on cards, dominoes, and dice," she said. "I don't understand why a man would want to kill himself for the reason you said."

"His condition is called 'intellectualization.' Emotions don't influence his thinking. He operates entirely on logic and reason."

"Is that a mental illness?"

"He'll be diagnosed as having a schizoid personality disorder even though intellectualization is a better term."

"Can he be helped?"

"Not easily. The problem with people like him is that their minds sidestep efforts to get them into emotional contact with the consequences of their actions."

Rows of daffodils provided a colorful greeting as we drove up the Ryans' gravel driveway to the rear of the house. The Ryan home had been built in a rural area on a half-acre lot decades before. Now, surrounded by apartments and newer homes on smaller lots, the land was more valuable than the old, white, one-story wood frame home sitting on it.

Mrs. Ryan was out the back door, wiping her hands on her apron before the car stopped. She called out a cheery "Hello" to us. She and Kathleen would talk with few pauses from this moment until we left Sunday afternoon.

It was a relaxing weekend. I watched baseball games on television with Mr. Ryan. Went for walk Sunday morning while they were at church. Played with Kathleen's nieces when the entire family gathered for Sunday dinner.

During the drive home Kathleen said, "I don't understand why I'm not getting pregnant. Would it be all right if I see a doctor to find out why?"

"Sure. Do you want to go to the university hospital?"

"No. I want to see a private doctor."

"Fine," I said, stroking her leg.

In mid-April, two weeks after my Menninger trip, I was working in my office when the phone rang. "Long distance, Al, line three."

"Thanks, Katy."

"Hello, Al. This is Marty Mayman. I'm sorry I wasn't able to call you last Thursday. We had to postpone our discussion of your application until this morning."

"That's okay. I figured something came up."

"Yes, several more important matters. But we did make our selections today. That's why I'm calling you now. The Director of Education asked me to inform you that the admissions committee acted favorably on your application."

"Son-of-a-gun!"

"You'll get a letter in a few days confirming the awarding of the fellowship. Plan on being here in time to start the program the first week in September."

"Okay."

"You understand that you must have your degree before you come, don't you?"

"Yes."

"Don't slow down or let anything keep you from getting it before September."

"I won't."

"Good." Mayman paused and then asked, "By the way, you didn't believe you were going to get the fellowship, did you?"

"No."

"That's what I thought. Please accept my personal congratulations and I'll see you in September. Good-bye."

"Thank you. Good-bye."

Fantastic! A post-doctoral fellowship to the Menninger Foundation. Me!

I picked up the phone and dialed home.

Fantastic. The Menninger Foundation.

"Hey, Kathleen, guess what!"

Chapter Five

Transitions

"Mayman's call came in the middle of your last semester at Michigan."

"Right, Sam. In mid-April."

"What did you do then?"

"I told Giora right away. He was very pleased. I would be the first person from the Michigan doctoral program in clinical psychology to go to Menningers. I telephoned my mother! I told her about the Fellowship. She was very happy for me. She felt very proud. We decided she should come to visit us early in the summer."

During my next supervision meeting with Giora I said, "I'd like to talk with you about my remaining time here. I expect to finish my dissertation and have my doctorate by June. Would it be all right for me to switch to full-time status during the summer until I leave at the end of August?"

He swiveled around to look out the window for several moments. Then he looked back at me and said, "Certainly. Two of the psychology interns will be gone during the summer. There will be plenty to do. You understand I'll have to get approval from Dr. Bostian and Dr. Waggoner."

"Dave will agree."

"You and Bostian get along especially well, don't you. You are on a first name basis with him. That is very unusual. How did that develop?"

"Before you came here I became curious about what was done with my reports of psychological testing. Bostian was the senior psychiatrist supervising most of the cases I tested, so I made an appointment to see him. You know it is common for the psychiatric residents and interns and psychology interns to go into psychotherapy with the senior psychiatrists..."

Giora nodded.

"When I walked in to Bostian's office, I saw he was halfway expecting me to ask if I could do therapy with him. But I

surprised him. I said, 'Many times you are the senior psychiatrist for patients I've tested. I would like to know what I could
put in my reports that would be useful to you.'"

Giora laughed.

"Bostian's eyes popped open, his jaw dropped, and he
rocked back in his swivel chair. 'My God!' he said loudly. 'I
don't believe it. I gave up on you psychologists long ago. And
now you walk in and ask what you can do to make your
reports useful to me. I don't believe it. I decided a long time
ago that you psychologists were off in your own little world,
not caring what the rest of us did with your reports. I skim
through them, but I usually don't find much I can do anything
with. I know you probably think they're important, but they're
not of much value to us.' He leaned forward and stared at me
intently. 'This is the first time this has ever happened in all the
years I've been in psychiatry. I can't believe it. A psychologist
has come to me and asked what he could put in his reports
that I'd find useful. It's astounding.' Then he rocked back in
his chair again and sat shaking his head in disbelief."

"You're right," Giora said. "I have to admit I've never done
that. How did you feel about his reaction?"

"I just sat there smiling. My attitude was that if I was a
competent professional person, I could adapt my work to the
needs of the people using it. I asked him again what I could
include in my report that would be useful.

"Bostian said, 'Al, I'm very interested in knowing the
patient's ego strengths. I want to know what we've got there to
work with. How much tolerance for self-reflection, capacity
for handling stress, and dealing with other people. Can you
provide me that kind of information?'

"I told him I could.

"He said, 'Thank you, Al. Maybe there's hope for you psychologists yet.'

"From then on he and I were 'Dave' and 'Al.' I had unexpectedly found a friend in high places."

Giora shook his head and chuckled. "You're an unusual
person, Al. You've got a very bright future ahead of you."

"Thanks. I hope so." I stood up to leave.

"By the way, Al, the report of psychological testing that you gave at the admissions conference on Thorson was very well done."

"Thank you. But you know what bothers me? Why is the patient never present at such an important conference? And why are patients never allowed to read the reports about them in their files? What if they disagree about something or want to correct a misunderstanding?"

"It's for the good of the patients. Attending the admissions conference would be highly distressing for them. Patients would be very upset hearing about their psychopathology or reading about it in their files. They are already emotionally disturbed. It is for their protection that they not be subjected to even more stressors."

"Oh."

I devoted myself to getting my dissertation research done. I felt more motivated than ever. I pushed ahead quickly.

"How long did the testing take, Al?"

"The test itself took from 25 minutes to an hour, Sam. Most of the subjects showed up at their assigned times. I scheduled makeup sessions for those who missed. I finished testing all 200 research subjects by the end of April. The last student couldn't get to any of scheduled times, so I went to his apartment on a Saturday morning. Then I went to work key punching the raw data from each test form onto computer cards."

"The old IBM punch cards?"

"State of the art back then. For the dissertation topic I'd chosen, I had selected my committee well. One of my committee members, James Lingoes, had written a computer program for factor analyzing my data. Doctoral students had free access to the university's computer for a certain number of hours. The key punching took me about a week. I got the computer printout of the factor analysis in mid-May. When I examined the numbers I felt relieved to see that the data validated my hypotheses. I met with Elizabeth Douvan, the head of my dissertation committee, to show her the results. We got along well. She was a slender, pleasant woman with graying light brown hair. She had been pleased to be my dissertation chairman because my topic was close to her area of interest. She had made valuable suggestions about ways to develop my research instrument. At the end of our meeting she gave me the go ahead to start writing up the research findings.

"Spring seemed especially nice that year. Walking to classes or back to the hospital, I enjoyed the fresh air. The morning sunshine felt very good after months of snow and ice. Colorful flowers sprung up everywhere. At school and at the hospital people were more friendly to me than before."

"Because of your Menninger fellowship?"

"I assumed so. It was a noticeable difference. People were friendly to me like they had been my first two years."

"What do you mean, Al?"

"When I started grad school we were all friendly, the faculty and students. But after I came back from Cleveland, when I passed different profs and grad students in the hall or got into the elevator with them, they were less friendly than before. Now, suddenly, they were friendly again. It wasn't a big deal."

Late in May I had my write up of my dissertation pretty well completed so I went ahead with the evening in-service meeting Laura had asked me to do for the nurses on her ward. I arrived early and took extra chairs from the conference room down to my office. Just as I finished arranging them I heard the nurses talking and laughing as they got off the elevator. At work Laura always wore her uniform. This evening she wore a short, tight, blue denim dress accented with a gold necklace and a gold bracelet. "Thank you for agreeing to meet with us," she said, touching my arm. "We've been looking forward to this evening."

She looks great.

No bra?

Doesn't look like it.

"What would you like to know about psychological testing?" I said to the group. There were five of them, counting Laura. "What questions do you have?"

Nancy asked, "Does mental illness affect a person's IQ.?"

"Not much. Only to the extent that a depressed person will get lower scores on items requiring physical performance."

"Is that why," Laura said, "you always report a verbal IQ and a performance IQ?"

"Yes, a discrepancy between them is useful information."

"What about a social skills IQ?" Laura teased, "or do psychologists only test abilities they're good at?"

Several nurses snickered.

"Good question," I said. I opened up my IQ testing kit. "These little boxes contain tests we use."

They leaned forward as I showed them how each test is administered and scored.

"What good is a performance IQ score?" one of them asked.

"It's an indicator," I said, fumbling with the little boxes trying to get them back into the kit, "of a person's eye-hand coordination."

Laura suppressed a laugh and turned her head.

"Can the ink blot test measure IQ?" Nancy asked.

"No, it's a projective test. By finding out how a person perceives the world we get information about his or her personality."

"How do you know?"

"A young Swiss psychiatrist, Hermann Rorschach, was fascinated by a party game where people would tell each other what an ink blot on a piece of paper looked like. He reasoned that when a person gives meaning to an ink blot, we get information about the person's personality. You can think of it as like a mental X-ray. "

"Can we look at them?"

"I'm not allowed to show them all to you, but I'll show you the first one." I opened up the packet. "These are replications of the ten ink blots that Rorschach made. What does this look like to each of you?"

"A bat!"

"I see a dead leaf."

"No, it's a butterfly!"

"It looks dead to me. A dead moth in a display case."

"Oh! Yes, I can see your moth. Can you see the bat?"

As they talked Laura looked at me, smiled, and crossed her legs.

Great legs. No stockings. She must hike, bike, work out. Lean, athletic, intelligent, playful, capable.

Remember why you are here.

"You see? Each of you is looking at the same splotch of ink and yet you each have different perceptions of it."

"But it does look like a moth!"

"To you," I said. "Have you heard the joke about the man who saw sexual organs in all the ink blots? When the psychologist said to him, 'The test indicates that you think about sex a lot,' the man said, 'what do you expect when you show me all these dirty pictures?'"

They laughed. "What's the right answer?"

"There is no right answer. It is just information about a person's way of perceiving the world. The big challenge for psychologists is to deal with our subjectivity in interpreting test results."

"What do you mean?"

"We always have to take into account that our perceptions of the people we test can be biased. Our minds, theories, assumptions, cultural upbringing, and so forth influence our perception of the people we test."

"Like an ink blot?" Laura said.

"Exactly. In fact, if you want to have some fun, skim through the test reports or diagnostic summaries written by a psychologist or psychiatric resident you know. You'll find them describing certain personality defects over and over. Once you find a favorite diagnosis, ask yourself how much the psychologist or psychiatrist seems to be talking about himself or herself. In other words, projective testing is a projective test. Sometimes the reports reveal more about the psychiatrist or psychologist than about the patient."

Laura nodded. "I've suspected that." She uncrossed her legs and sat up. "We must stop soon. Nancy and Kim have to return to duty."

"Keep in mind," I said, "that psychological tests are like any tool. Their value comes from the skill of the person using them."

Laura looked into my eyes and smiled. Then she stood up. "Thank you for meeting with us this evening."

The nurses thanked me and left my office talking and laughing. I followed Laura to the door. She paused to smile at me again. I put my hand on her back. I felt a strong charge of energy when I touched her. She felt it too. "Oooh!" She said, pursing her lips. She looked at me. "Thank you again."

She's so beautiful.

"And tomorrow I have some reading to do," she said.

"What kind?"

"I'm going to read your psychological reports about the patients on my ward!"

I laughed out loud and said, "I love it!"

When I got home Kathleen said, "Nate Caplan called. He is here in Ann Arbor for a few days looking for a home to buy. They'll be moving here in July."

"Great! He got the job at the Social Research Institute?"

"Yes. We had a nice talk. I invited him for dinner Friday. I knew you wouldn't have any games then. It will be nice to see him again."

"It will. We have the greatest laughs together. I still think it was funny when he came here for a visit after we were married and I thanked him for giving us a bud vase that came with water in the bottom."

Kathleen blushed. "You aren't supposed to say anything if a person does that."

"He thought it was funny, too. We all knew he took it from his house before he left for the airport so he'd have a wedding present for us."

"You embarrass me."

"Sorry."

"How is the house hunting going?" I asked Caplan as he sat down at my desk with his bottle of beer. I sat on the couch while Kathleen prepared dinner.

He's putting on weight. He's pale, out of shape.

"I've narrowed it down to two," he said. "This is the best time of year to buy a home in a university town."

"What are they like?" Kathleen asked from the kitchen.

"You know we need a four bedroom home with a basement and a den, and it has to be near a school. The nicest one is about fifteen thousand more than the other, and they won't be moving until July. The one with the best location is available now, but it needs painting and the basement needs finishing."

"That can be expensive," Kathleen said.

"If you contract the work out. Did you know my father was a building contractor?"

"No," she said.

"I worked for him summers. I could do the work myself." As Caplan took a drink from his beer bottle, he tilted back and looked around the room. He smiled when he saw the bud vase he gave us. He looked at a straw basket filled with artificial flowers sitting next to the vase. "That is a colorful arrangement of autumn colors." He peered at the flowers. "What are these made of?"

"They seem to be wood shavings," I said.

"A friend of Al's gave it to us as a wedding present," Kathleen said, "when he came to visit us last year."

"We were in the same sensitivity training group at Bethel, Maine," I said. His name is Larry MacDonald. He's an undergraduate at the University of Illinois. He has our kind of humor."

Caplan shook his head. "The world can't handle too many of us," he said.

"It'll have to," I said. "Tell me how your Chicago research turned out."

"You know we were studying ways for outreach workers to influence juvenile gangs. We were looking for a method to change the reference group norms of teenagers with dyssocial personalities."

I nodded.

Caplan saw a box of crayons at the side of my desk. He opened it, poured the crayons out, and took a piece of typing paper from the stack.

"A worker would go hang around a neighborhood," he said. "He would gradually make friends with gang members. Once his influence was established, the aim was to get the gang to stop stealing, robbing, mugging, using drugs and such while getting them to be more interested in school, sports, and jobs."

Caplan started drawing while he talked.

"At first the results seemed disappointing. In every gang there seemed to be one youngster who would gravitate to the street worker. This kid would have all kinds of problems and get the worker very involved. So much so that up to 60% or 70% of the worker's time and effort would go into this one kid."

Caplan drew rapidly.

"The gang would benefit from getting an empty store for a club place, tickets to ball games, and free meals without the gang leaders being hassled by the worker. But when we looked at the actions of the gang members, we discovered a beneficial effect. We saw that the one kid was like a "bait animal" hunters in Africa use to lure lions into a trap. The kid draining the time and energy of the worker was not showing much change, but the kids standing around listening were showing improvement."

Caplan sorted through the crayons, found the one he wanted, and continued making rapid strokes.

"The research team discussed this unexpected development. We created a technique we called 'loud talk.' It was our version of what happens in prisons. When a prisoner wants the guards to know something but doesn't want to be known as a squealer, he'll talk loudly to another prisoner within earshot of a nearby guard."

Kathleen set dishes of steaming food on the table and wiped her hands on her apron. "Dinner is ready," she said.

"We trained our street workers to talk to the 'bait animal' in a way so that the other gang members could overhear." He grinned. "This led to more changes in the gang than when the worker directed his remarks to all the members."

He signed the drawing and shoved it toward me.

"Al, was Caplan an artist?"

"Yes, he was, Sam. And good with both water colors and oil. It was his way of relaxing. His apartment in Chicago was filled with his works."

"What did he draw for you?"

"It was a landscape scene done in the style of Vincent VanGogh. I still have it. What is especially fascinating is that few years ago it gave me a 'woo-woo,' you know, a Twilight Zone experience."

"What was that?"

"I'll show you."

Al gets up, goes inside, and returns with a framed picture. "Here. Tell me, what do you see?"

"This isn't a projective test, is it?"

"No," Al says, laughing.

"All right, then. The picture is of a large, snow-capped mountain with a river in the foreground. The mountain is forested up to the snow line. The river runs from one side of the picture to the other in front of the mountain. Three sail boats are moored on the far side—the mountain side—of the river. On the viewer's side there is a grassy bank and pilings of different heights. At the top right of the picture there is a blazing yellow sun. Opposite, at the top left there is what looks like a full moon. The coloring of the entire drawing is rich and almost shimmering in places. But what about this was a Twilight Zone experience for you, Al?"

"You remember where I lived before I built my home."

"In a houseboat about a mile down the river from here."

"You remember how I watched the Mount St. Helens eruption from my living room."

"Yes, you wrote about it in *The Survivor Personality*."

"In 1981, the year after the eruption, I went for a walk early one summer morning. I came back and paused on the river bank to breathe in the cool air and enjoy the sunrise. I felt the warmth of the morning sun to my right in the east. A full moon was hanging over the horizon in the west. With soft eyes I looked at the pilings securing the moorage in place, the sail boats in their slips in the moorage across the river, and Mt. St. Helens in the distance. I observed that a mountain that used to look like a rounded scoop of vanilla ice cream was now a broken-top mountain. At that moment the hair stood up on the back of my neck. A wave of adrenaline surged through me. My heart pounded. I sucked in a deep breath."

"Wow!"

"Mega wow! It was Caplan's drawing! I was living in his drawing! Notice that he drew a *broken-top* mountain, not a rounded one. The scene didn't exist until 15 years after he drew it."

"That's incredible. I've never heard of anything like this."

"I hadn't either. I sent a color copy of the drawing to Theodore Wolff, the art editor for the Christian Science Monitor. I asked him if he'd ever run across a case of precognitive art. He wrote back and said he hadn't."

"That is incredible. Before you go on, when Caplan told you about his research he used several terms I'm not familiar with. He mentioned 'changing reference group norms for teenagers with dyssocial personalities.' What did he mean?"

"He was referring to a personality condition we'd find in some inner city teenagers when we tested them at the juvenile court in Cleveland. Their criminal actions were not from emotional disturbance, lack of conscience, or antisocial tendencies. Psychologically they were mentally healthy and had a healthy conscience. The problem for the community was that their code of conduct came from the norms of a subculture that condoned predatory actions against the larger society."

"Can you give me an example?"

"Sure. A strong teenage boy would hang around on a street corner and let himself be picked up by a homosexual man driving an expensive car. When the man drove them to a secluded place, the teenager would beat him up, steal his money and jewelry, dump him out, and drive the car back and abandon it."

"I see. With little risk to the teenager because the man wouldn't dare complain to the police."

"That's right. For the boys it was a way of getting money that was condoned by their primary reference group. The group was dysfunctional in society. The term 'dyssocial personality' let us describe a psychologically healthy teenager who acted in ways that would indicate a defective conscience in someone else."

"I understand. That is why Caplan's project in Chicago was to try to change the code of conduct of a gang instead of trying to change an individual."

"Right, Sam. The approach was well thought through and they did get some positive results. After two years, however, Caplan was tired of living in Chicago and could write up the results anyplace. I looked forward to his moving to Ann Arbor.

"In the meantime, the first two weeks in June were very busy for me with teaching, my dissertation, and athletics. My volleyball team, Psych O, as usual, played McKeachie's team for the championship."

"Psych O?"

"The psychology department had six volleyball teams. McKeachie played on the original Psych A with John Milholland, Clyde Coombs, Warren Norman, and several other professors. Mine should have been Psych F, but when Dick Schmuck and I formed the team in 1962 we decided that naming it Psych O was more fun."

"Just how big was the psychology department?"

"There were about 150 faculty and 150 graduate students at that time."

"One student per faculty? I've never heard of such a low student-teacher ratio."

"Remember, this was a research department. There were only seven or eight full-time faculty members. Most of the faculty taught part-time and did research the rest of the time. The clinicians had positions at hospitals or clinics as well as their private practices. Those in industrial or social psychology had positions in industry or with the state. Those who were experts in physiology, perception, motivation, and so on worked for private centers or had their own research facilities. The big benefit was that with about 300 faculty and students we could field teams for every intramural sport—basketball, football, tennis, softball."

"Al, you told Mayman that McKeachie had lots of game balls from no run, no hit games. He must have been a good softball pitcher."

"He sure was, Sam. Fast pitch. Only the math pitcher came close to being as good. I'll give you an example of just how good McKeachie was. Several times only eight of our players showed up for a game. When that happened, Dick Schmuck and I played the outfield by ourselves. After McKeachie would get the signal for the next pitch from the catcher, Warren Norman, he would put his hand behind his back before he started his wind up. He held the ball in way that let Dick and me see if the pitch would be fast or slow."

"What good would that do?"

"I can tell that you're not a softball player. If it was to be a fastball, we'd break left just as he pitched. For a slowball we'd break to the right."

"I see. When a ball is pitched slow the batter swings too soon and the ball goes to left field. A fast pitch would be more likely to go to right field."

"Yes, in our league anyway. That's why we usually won even with only eight players. We were good."

"It seems that you had many roles with McKeachie."

"That's true. He was my mentor in graduate school, an opponent on the volleyball court, a player on my softball team—I was the captain—a teaching colleague, my department chairman..."

"He was author of the textbook you wrote the manual for."

"Right, and a friend as well. Our team won the softball championship and with that the all-school championship. I typed out a list of all the players on all the teams and had it framed. I took it to his office so it could sit along side the championship trophy. He was very pleased."

"And you felt pleased at doing something for him that was so important."

"Yes, I did. I took the time to do it even though I was writing my dissertation and had to turn in grades for the seniors in my personality course two weeks before graduation. The first week in June I gave an early final exam to the class, graded term papers, and turned in their grades. Then, because we still had several class meetings scheduled, I did something unusual. I had the class members take turns coming up front in small groups to interview each other and discuss what they learned from their study of mentally healthy people. We had a great time. At the last class meeting I received a rousing ovation."

"Congratulations."

"By this time I had finished the final draft of my dissertation and scheduled my oral defense. Kathleen did a terrific job. Sometimes she would type almost all night to get a revision done. This was before the days of word processing."

"Were there any problems finishing up?"

"Nothing major. It took me about 100 days from the time my committee approved my topic to develop the research design, do the testing, analyze the data, write up the rough draft, get it critiqued by committee members, and produce the final version."

"That's amazing."

"The only hitch occurred when I ran into one of my committee members, professor Joseph Adelson, on campus one afternoon early in June.

"He said, 'I've been having second thoughts about being on your committee. I want to resign from it.'

"'I don't understand why,' I said. 'Is there something about my research you dislike?'

"'It isn't that,' he said. 'I'm your ex wife's advisor.'

"He spoke in a way that implied I should know what he was talking about. I didn't, but I agreed to his request. I went immediately to speak to Douvan. She said that dropping Adelson would not hold me back. This was not an unusual development. I'd still have four committee members and that was sufficient for university requirements. She told me to get a petition from the department office and fill it out for her to sign."

"How did the oral defense of your dissertation go?"

"It was easier than I expected. I had stayed up late trying to anticipate any question they might ask. I was ready for a grueling session, but they spent most of the time talking with each other. After forty minutes Douvan asked me to leave the room. I heard them talking and laughing as I waited. Elton McNeil was on my committee. He could have been a stand up comic.

About five minutes later Douvan opened the door and asked me back in. She smiled and extended her hand. "Congratulations," she said. "You have passed your dissertation

defense. I am very pleased to have you as a professional colleague, Doctor Siebert."

Yay!

Each of the committee members shook my hand. It was an
exciting moment. McNeil laughed. "We all agree," he said,
"you have learned how to pile it as high and deep as anybody
else."

I laughed.

On the way home I stopped at a market and bought a potted
yellow chrysanthemum for Kathleen. When I handed it to her I
said, "Thank you for your constant support and all the work
you've done o help me get through school. I feel blessed to
have you as my wife."

She blushed. "I help you because I love you. Do you want
some tea?"

That evening we celebrated by going to a German restau-
rant with several friends. Later that night, in bed, I petted
Kathleen a long time. Our love making was tender, slow, and
satisfying.

After breakfast Kathleen came and sat in my lap. She gave
me a kiss and a hug. "I liked last night," she said, blushing
slightly. "The gynecologist told me she couldn't find a reason
why I'm not getting pregnant. She said she wants a urologist
to examine you. She gave me his name and address." She
paused and looked at me. "Would you be willing to go see
him?"

"Sure."

"Only if you want to."

Chapter Six

Commencing

Saturday afternoon I walked over to the apartment of another psychology graduate student to attend a party celebrating the end of finals. Kathleen, as always, had declined to come with me. The party was in full swing. Over 25 people were crowded into a one-bedroom apartment. Every one talked loudly because the music was loud. I nodded to several friends and said "Hi" to others as I threaded my way to the kitchen counter with the six-pack I'd brought.

Gary and Janet, two clinical students, saw me. "Hey, Al! Or should we say *Doctor* Al now."

"Yuk."

"How do you feel about going to Menninger's?" Janet asked.

"It's a fantastic place for advanced training," I said. "I'll have two years with some of the best clinical psychologists in the world."

Gary asked, "Will you do any teaching?"

"I don't expect to."

"I like being a teaching fellow," Janet said. "What is your secret Al, to always getting such good evaluations? I saw the department printout. You got a rating of 4.9."

"There is no secret. The two most important principles I have learned are, first, keep getting evaluations from students and learn from what they tell you. Second, if I present an idea to students and they don't get it, then either it wasn't a good idea or I didn't present it well. There is nothing wrong with the learner."

Janet nodded. "I like that."

"I wish our government would learn to stay out of wars," Gary said.

"What do you mean?" I asked.

"That incident in the Tonkin Gulf last year," Gary said. "Our military set that up as an excuse to go to war. Now we're sending troops into Vietnam."

Janet looked at me. "Al, what do you think about the fight against communism?"

"I don't agree it will be defeated with military action. I was over at the Michigan Union when Kennedy proposed creating the Peace Corps. I like that approach better. Besides, our government doesn't seem to understand what is going on with communism."

"What do you know about communism?" Janet said.

"I wrote a term paper on it when I was a senior in college. Communism is not a political party. To be a member a person has to go through an indoctrination. He has to join a secret cell, a small group of other communists, and confess to them any reservations or doubts. In public he has to speak the party line or get labelled a capitalist lackey."

"That sounds like Festinger's research," Janet said, "in reduction of cognitive dissonance. When a person publicly states views he doesn't believe, he begins to believe what he is saying."

"If you don't pay him much," Gary said. "If they are paid a large amount, the reduction in dissonance doesn't happen."

"What do communists believe?" Janet asked.

"That people in the United States," I said, "and other western countries are infected with capitalist ideas, ideas the communists are dedicated to eliminating from the planet for the good of the working class. It's scary. I remember reading the Congressional testimony of Dr. Frederick Schwartz, a psychiatrist. He said paranoic self-deception is at the heart of communism."

"What is paranoid about their thinking?" Janet asked.

"Their fear of becoming infected with capitalistic ideas coupled with feeling justified to use any means for purging the human race of such ideas. After the second world war they slaughtered thousands of Polish officers and soldiers and buried them in mass graves. They saw themselves as destroying infected animals, not as killing human beings."

"Maybe I'd better study paranoia," Gary said, "if they intend to eliminate me."

"There isn't much published on paranoia," I said. "When I took the seminar on the psychoses I was able to read through everything about paranoia in the psychiatric literature in one evening at the library."

"I wish reading the schizophrenia literature was that easy," Janet said. "There are thousands of articles and books about it."

"What do think schizophrenia is?" Gary asked Janet.

Janet shook her head. "It's a mysterious disease. Every researcher has a different explanation. There are at least ten different kinds, all with different symptoms."

Gary said, "I just read that schizophrenics come from families that put them in a double-bind. You know, would say one thing while acting the opposite way."

"Give me some examples," Janet said.

When Janet and Gary started discussing theories of schizophrenia, I edged away.

Robinson came over, sipping a beer. "When does summer softball start?" he asked.

"In two weeks."

"You taking time to relax? Get some R and R?" he asked.

I laughed. "Yes. I even watched a movie on TV the other evening."

"What was it?"

"The *Last Time I Saw Archie*, starring Robert Mitchum and Frank Sinatra. It was a comedy about two privates in the army. Mitchum—Archie—went around the base with a clipboard making notes and check marks. He never said anything to the sergeants or officers, but he acted like an investigator. The sergeants and officers started giving him special privileges. They gave him a private room in the barracks and his own jeep. It was hilarious."

John laughed. Then, noticing an attractive grad student standing by herself, he said, "Excuse me. I have to circulate."

I moved over to an open window to get away from the smoke.

As I stood listening to several nearby conversations, a woman in her early 20s came over to me. "Hi, I'm Kerri," she said. "I'm a graduate student in social work." She held out her hand to shake mine. "What's your name?"

Not an athlete but not in bad shape either. Couldn't hold up on a long hike.

"I'm Al."

"Pleased to meet you Al. What's your major?"

Don't tell her it's clinical, that turns people off.

"Psychology."

"What area?"

"I do some teaching." I reached over to an end table and grabbed a handful of nuts.

"You didn't answer my question! What's your area?" she said, insistently.

Oh, well.

"Clinical."

She pulled back. Her eyes narrowed. She stopped smiling. "Do you think most people are mentally ill?" she asked.

"No, the only time I see mental illness in people is when I'm at the hospital wearing my long white coat. Out here in real life I think everyone's just fine."

"Whew! That's a relief," she said, smiling again. "I read in a book for a paper I had to write that psychiatrists see mental illness in everyone. It was a big research project. The book I mean, not my paper. Have you read it?"

"Probably. What is the title?"

"Mental Health in the Metropolis."

"Was Srole the editor? Leo Srole?"

"I think so."

"Yes, I've seen it."

"They found symptoms of mental illness in everyone, even the few people they put in the 'well' category." Kerri made a long face. "That is depressing!"

"I know what you mean. And that helps explain why I tried to avoid your question."

"Why did you?"

"When I was a boy people would talk to me—strangers on busses, people I mowed lawns for, neighbors. They would tell me all sorts of personal things. But now, when people find out I'm in clinical psych, they're often afraid to open up."

"People are afraid of someone who might see mental illness in them."

"I know."

"Why did you pick clinical as a major?" she asked.

"I had to choose something. When I came here I wanted to be a teacher. But they said I couldn't major in teaching psychology."

"Do you like being in clinical?"

"In many ways I'm not really in it. I mastered it because it was necessary. Why did you choose your major?"

"I want to help people," she said.

"Why?"

"So their lives are happier. But I know I have selfish reasons too."

"What do you mean?"

"I just read *Atlas Shrugged* by Ayn Rand. Have you read it?"

"No."

"You should. She gets you thinking about the selfish reasons behind all our actions and how much harm people cause when they don't admit their selfish motives. That's why I'm trying to see my selfish reasons for wanting to help people."

"Hmm. Sounds interesting."

Kerri looked at her empty plastic wine cup. "I need a refill. See you."

"See you," I said.

I slipped out the door and went home.

I decided to catch up on long overdue correspondence. I spent the rest of the afternoon and part of the evening at my desk writing to fraternity brothers, relatives, and friends.

Kathleen brought me a cup of tea and some chocolate brownies. "I've never seen you write so many letters."

I put my arm around her hips and pulled her closer. "I want to let my friends know I made it! I'll also send a notice to my college alumni news magazine."

She touched the letter on top of the stack. "Tell me more about this man you call 'The Ranger.' I know you were in the army with him. You said his real name is Crews?"

"Right. I met him when he was the ranger assigned to our medical company. Have you ever met someone and you immediately became friends for life?"

She nodded. "My friend Rachael. She worked at the court with me."

"It was like that with Crews and me. He was a sergeant in the Rangers. Now they're called Green Berets. He is about 5'9", very strong, and the most cheery tough guy I've ever known. He grew up in San Francisco drinking and fighting. He was the same in the army. He'd come to me for a hangover cure on Sunday mornings and tell me about his exploits. He'd win fights with the toughest guys in camp. On maneuvers he was superb at surviving on his own and accomplishing secret missions. The name 'The Ranger' fits him perfectly. If my life was ever at risk, he'd be the one I'd want by my side. We hung out together evenings and weekends. Sometimes on a hot summer day we'd go to the camp beer garden and sit outside in our shorts in a heavy downpour and drink beer. We always laughed a lot."

"What kind of work does he do?"

"The last I heard he was working for the San Francisco library as bouncer in the Mission Street branch."

"Why would they need a bouncer?"

"To keep drunks and winos from camping inside. But he's probably doing something different now. Say, will you do something?" I showed her a hand written letter.

"What is it?"

"Please type this letter to Mayman's secretary, Mrs. Falley. My letters have strikeovers and I want this to look professional."

"What is it for?"

"I want to get the name and address of their local paper."

"Why?"

"I read in *Consumer Reports* that it's a good idea to subscribe to the newspaper in the city you're moving to."

"Why should we do that?"

"We'll learn about the community and read ads of apartments for rent."

"We can't rent a place without looking at it."

"No, but when we arrive to go apartment hunting we'll know what's in the ballpark for rents, which apartments are dogs because they haven't rented, and ones newly listed. Besides, it will give you more crossword puzzles to work."

"Would you like some tea?"

"Sure. I've been thinking, how about us treating ourselves to a little vacation. What about a weekend trip to Canada? Would you like that?"

Kathleen smiled like a little girl given a wonderful present. "I would!"

"Did you graduate in June, Al?"

"Technically, no. I didn't pass my oral defense in time for the paperwork to get turned in for the June commencement ceremony."

"But you did have your doctorate."

"In every way except for the commencement ceremony. The Rackham graduate school notified me that my doctorate would be conferred at the next commencement in December."

For our celebration trip Kathleen and I decided to go to Windsor, Canada. It had been an intensive two and a half years for us. It felt good to have time to walk in parks and visit museums. We toured a liquor factory and went to various stores. We discovered a leather shop where I bought a briefcase as a graduation present to myself. Kathleen bought me a matching key case.

Back home we enjoyed ourselves more than ever. We went to dinner with friends. We went for walks. Some evenings Kathleen would sit on the couch and I'd put my head in her lap while we watched television.

At the end of June my mother arrived for her visit. She slept on the couch and never complained about feeling the metal bars underneath. She and Kathleen got along very well. One thing about her visit stands out. During dinner one evening she said, "I suppose it is all right to tell you now, Al. When you graduated from high school, your school counselor called me at work and told me to not encourage you to go to college."

"What?"

"He said you were not college material. He told me to not push you to go to college. He said you would fail and it would cause you emotional harm."

"No kidding?"

"I didn't tell you. I wanted you to find out for yourself if you could succeed or not."

"Thank you. Thank you very much." I laughed. "If high school counselors kept records on how well their predictions turned out, I would certainly be counted as an error for him!"

"Yes, you would."

"But you know, this makes me appreciate even more what a fantastic country we have. Where else in the world could this have happened? Dad was a truck driver. After he got sick and died you went to work as a ward clerk in a hospital to raise Mary and me. And now here I am, getting a doctorate from one of the best universities in the nation and heading for a post-doctoral fellowship at the Menninger Foundation. You sure did a wonderful job with us, Mom."

She smiled and got tears in her eyes. She always did when I praised her.

"It sounds like your mother was quite a person, Al."

"She was, Sam. By working to upgrade her skills, she became the office manager for three surgeons. She raised us to be self-reliant. I especially appreciate that she always left my mind alone."

"What do you mean by that?"

"She never demanded that I think or feel a certain way. I was always free to think or feel or daydream as I wished. She and my sister talked all the time. I think that is why I operate non-verbally better than verbally."

"What do you mean?"

"Growing up in my home I seldom had a chance to finish sentences. My mind would wander while they talked. I got along by observing and acting non-verbally."

"So that's why psychology is so natural for you. You grew up being an observer of people."

"I guess you're right. I never thought about that."

"When your classes were finished did you start working full-time at NPI?"

"Yes, as of July first. Giora had everything arranged. At rounds Bostian announced that I'd received my doctorate and that I was now full-time. The whole group applauded. I went to central supply and ordered long white coats with my name and degree stenciled on the pocket."

"What was the relationship between the psychologists and the psychiatrists at NPI?"

"It was good. Giora was very effective as the head of the psychology department.

"But the psychiatrists were in control."

"Very much so. Psychiatry based its power on employing the medical model for mental cases. Psychologists were seen as paraprofessionals, as a sometimes useful resource."

"Al, explain what the 'medical model' is."

"Sure, Sam. We start with a person thinking or feeling in ways that upsets and bewilders others. To employ the medical model means that the person's thoughts and feelings are said to be 'symptoms' of 'mental illness.' The person is called a 'patient.' A 'therapy plan' is developed to 'treat' the person's 'illness.' It's a belief system copied from the treatment of physical illnesses."

"This helps explain your response to the woman at the party. You weren't looking at her from a medical model perspective."

"No, I wasn't."

"But you knew she would think you were looking to diagnose her if you said your specialty was clinical psychology."

"Right. That was my experience with most people."

"Okay, what happened after you started working full-time?"

"My salary tripled because I also moved from the masters level pay scale to the doctoral level. My testing load increased, and I participated in more NPI activities. Even so, I felt like I had almost nothing to do."

Up until then I had been teaching half-time, working at the hospital half-time, carrying a full load of graduate courses, doing my doctoral work, and coordinating the Psychology department's athletic competition.

All of a sudden everything was done. My dissertation was completed. There were no more classes to take and none to teach. No more course assignments, papers to grade, or late-night writing. I had more time than I was used to. My energies were freed from the many responsibilities that had occupied me for the previous two and a half years.

At first I made unnecessary trips to the hospital cafeteria and other places in the hospital so that people could see the new "Siebert, Ph.D." stenciled on the pocket of my long white coat. Considering all the years I had spent in school feeling out of place because I wasn't interested in the subjects, was poor at memorizing, and had spelling problems, I was elated about my doctorate.

At my next meeting with Giora I said, "Now that I have some extra time, I have a small research project I'd like to do. Will you please help me arrange to purchase a color-blind test and a full-spectrum light?"

"What do you want those for?" he asked.

"I went to a lecture on the genetic basis for color blindness and color deficiency last winter and heard something that got me thinking. Color blindness is transmitted with the male chromosome. One man in 20 has a color vision defect, almost always for red and green, but only one woman in 400 does."

"I'm not following you."

"Clinical psychologists may be interpreting some projective test results incorrectly. When a man does not respond to colors on the Rorschach, this is interpreted as weakness in his emotional integration. I went to the library and searched the clinical psychology literature. There are no studies reported where males who gave no color responses on the Rorschach had been tested for color blindness. This disturbs me. All across the country thousands of males are given the Rorschach every year, and yet the ones who give no color responses are viewed as having personality defects."

"I never thought of that."

"I talked with Dan Weintraub about how I could do color vision testing with a patient if it seemed indicated. He says I need a set of color vision testing plates and a full spectrum lamp."

"Why do you need a full spectrum lamp?"

"To avoid what happens when you go into a department store to purchase a sweater or a shirt. Under the artificial light it looks fine, but when you go out in the sunlight it looks different. Sunlight is full spectrum."

"I don't have funds available in the Psychology budget," he said. "But I like your idea. I'll back you up if you want to submit your request to Dr. Waggoner."

Raymond Waggoner was chairman of the psychiatry department. We hardly ever saw him. He was busy doing whatever chairmen do and working toward becoming president of the American Psychiatric Association. I went to see his personal secretary. When I promised her I would not need more than ten minutes, she found a way to work me in to see him several days later.

At the appointed time I went up to his office on the seventh floor. I'd never seen it before. Waggoner remained seated at his desk when I walked in. He was a large man with thinning hair. His shoulders slumped over from years of sitting. Thick glasses accentuated the dark circles under his eyes.

His office was very large with a nice view of the Huron River and park. It had thick, wall-to-wall carpet. The dark wood desk, book cases, conference table, and chairs were expensive looking. In a separate area I saw several padded chairs and a short couch.

That must be where he interviews private patients and their families.

Waggoner said, "I understand you will be leaving here to start a post-doctoral fellowship at the Menninger Foundation."

"Yes. It starts in September."

"Congratulations. You will receive an excellent education there. I've been on several panels with Dr. Hall. He runs a fine training program for analysts. What is this request of yours?"

Waggoner listened attentively to my explanation. He asked several questions. Then he said, "I'll let you know next week." Our meeting took about five minutes.

Six patients, an aide, and several residents got onto the elevator at the sixth floor. The patients and the aide crowded together in the back. I looked at the patients.

Look at how uneasy they are, how they study us. They're tense, uneasy. Why is there so much emotional distance between us?

The next week I received a memo from Waggoner saying he authorized the purchase of the color plates but not the lamp. His personal secretary took care of all the paperwork for me.

Being full-time, I now attended rounds every morning and tested more patients. One morning Bostian began the meeting saying, "I regret having to announce that Dr. Ferris, a psychiatrist with the outpatient service, shot and killed himself last night."

People gasped. "Oh, no!"

"He'll be missed by those of us who knew him," Bostian said, shaking his head. "It's unfortunate that the stress from constant exposure to emotional disturbances in others can become overwhelming. Services will be held Wednesday morning. All right, let's proceed."

I whispered to Lois, "Did you know him?"

"He consulted on several of my cases. He was a nice man, sensitive."

Several weeks later Frank Moran stopped me after rounds. "Al, I'd like for you to come to my office this afternoon when I meet with one of the patients you tested."

"Which one?"

"Tony Rico. I'll be telling him about our diagnostic findings and our recommendations. His wife will be there."

"I'd like to! This may surprise you, but I've never observed a psychiatrist talking to a patient about the results of a diagnostic workup. Lois Jackson did the case work?"

"Yes, she'll be there too."

Frank wasn't in his office when Lois and I arrived. She and I sat in chairs along the wall. An aide brought Tony and his wife in. They sat in two chairs in front of Frank's desk. The aide waited by the door.

Tony was a 21-year-old, unemployed, auto factory worker. He'd gotten into a fist fight with his father, beaten him up, and taken off in his father's car. The father called the police. They found the car and arrested Tony for auto theft. The judge sent him to NPI for psychiatric evaluation.

Frank looked upset when he walked in. He sat down and said, "Tony, your behavior is sick. We can treat your problem, but you must accept that you're mentally ill before we can help you."

Frank's voice is tight. This isn't like him.

Tony shook his head. "I'm not a crazy person."

"You are mentally ill! You must accept that."

"No, I'm not! You doctors are crazy if you think I'm nuts!"

"We've argued about this before. You must believe you're mentally ill or we can't help you."

Tony's face got red. His nostrils flared and he breathed faster. "I'm not mentally ill!" His wife reached over and put her hand on his arm.

"Yes, you are!" Frank said.

"No, I'm not!"

"Yes, you are!"

"No!"

Lois and I looked at each other. Frank gave up. Everyone sat in silence. Frank said, "The meeting is over." He nodded to the aide to take Tony back to the ward. His wife left with them.

Frank sat with his head down. Lois and I left without saying anything to him. We had to wait for the elevator.

"Lois," I said. "Do psychiatric residents yell at their patients like that very often?"

"It happens, but I've never seen it that bad before."

"I've got to tell you something."

"What is it?"

"I'm shocked by what I just witnessed."

"Why? The first thing a psychiatrist must do is convince the patient that he's mentally ill."

"That's what I'm shocked to learn. During graduate school I read hundreds of articles and books on psychotherapy. None of them mention what we just saw! The research reports about psychotherapy are silent about a *major* variable!"

"I'd not thought about that. You're right."

"When we read a case study, do we know if the patient was told to believe he or she is mentally ill?"

Lois shrugged. "They never say."

"This means that most reports about psychiatric treatment are badly flawed!"

"Al, do you agree that Tony is mentally ill?"

"He's a kid with poor control over his impulses, but I've seen many like him. At the juvenile court where I worked, he would be typical. He's okay. His father used to beat him when he was a boy."

"He told me."

"This is a case of another dumb parent not realizing that one day his son will be bigger and stronger and may decide to get even. No, Tony doesn't have a mental disorder."

"I feel the same. Why did Frank get so angry?"

"I'm not sure. I'll ask him."

At rounds several days later Laura Stevens began her ward report saying, "Tony Rico eloped from the ward at 7:20 yesterday evening."

"How did it happen?" Bostian asked.

"He hung around near the door," she said. "He bolted out when we let a visitor in. We notified hospital security, but they couldn't find him."

"Did you notify the police?"

"We notified the court because he was a court admission, but not the police. He's not considered dangerous."

I whispered to Lois Jackson, "The poor guy is probably hiding, afraid the police are looking for him. I wish I could tell him he doesn't have to feel like a fugitive."

After rounds I saw Frank walking away with his head down. I hurried and caught up with him. "Hey Frank, may I ask you a couple questions?"

He looked up, startled. "I suppose so." He drew himself up as though getting ready to be "Doctor."

"What happened the other day in your office? You seemed uptight. What's going on?"

Frank let down a bit and took a deep breath. He shook his head. "Al, I'm trying to do what my supervisor tells me, but I don't like it. When I ask questions about why I should talk patients into believing they're mentally ill, he tells me to work it out with my therapist."

"I heard that you've been warned to be more cooperative."

"This is confidential."

"Sure."

"I met with my supervisor before that session with Tony. That's why I was late. He told me that my 'case' was discussed at a senior staff meeting. He said if I didn't work out my problems and my resistance to the program, they would drop me."

"That's a heavy duty threat."

"I tried to do what he said with Tony, but I hated it. I'm worried. If I get dropped from here it would be difficult to find another residency. I may have to give up psychiatry altogether. That's a lot of years wasted. I've taken out loans..." He became thoughtful. Then he realized I was still standing there. "Thank you for your concern," he said, and walked away.

What's going on here? All these things going on that were never taught to us.

I returned to my office. I spent the rest of the morning outlining my report of a patient I'd tested. Then I set up the transcriber and began dictating my findings. "Okay, here we go. But before I tell you about the patient I tested, I want to tell you a funny story I read in the *Reader's Digest*. Pretend you're still working, but just sit and relax while I talk. There's this minister who..."

After lunch I sat at my desk, but I had nothing to do.

Here's a chance to look ahead.

I opened the file with the Menninger program materials. I reread the description of the Program Philosophy.

"I have it here, Sam." Al opens the folder, searches through it, and takes out several pages stapled together. "It says, 'The specific goals of the program are to foster a searching curiosity about clinical processes that will generate new research into the nature of these processes. The program allows Fellows a two-year "moratorium" in which they are free to re-examine and reintegrate their theoretical, clinical, and professional skills.'"

"I'm not clear why you decided to reread their statement of program philosophy, Al. After talking with Frank were you starting to have doubts?"

"Not then. At that time Frank's problem was just an incident with no special meaning. I hadn't looked at the program philosophy since Mayman sent it to me in March. Now that I was going there I wanted to start preparing myself."

I tilted back in my chair.
Two years to think things through.
I could start now. But where? How?
Brainstorm a list of questions.
Okay.
I took a yellow legal pad from a drawer and started writing a list of questions.

Why are mental illnesses so difficult to cure?

Why is schizophrenia such a puzzle? Why are there so many kinds?

Why do people label each other and call each other names instead of finding ways to resolve their conflicts?

Why do parents beat their children?

If everyone wants a peaceful world, why is there so much fighting and killing?

Why do people kill themselves with alcohol, drugs, smoking, and overeating?

Why is the human race killing the planet that supports its life? Why don't people work together to revitalize and nourish the planet?

Things aren't working right. Why not?
Why? Why? WHY!?
In the mid-afternoon I went to the cafeteria, bought a carton of milk, and took it back to my office to drink with the chocolate chip cookies left over from lunch.

How do we get from where we are to where we would like to be?
What can be done to get people to change?

But isn't that part of the problem? Everyone seems to think that others have to change for things to be better.

I threw the milk carton in the waste basket, then folded my paper lunch bag and put it in my briefcase.

Observe yourself! You're doing the same as everyone else, thinking the solution is for others to change.

That's right. I am!

So take a look at yourself. How might you be responsible for the world not working well? What if you are the one who needs to change?

Okay, but where do I start?

What's the key question?

What don't I understand about me that's keeping the world from working well?

Yikes! Look at the time!

I had become so preoccupied with my questions I was almost late to the softball field for our pre-game warm up. I had to be there because I had the bats, balls, and catcher's mask in an old duffel bag in the trunk of my car.

Chapter Seven

Questions

Several days later Kathleen noticed that I came back from a bike ride with a paperback book. "What book is that?" she asked.

"*Atlas Shrugged*. I was over by that used-book store with the blue front door and decided to get a copy. Have you heard of it?"

"I've heard of the author. Her first name is spelled AYN."

I took the book to my office the next day and read it all morning. At lunch time I went up to the cafeteria and bought a carton of milk. I walked back to NPI and stepped into the elevator with one of the residents. From down the hall someone yelled, "Hold the elevator!" I reached my arm out. When the doors closed on my wrist the rubber safety bumpers automatically opened the doors. The resident behind me said, "Be careful! You could lose a hand that way."

That's eight out of nine.

Rod Baker, a second-year resident got into the elevator. As we started down, Rod said to the other resident, "these patients should be more cooperative. They should accept that they are ill. A woman I am committing to the state hospital is demanding to be taken to court for her hearing. And she says she wants me there to testify! We can't spare aides to take patients to court hearings. I can't take time to go to court every time I have someone committed. I told her it would be much better for her if she didn't fight the commitment and went to the state hospital willingly."

Here it is again. Another aspect of treatment never included in journal articles or textbooks. What is going on here?

Back in my office I read *Atlas Shrugged* all afternoon and the next day as well. I was fascinated by the way Rand, through her characters, showed the many ways that selfish motives or denial of selfishness influences what people do. I read so intently I ate almost half of the bag of semisweet chocolate chips I kept in the back of my desk drawer.

The role of selfishness was never covered in my psychology courses. I've got a lot more learning to do.

The next time I checked my mail box I found a package with the color vision test plates. I started using them with every male I gave psychological testing to.

"What results did you get, Al?"

"None. I never had a male patient who didn't show some color responses to the Rorschach. I gave the color vision test to gain experience. Giora had me explain what I was doing at the meeting of our psychology group at the hospital, but none of them ever borrowed the plates. It wasn't a big deal."

The first week in July I received a letter from Sydney Smith at the Menninger Foundation. He said Mayman was leaving to become a visiting professorship someplace. Smith was appointed acting director in his absence. That was fine with me. Smith and I got along well. Summer softball had started. McKeachie was in top form. I knew we had a good shot at the summer league championship.

At NPI I continued going to rounds, testing patients, and dictating my reports, but I became increasingly preoccupied.

Everyone is motivated by selfish reasons.

But people are seldom aware of their selfish motives. They justify pain or harm they cause with statements like: "I was just trying to help you," "I meant well," or "This is for your own good."

How I could I explore this? Research how blind people are to their selfish motives for helping others?

Several days later I was walking in the second floor hallway when I saw a female patient leave Rod's office. Rod came out into the hallway, placed his hands on his hips, and watched her walk toward the elevator. He shook his head.

"What's wrong, Rod?"

"That patient refuses to believe I'm acting for her own good."

Here's a chance to experiment!

"Are you?"

"Of course."

Think fast, probe for selfish motives.

"By working with her, aren't you learning how to be a psychiatrist?"

"Yes."

"Won't you enjoy the prestige, money, and working conditions that psychiatrists have?"

"Yes."

Rod looked at me with caution as I continued. "If you succeed with her, won't the nurses and supervisors think well of you?"

"Yes."

"If you help her, won't you gain her appreciation?"

"Probably."

Fantastic! Listen to this! Keep going.

"If you can get her out of the hospital, won't that help reduce your taxes?"

Nodding, he said, "indirectly."

I can't think of any thing else.

Okay, wrap it up.

"And you want her to believe that you're working entirely for her own good?"

He clenched his jaw. "But I am!" He swirled around, walked back into his office, and yanked his door shut.

That is amazing! And he's one of the better residents!

You have a big job ahead.

I went back to my office.

Where does this self-deceptive unselfishness come from?

What is the pattern here? I don't understand.

Something is going on that is much different from what I've been taught. What is it?

Look inside. If I am responsible for the world not working well, what don't I know about myself?

And so it went. During the first two weeks in July I became increasingly preoccupied. I became sensitive to selfish reasons behind the actions of people all around me. I went for long walks by myself.

One afternoon I came home from work and saw that Kathleen's eyes were red.

"What's wrong Kathleen?"

"Nothing."

"Your eyes are red."

"I've been crying."

"Why?"

"You don't talk to me enough. I want to know what you do at work. I want to know what you spend so much time thinking about."

"I've told you before that just going through the day is tough enough. I don't want to go through it again when I come home."

"But you've been sitting and thinking so much lately and taking long walks. Why won't you tell me what you're thinking?"

"You get upset when I tell you what I really think."

"No, I won't. Please tell me."

She's asking for it. Show her you are right.

"I've realized that everything people do has selfish motives. There's a selfish gain behind every action."

"People shouldn't be selfish."

"Everyone is selfish whether they realize it or not. You are."

"No, I'm not!"

"Yes, you are. You have selfish reasons when you type for me and cook and sew and..."

"No! I do that because I love you."

"I know you love me, but you keep me attracted to you by doing those things. And you like living with me and being able to tell friends you're married to a doctor."

"No. I do those things because I love you." She buried her face in her hands. Tears dripped down her cheeks.

"I agree that you love me, but you also have selfish reasons."

"I'm not a selfish person. I help you because I love you." She started sobbing.

Back off.

"I know you're not selfish. I know you love me." A while later I said, "Let's drive down to see your parents next weekend. I know you'd like to see your mother before we move to Topeka. Smith said in his letter that my fellowship starts September 7th. That means we should arrive there the last week in August to find an apartment and settle in."

Kathleen dried her eyes, stood up, and went to the kitchen to make herself a cup of tea.

Congratulations smart guy. You proved you were right. Proud of yourself?

No.

I left the house and went for a walk. My mind struggled trying to make sense out of it all.

All behavior is motivated, so what motivation prevents people from being conscious of their selfish motives? Why do people have to hide their selfish motives from themselves? Where does it start?

What mechanisms are operating?

Could there be defense mechanisms Freud didn't discover?

Try that route.

Okay. A defense mechanism is unconscious, is automatic, and distorts reality.

All right. So what are the defensive behaviors I'm spotting? To give help when none has been asked for.

What is defensive about that?

How about to force help on a person who doesn't want it?

Okay.

Giving the recipient of help no choice.

The one book Freud wanted to be his legacy to the human race is *The Interpretation of Dreams*. He revised it eight times. I took my copy to my office at NPI and read through it searching for clues about ways that defense mechanisms operate.

I'm beginning to see what he was talking about. Unconscious distortions trace back to things that happen in childhood.

What comes to me? What was I told as a child?

I asked my mother, "How do I get people to like me?"

She told me, "Follow the Golden Rule. Do nice things for them. Help others and they will like you. Don't brag about yourself. If you think too much of yourself, other people won't like you."

I looked for ways to help others so they would like me.

What is the selfish gain from helping others? From being charitable?

You feel good. You like yourself.

Okay, good feelings result. Feel good, worthwhile, likable.

Okay, so the inner payoff of "charity" is good feelings.

It builds self-esteem.

No! Not self-esteem. Not conscious self-esteem. It is indirect.

The person gets feelings of esteem in a disguised way.

But why does it have to be indirect, disguised?

If parents can raise a child to not think well of himself or herself, to depend on them to supply the needed esteem, then there is a hook in the kid.

And the adult.

Right.

If a person can be raised to not have high self-esteem, he can be manipulated by others because of his need.

Which means...

If he has high self-esteem, he can't be manipulated.

And people can't handle that!

Right. Listen to how people talk about the way Cassius Clay brags about his boxing prowess.

They say, "No one should talk like that. He needs to be brought down a few notches."

Right.

They want to tear him down. But why? He is right! He is the greatest!

Why can't people remain silent? What motivates this automatic reaction?

They don't want him to say it. They want him dependent on them for expressions of his worth. But notice, when a person is depressed or speaks poorly of himself, the automatic reaction of people is to build him up!

I jumped when the phone on my desk rang. "Dr. Siebert?"

"Yes?"

"This is Dr. Waggoner's secretary. Could you see Dr. Waggoner at two o'clock this afternoon?"

"Yes."

"Fine. We'll see you then"

I wonder what the Chief wants?

I peered around his door. "Dr. Waggoner?"

"Come in, Dr. Siebert. This is Dr. Cannicott, Dr. Stanley Cannicott. He's from England."

I nodded at the other man and said, "Howdy."

Cannicott smiled and shook hands with me.

Short, solid build, physically strong. Could play rugby. Nice smile, good eyes. He looks English.

"He agreed," Waggoner said, "to come over for a month on a grant I obtained to do some research here on a new electroshock technique he developed. You're going to set up the research design, do the testing, evaluate the results, and give us the data we need to publish a paper on his method."

Mercy. Just like the army.

"You will now do this."

"My testing load will need to be reduced."

"That will be arranged. This can't take more than a month. You must be finished before the end of August. You'll use patients at Ypsilanti State Hospital and Mercywood, the private psychiatric hospital at the edge of town. Cannicott will tell you about his technique. I visited his hospital when I went to England for an international conference. I want you to obtain statistical verification of Cannicott's clinical success."

"All right."

I took Cannicott down to my office. He appeared to be in his late forties. He had a ruddy complexion and short brown, graying hair. "You look like you spend time outdoors," I said. "What do you do away from work?"

"Mountain climbing is my avocation. No tonic better than a weekend in the Alps. When I was younger I helped train the RAF mountain rescue teams."

I believe that.

"Have you witnessed shock treatments?" he asked.

"Yes, at the state hospital. They herd all the patients into a room before breakfast and lock the door. The patients are frightened and scared. Then the aides bring out one person at a time—those scheduled for shock treatment. They get zapped and go into a convulsion. They're placed on a stretcher with wheels, run down the hall to the sleeping area, and flopped onto a bed. Soon the room is filled with patients moaning, crying out, and thrashing around as they recover from their brain concussions."

"Bad show isn't it?"

"Yes, it is."

"The unilateral treatments don't affect the poor blokes that way."

"Unilateral? One-sided?"

"Yes," he said, "you know the traditional method for inducing convulsions?"

"The nurse holds a rubber strap across the patient's forehead so that metal discs make contact on each side of the forehead. Then the doctor presses the button."

"It's called bilateral," he said, "because the electric current goes through both frontal lobes. Why do we physicians give shock treatments?"

"Someone noticed that people having epileptic seizures recovered from depression."

"During the second world war an Italian army doctor was interned with many captured soldiers. He saw some lads become badly depressed, giving up living. He obtained a long electric wire and would sneak up behind one of these poor chaps. He would quickly reach around and jam the bare ends against the chap's forehead. It worked. Normal house current for one or two seconds and the chap would have a seizure. Saved many lives, he did. These frilly $800 dollar machines are unnecessary. Fluff. Only makes money for the engineers. We could use that money for better work back at my hospital. Do you know why we physicians use electricity?"

"The electricity controls the seizure best," I said. "Drugs are stressful and difficult to control. Tell me more about your unilateral treatment."

His eyes brightened. "It induces the seizure by putting the current through the non-dominant hemisphere of the cerebral cortex. Our electrodes must be held by hand. It's a bother but we do it. One contact goes on the forehead, the other slightly behind and above the ear on the same side."

"You avoid damage to the dominant hemisphere that way."

He nodded, pleased that I understood what he was saying. "With unilateral the chap has the benefits of the seizure without the usual confusion or brain damage. Depressed business-men drive to my hospital in the morning, have their treatment, eat a light breakfast, and drive off to go about their day! You never see that with bilateral! Unilateral can be used with people who earn their livelihood with their minds—doctors, accountants, professors. They show no mental impairment!"

"That's fascinating."

"With unilateral they have almost perfect memory within moments of waking up. Bilateral is different."

"I know. Patients don't know where they are, who their doctor is, what the date is. It's pitiful."

The next day I outlined my proposed research design to him. "We'll use a control group and an experimental group. We'll match them according to age and gender. I would like to use four short tests in our experiment. A test of recent memory, a test of short-term memory, a test of abstracting abilities, and a visual-motor test. Brain damage will show impairment in the first three. We should include the last to see if the unilateral has a negative effect in the visual or motor areas of the cortex."

"Of course! Jolly good!"

"For the abstractions I'll use questions from an old IQ test. For example, in what way are a dog and a lion alike?"

"They're animals."

"Right. In what way are a coat and dress alike?"

"Clothing." He smiled and nodded his head.

"A wagon and a bicycle?"

"Ride them, transportation!"

"Right. A brain damaged person gives concrete responses. He or she can't make the abstraction. They would say that a dog and a lion both bite, have teeth, are furry, have four legs, have tails, or something like that. Even under questioning they cannot think in abstract ways."

He nodded his head with vigor and grinned. "We're con-crete removers!"

"I guess we are!"

"Five unilateral treatments are enough for most people," he said.

"Fine. I'll build our research design around a series of five treatments for subjects in both the experimental and the control groups."

We went upstairs to present our research plan to Waggoner. He approved it but cautioned us. "Remember that you're guests in the facilities and must not interfere with any hospital procedures or treatments."

"Dinner smells nice," I said to Kathleen. I kissed her on the neck and put my hands on her breasts.

She handed a raw carrot to me over her shoulder. "Here, chew on this."

"I saw the urologist today. He told me my sperm count is too low to start a pregnancy."

"Oh, no!" She winced.

"He told me about several possibilities. He prescribed a drug for me to take. He said it helps some men build up their sperm count."

"Did what he say upset you?"

"It's just information. It explains why I've never gotten anyone else pregnant."

Kathleen blushed. "Don't you want to have a baby?"

"Sure, honey. I've expected we would. And I know how much you want one, so I'll do my best to cooperate. Want to go practice?"

Her cheeks got red. "Not now."

"I'm going to be busier than I expected with this new research project at work. Will you please call several moving companies to get estimates for moving us to Topeka?"

"All right."

After dinner I dozed with my head in Kathleen's lap. She said, "Do you still want to go to my parents' home this weekend?"

"Mmmph."

"Was that yes?"

"Uh-huh."

"I'm looking forward to seeing my mother again. It's been three months since we were there and we'll be moving to

Kansas soon."

"You're right. I'll enjoy going to see them."

"Only if you want to."

Dang. Why I am forced to play this game?

We left early Saturday morning. The weather was clear and dry. We didn't talk much. Kathleen read me the ads for apartments and homes for rent in Topeka. After she finished reading, she knitted on a sweater for one of her nieces.

Rand showed how people will force help on people who haven't asked for it. They say, "I'm doing this for your own good." The recipient is forced to accept unwanted help.

Motives?

Well, what feelings might the donor gain?

They feel good about themselves. Feel needed? Valuable from helping the unfortunate?.

But deny they have such feelings?

Right.

But at other times they feel unappreciated. They coerce others into complementing and praising them. Let's call that behavior "tax collecting."

Sounds good.

Okay. So there is a...a...a Robin Hood complex with the key defense mechanisms being "charity" and "tax collecting." The hidden motivation behind charity forced on others—"I'm doing this for your own good"—is indicated when the target person is not allowed the freedom to not be helped.

You've got a lot of work to do to stop doing these things yourself.

I know.

Stop helping people who haven't asked for it, giving people unasked for advice. Stop being so vulnerable to put-downs, being so concerned about what people think about you.

But how?

Esteem is the key.

We arrived at the Ryans' place about noon. Mrs. Ryan came out the back door, smiling, waving, wiping her hands on her apron. I wanted to keep on with my thinking. Mr. Ryan agreed to let me mow the backyard. I filled the mower with gas, checked the oil, started it, and began mowing the edge of the yard.

So how can you escape from being manipulated, from being used, and from playing emotional games with people?

By understanding my selfish motives better and by taking my need for esteem away from the control of others.

How do I do that?

By allowing myself to have high self-esteem.

That computes. Do it!

What would be the highest possible statement of self-esteem you could come up with?

I am better than everyone else?

No.

I am more valuable than anyone else?

Close, but "more" is a relative term. You can only be more by comparing yourself to others, like being graded on the curve in a class.

I am the most valuable person on earth?

That's still relative. It needs external support. Make the statement independent of what others think or feel about themselves. You must avoid the contrast effect.

How about "<u>As far as I am concerned</u> I am the most valuable person who will ever exist!"

That would work. Fantastic!

Right, it's a conscious feeling that many people could have and not cause problems. Who cares if another person thinks it too? If they do, fine, good for them. If they don't, then tough.

But dangerous!

True. Dangerous because they will feel threatened. If they believe there's only so much esteem to go around, if you have too much, their supply is threatened. They have to take yours away.

For your own good, of course.

Right. And then demand appreciation for having saved you.

The lawn was finished but I wasn't. I found a pair of hand shears in the garage and started trimming edges.

Okay, so the feeling "as far as I am concerned I am the most valuable person who will ever exist" is a tool. It can be used to break free from the hooks and games and manipulations that both <u>you</u> and others are into.

But a lot of people won't like it.

For sure!

So keep your mouth shut.

Right.

Hey!

Maybe the need for high esteem is why people claim to be Jesus, Cleopatra, Napoleon...

Wow! That's big.

Maybe if their self-esteem has been driven way down, there's a homeostatic mechanism that tries to rescue it!

Okay, that computes. Keep going...

A person knows that Jesus, the Virgin Mary, Napoleon, receive high regard.

"Ow!" The top of my head bumped into the thorny stem of a rose bush.

That hurts!

I rubbed my head, then checked my fingers for blood.

Pay attention, you klutz.

So the mind matches up the feeling with the image and the name. They feel fantastic—wonderful, highly esteemed.

And what happens? Other people declare that to be the <u>sickest</u> of ideas. Then, claiming to act unselfishly for the person's own good, they lock him up and use every means possible to drive such thoughts and feelings out of his mind. They can't let him walk around free if he feels too much self-esteem.

The shrinks are impelled to action. They must cure him of his "paranoid schizophrenia."

And what is their success rate?

<u>Below</u> chance.

And then they blame their lack of success on the patient.

Right. They tell the public, "He's so sick he's beyond help. The best we can do for the poor soul is to keep him in a protected environment."

God, I may puke.

That's enough for now. Back off. Let this set for awhile.

I put the tools away and went inside to watch TV.

I didn't talk as we drove back to Ann Arbor.

"Al, are you all right?" Kathleen asked.

"Sure. I just have a lot on my mind."

"Please tell me what you think about so much."

"You don't like to hear about some of the things I think. I'm sorry you're concerned. I've got a lot on my mind. Everything is okay, really."

"Are things all right with the research project? All right at the hospital?"

"Yes. The testing is going very well. It is obvious we will get significant results to validate Cannicott's work. Mrs. Martin, the records department supervisor, talked with me about how to be better at hiring people. Bostian told me my testing reports are very helpful."

"You always speak well of him. Do you like Dr. Bostian better than the other psychiatrists?"

"I do. He's an excellent supervisor. He has more common sense than the others. Do you want to come and watch the softball game tomorrow? It will be a good one."

"All right." She looked out the window. "It certainly got dark early."

I glanced at her and smiled. "It might not look so dark if you took off your sun glasses."

"Oh!" Kathleen blushed and laughed at herself as she removed them.

Stanley and I went to each psychiatric facility on Waggoner's list and established our contacts. We learned when each facility conducted shock treatments and wrote out a schedule for ourselves. We were given pass keys to each hospital so we could come and go as we wished.

By the end of July our research was underway. Cannicott interviewed each patient scheduled for ECT to verify he or she was depressed and I conducted the memory testing. We went from place to place in my car. Almost every time we entered one of the hospitals, he would announce cheerily, "Here come the concrete removers!"

The research went smoothly. After our routine was established Cannicott taught the physicians how to hold the electrodes. I made sure they were used on the correct side of each patient's head.

"What would the correct side be, Al?"

"We ran across several left-handed patients. With them, if the electrodes were used on the right side of their heads, the negative effects would have been as bad or even worse than the bilateral method. The dominant hemisphere of your brain is on the opposite side of your handedness. If you are right handed, the left side of your brain is dominant. This meant that for the right-handed patient the electrodes would be placed on the right side, for left handed on the left side. That's why we questioned each patient about which hand they used."

"It sounds like you and Cannicott worked very well together."

"We did, and we spent lots of free time together as well. One Sunday Stanley and his wife Shirley came over to our apartment. We ate watermelon out in backyard. They'd never eaten watermelon before. We all had fun spitting the seeds out. Afterwards we went inside, washed up, and drank the bottle of wine they'd brought. During the next several weeks we got together for dinners, picnics, and short sight-seeing trips."

Kathleen and I talked about what to do about the moving estimates. They were higher than we expected. I told Kathleen, "The information packet Smith sent me says they have a credit union. My stock is only worth about $500. Let's keep that in reserve and try to get a credit union loan to cover our moving costs. How does that sound?"

"It's all right with me."

"Good. Please type a letter to Karren Falley for me asking how we can do that. It's the sort of thing she would be arranging."

Chapter Eight

The Mother of the Second Savior

In early August Laura reported at rounds that an 18-year-old girl had been brought in by her parents during the weekend. Bostian asked Marcene Gibbons, the psychiatric resident in charge of the patient, for a report. Marcene said, "The parents told us that Molly claims God talked to her. My provisional diagnosis is that she is a paranoid schizophrenic. She is very withdrawn. She won't talk to me or the nurses."

Bostian looked at Laura.

Laura shook her head. "Unresponsive," she said.

Each morning we heard that Molly would not talk to anyone. She refused to go to recreational therapy, occupational therapy, or any ward activities. She stopped talking to her doctor. After two weeks of such reports Bostian said to Marcene, "This patient is not responding to our treatment milieu. She is so severely withdrawn you should start the paper work to have her committed to Ypsilanti State Hospital."

Most of the staff nodded in agreement. One of the supervising psychiatrists said, "Molly is so severely paranoid schizophrenic she will probably spend the rest of her life in the state hospital."

I remained silent, thinking.

Siebert, here might be a chance to test out some of these ideas.

I don't know. Experimenting with patients is…

What is there to lose? Right now she is headed for a lifetime in the back wards.

Okay. We'll give it a shot.

After rounds I asked Marcene for permission to interview Molly and do a few psychological tests before she was transferred. Marcene agreed.

I went up to the ward office and arranged with Laura to see Molly. "I'd like to interview her on the ward," I said. "She is familiar with it. She might be too uncomfortable if we went down to my office."

"How about interviewing her in the ward dining room at ten a.m. tomorrow? I can make sure you have privacy there."

"Sure. Thanks."

That night I mentally prepared myself for the next day.

McConnell has always emphasized that behavior is determined by it's consequences. What questions would help me explore the links?

I developed four questions and fixed them firmly in my mind:

What would happened if I just listened to her and don't allow my mind to put any psychiatric labels on her?

What would happen if I talked to her believing that she could turn out to be my best friend?

What would happen if I accepted everything she reports about herself as being the truth?

What would happen if I questioned her to find out if there's a link between her self-esteem, the workings of her mind, and the way that others have been treating her?

Laura brought Molly into the ward dining room. She was about average height with brown, shoulder-length hair and a pale complexion. She looked slightly overweight. Face and figure about average. Shoulders slumped. A plain looking young woman—almost dowdy. She wore a faded, shapeless cotton dress. Molly glanced toward me when Laura introduced us, then dropped her eyes.

She seems frightened and lonely.

Her mind is on me so I know she isn't self-absorbed.

As Laura left the room I seated Molly in a chair at the end of a table. I sat on the side. I placed a blank piece of paper and a pencil before her. "I'm going to show you some cards with designs on them," I said. "Please copy each design on the paper as well as you can."

I wasn't really interested in how well she could draw, I just wanted her to become comfortable with me. I sat relaxed and quiet. When she finished a drawing I'd say, "Good," or "That's fine," or "Okay, here is the next one."

Next I gave her a test arranging blocks to match designs on cards. She followed the instructions accurately and worked at a good speed.

She's not depressed. No obvious neurological problems.

Molly looked up at me.

There she is.

"Hello."

She blushed and ducked her head.

I like her. She's like a skittish cat that wants to come close but is cautious and poised to run.

"Molly," I said softly.

She kept her head down.

"Molly."

She looked up at me.

"I'm curious about something, why are you here in a psychiatric hospital?"

"God spoke to me and said I was going to give birth to the second Savior."

Keep your mind silent. Be a friend.

"That may be, but why are you here in the hospital?"

Well said—matter of factly. "So what else is new?"

She was startled. With a somewhat puzzled look on her face she said, "Well, that's crazy talk."

"According to whom?"

"What?"

"Did *you* decide when God spoke to you that you were crazy?"

"Oh," she said. "No, they told me I was crazy."

"Do you believe you are crazy?"

"No, but I am aren't I."

That wasn't a question. It was an assertion so it has self-esteem attached and would be defended. Try to get the self-esteem away from it.

"If you will put that in the form of a question, I will answer you."

She wrinkled her forehead. She stared at me. "Do you think I'm crazy?"

"No, I don't."

"But that couldn't have happened could it?"

"As far as I am concerned you are the only person who knows what happens in your mind. Did it seem real at the time?"

"Oh, yes!"

Help her check this out—how real it seemed.

"Tell me what you did after God spoke to you."

"What do you mean?"

"Did you start knitting booties and sweaters and things?"

She laughed. "No, but I did pack my clothes and wait by the door several times."

"Why?"

"I thought I would be taken some place."

"It wasn't where you expected, was it!"

She laughed. "No!"

Empathize. Really put yourself in her place now.

"One thing I'm curious about..."

"What?"

"Why is it that of all the women in the world, God chose you to be the mother of the second Savior?"

She broke into a big grin. "You know, I've been trying to figure that out myself!"

Very good!

Okay, we have a good conversation going now.

Let's see what led up to this.

Look for feelings after events.

"Molly, what was happening in your life before God spoke to you?"

It took about thirty minutes to draw out a sequence of events. She was an only child. She wanted her parents love, but they didn't give her much. Only once in a while. Just enough to give her hope she could get more.

She would come home from high school and volunteer to help with the housework, the cooking, and the dishes. But her mother rarely showed any appreciation. Her father had been a musician, so she took up the clarinet in high school. She thought this would please him. Her senior year she was chosen to be first chair in the high school orchestra.

"I was excited," she said. "I believed my father would be proud of me. When he came home that night I told him. But he got angry. He picked up my clarinet and smashed it across the kitchen table. He yelled at me, 'You'll never amount to anything.'"

"How did you feel after that?"

"Awful. I cried and cried. I knew my parents didn't love me."

"What happened after you graduated from high school?"

"I spent the summer with my boyfriend. At the end of summer I went to nursing school and he went to a university in a different city."

"Why did you chose nursing?"

"I thought the patients would like me for all the nice things I would do for them."

"What was nursing school like for you?"

"I kept to myself. I didn't make friends with other student nurses except for one. We had to study a lot. The third term I got my first clinical assignment. I was really looking forward to it." Molly looked down.

"What happened?" I asked.

"The two women in my room criticized me." Molly's face twisted in pain. "I couldn't do anything right for them."

"How did you feel when that happened?"

"Like the world was falling in. It was horrible." She dropped her head. "I ran away from school. I took a bus to where my boyfriend was at college. He came and met me at the bus station. We went to a coffee shop to talk. I said I wanted to come and live with him, but he said he wanted to date other girls. He said we could still be friends, but I should go home and write to him."

"How did you feel after that?"

"Awful lonely."

"What did you do?"

"I left school and went back home."

"How did your parents feel about that?"

"They didn't want me there."

"And you felt..."

"Lonely. I stayed in my room most the time."

"So your dad and mom didn't love you. The patients were critical. They didn't like you. Your boyfriend just wanted to be friends. Your parents didn't want you to come back to live with them."

"Yes, there didn't seem to be anyone in the whole world who cared for me at all."

"What an awful feeling. And then God spoke to you."

"Yes," she said in a soft voice.

"How did you feel after God gave you the good news?"

Molly looked up with a warm inner radiance and smiled. "I felt like the most special person in the whole world."

There it is! Fantastic!

"That's a nice feeling, isn't it?"

"Yes, it is."

Sounds of the kitchen crew getting ready for lunch became louder.

"It's almost noon. We must stop now."

As we stood up she reached out and touched my arm. "Please don't tell them what we've been talking about," she pleaded. "No one seems to understand."

Kiddo, you are so right. And I don't want them to find out about this either. Not yet anyway.

"I know what you mean. I promise not to tell if you won't. I mean that."

You're not supposed to do that.

Fuck the rules.

"I promise."

We walked out of the dining room.

Amazing! My experiment worked!

I didn't let my mind diagnosis her or label her. I empathized with her experience and accepted it as her reality.

When I questioned her the sequence came out. Extreme loss of love—of esteem—seemed to trigger a homeostatic mechanism. It rescued her esteem.

Then when that emerged, no one could handle it. They automatically viewed her as sick and have been impelled to try to drive the idea and the feeling of being the most special out of her. Everyone certain they are doing this for her own good.

Fantastic!

Yeah. Now what do I do with it?

Two days later I was walking through the closed ward to pick up a patient scheduled for testing. Molly walked up to me and put her hand on my arm. I stopped and looked at her.

"I've been thinking about what we talked about," she said. "I've been wondering. Do you think I imagined God's voice to make myself feel better?"

Holy cow! I didn't intend to do therapy, but she seems to see the connection.

Be careful Siebert.

What?

Be practical.

Right.

"Perhaps," I said, and shrugged.

Why not? If there really is an old fashioned God who does things like this, then HE is watching! I don't care what the other doctors and nurses do. I am not about to give her a rough time!

I mentally looked upward to whoever might be listening.

I am her friend! Right?

At rounds during the next week Laura reported that Molly was talking to people, participating in ward activities, wearing nicer clothing, and putting on makeup. The plan to commit her was postponed.

Bostian said to us, "This may be a case of spontaneous remission. You can never predict when it will happen."

Fascinating. A patient they can't cure suddenly gets better and they see this as happening all by itself. Why aren't they curious? Asking questions?

Use the scientific method. Look for opportunities to confirm or disprove your speculations.

Chapter Nine

Shocking Discoveries

About the time we completed the first patients receiving five unilateral ECT treatments at Mercywood, the private psychiatric hospital, I ran into a surprising development. When I went onto the women's ward several patients scheduled for electroshock said, "Please have them give me the good kind." The patients, observing differences in each other after shock treatments, had figured out that two different methods of treatment were being used. The unilateral method was clearly less damaging. After that I felt bothered when I had to assign a new patient to the control group, the group receiving traditional ECT.

"Al, did you talk to Kathleen about Molly or the unilateral ECT results?"

"A little. I told her about how much better the unilateral was. When I tried to talk to her about Molly, however, she just stared at me, so I dropped the subject. During the first several weeks of August, my mind was really churning. My interview with Molly and the effect it had on her were so totally unexpected. I felt thrilled but frustrated. There was no one to talk to. I went for long walks at night. I didn't sleep well because I was very excited and my mind was working hard trying to make sense of everything. I'd get up at 2:00 or 3:00 a.m. and soak in a tub full of hot water to try to relax."

When I got home one afternoon Kathleen started in again. "Please talk to me. Tell me what you're thinking."

"How can I? You don't want me to say anything you don't want to hear. I've made an important discovery. I've stumbled onto some incredible insights into how the human mind works. I have some glimpses of how the world can work better, but I don't understand things well enough to explain what I see."

Tears came into her eyes. "You come home late in the evening. You go for long walks late at night. You get out of bed at three in the morning and soak in the bath tub for hours. You don't tell me what you are thinking about. Please talk to me more."

Don't do it!

"You can't handle it."

"Yes, I can."

"Okay, but you won't like it."

You're making a mistake.

"I discovered that a person can break the control others have over his self-esteem by thinking, 'As far as I am concerned I am the most valuable person who will ever exist.'"

"No one should think that."

"But it works."

"Only Jesus can think that." Her face became disfigured with a mixture of distress and horror. It pained me to see the effect of my words on her.

"Everyone thinks it at some level," I said.

"No. No!"

"Yes! And when they aren't consciously aware of it, they do deceptive, manipulative things to build up their esteem and control other people's esteem."

She lowered her eyes and shook her head. "No!"

"Yes! Look, if Jesus really thinks well of himself, he doesn't care what anyone else thinks. Look at how successful I was with the young woman I told you about, the one who said God spoke to her. I didn't care what she thought about herself, so I could talk to her as a real person. It works. It's a useful idea."

"No! No one should think that."

"Yes. Just let yourself think, 'As far as I am concerned I am the most valuable person who will ever exist.'"

She buried her head in her hands. Tears ran down her face. She started sobbing.

I got angry. "Kathleen, may I make a suggestion?"

"What?"

"If you can't handle the answer, then don't ask the question! I don't like it when you ask me a personal question with the hidden qualification, 'But don't say anything I can't handle.' It's very distressing to people who want to be honest."

Back off! You proved your point. Feel good about it?

No. I shouldn't have given in. But I was right. She couldn't handle it.

You didn't have to do that.

Well, maybe she'll stay off my back now.

She picked up her purse and started out the door. "I'm going to church."

"At this time?"

"I want to talk to the priest."

Good. Maybe he'll be able to reassure her.

A 25-year-old male was admitted to NPI with the diagnosis "acute paranoid state." I obtained permission from his resident to interview him.

I took the man to my office and had him sit down. "Why are you here in the hospital?"

He clenched his jaw. "My wife and family say I don't think right. They say I'm talking crazy. They pressured me into this place."

"You're a voluntary admission aren't you?"

"Yes. It won't do any good, though. They're the ones who need a psychiatrist."

"Why do you say that?"

"I work in sales in a big company. Everyone is out for themselves. I don't like it. I don't like to pressure people or trick them into buying to put bucks in my pocket. The others seem to go for it. Selfish, clawing to get ahead. My boss says I have the wrong attitude. He rides me all the time."

"What's the problem with your family?"

"I talked about quitting and going to veterinarian school. I like animals. I'd like that work. My wife says I'm not thinking right. She wants me to stay in business and work up into management. She went to my parents and got them on her side."

"I still don't see the reason for your being here."

"They're upset because I started yelling at them how selfish they are. My wife wants a husband who earns big money, owns a fancy home, and drives an expensive car. She doesn't want to be the wife of a veterinarian. They can't see how selfish they are trying to make me fit into a slot so they can be happy. Everyone is telling me what I should think and what should make me happy."

"So you told them how selfish they are?"

"Yes. They couldn't take it. They insist they're only interested in my welfare." He leaned over and held his face in his hands.

This confirms the blind selfishness behind "Charity," but where does the paranoid diagnosis come from?

"Did you tell the admitting physician about them trying to make you think right?"

"Yes. Everyone's trying to brainwash me. My wife, parents, the sales manager. Everyone's trying to push their thinking into my head."

There it is! The resident hears him saying, "people are trying to force thoughts into my mind," and this is seen as a symptom of paranoia. Amazing. The truth is diagnosed as sickness.

"How do you feel about all this?"

"I'm angry. They say they want to help me, but they don't care about me. They're all selfish. Afraid I'll upset their little worlds. I shouldn't be here."

"What has your doctor said?"

"He doesn't listen. He says I must believe I'm mentally ill. It's crazy."

I'm beginning to see that.

We talked for awhile about what he thought he would do about his situation. Then I took him back to the ward. Several days later he signed himself out. Lois said he took off for California.

This is amazing. Perhaps there is something to the title of that book I've seen in the library, The Myth of Mental Illness *by Thomas Szasz. I wonder why no instructor ever assigned it or mentioned it?*

Cannicott used my office when he needed a place to work. He read some of my books and asked questions about psychological testing. He wanted to take the Minnesota Multiphasic

Personality Inventory, the MMPI, so I administered it and scored it for him.

"Here is how your psychological profile looks," I said.

"What does it show?"

"This is as healthy a score as you can get."

"How do you know?"

"It is a typical score for an educated male."

I opened a drawer and took out a folder. "Here, I'll show you something. Your profile and mine are almost identical."

He compared the two. They were amazingly similar.

"How do you know I didn't fake the answers?"

"The test is built to spot that." I opened the MMPI handbook. "Here are examples of what happens if a person has mental or emotional disturbances and tries to look healthy. Here is how it looks if someone is healthy and is trying to look sick, such as a soldier bucking for a psychiatric discharge. Even professionals can't fake it."

"They can't?"

"No. We covered that in a course I just took. When mental health professionals try to produce the profile of someone with paranoid schizophrenia, they can't do it. Their results come out in a saw-tooth pattern. Much different from the pattern of actual patients."

"What if I marked it at random?"

I turned to a different section of the manual and pointed to a chart. "It would look like this. The validity scales spot that."

"Impressive it is." He looked at me. "Al, our month in the colonies is ending. The Mrs. and I must return home. You know that Waggoner wants more patients tested."

"I promise to continue testing."

We parted with a vigorous, double-handed handshake.

The loan from the Menninger credit union came through. Smith co-signed for us.

I played my best softball ever. In one game we were ahead by two runs in the sixth inning. The other team had two men on base with two outs and their best batter at the plate. I was playing deep in left field to make certain the batter didn't hit one over my head. McKeachie pitched a fast ball to the inside corner. The batter swung fast. He connected solidly and hit a long line drive into foul territory down the left field line. The moment he swung I sprinted at top speed toward the foul line. In my cells I felt that my sole purpose for existing on this planet was to catch that ball before it hit the ground.

Time slowed as my body accelerated to the one spot where my glove would intercept the trajectory of the ball. I raced across the foul line, leaped with my body fully extended. I caught the ball backhanded.

Tuck and roll.

I pulled the ball into my stomach so it would not fall out of my glove when I hit the ground. I tucked my left shoulder underneath, rolled into a parachute landing fall, and ended up on my back.

My momentum had carried me into the unmowed tall grass at the edge of the playing field.

Show the umpire.

I knew the umpire would need to see that I hadn't dropped the ball. I quickly extended my left arm from up out of the tall grass to show everyone that the ball was still in my glove. Everyone on both teams and all the spectators yelled, applauded, and cheered. When I jogged in from the field I was mobbed by my teammates rushing up to shake my hand and pat me on the back. McKeachie beamed. "That was a fabulous catch!" he said. Even the batter shook my hand.

I felt happy driving home, very good.

When I went to bed that night, I fell asleep quickly.

I'm lying in bed on my left side. My head is propped up on my left hand. Laura is lying next to me with her eyes shut. She's nude. With my right hand I caress her body. It is a caress meant to comfort, not to arouse. I stroke her stomach, hips and thighs. Then back up to her stomach, her breasts, neck, and shoulders. She seems unhappy. I want her to feel better. Her soft, moist lips part for me. I lean over. I move my lips close to hers…

"…and remember," a male voice says, "when you take our nonstop flight to Miami, you can fly now and pay later."

What?

It's my clock radio.
I've been dreaming!
That goddamn clock radio! It ruined my dream!
"Now for the weather. Today's high in the Detroit area will be..."
Damn! Just a few more seconds!

Mercywood physicians did their shock treatments before 7:00 a.m., so I had to shower fast and get going. As I dried off, Kathleen asked, "Do you want me to fix you a lunch?"

"Sure, if you hurry."

"I'm out of lunch meat. Will fried egg sandwiches be all right?"

"Okay."

She slipped on her robe and went into the kitchen. While I shaved, Kathleen started the eggs frying. As I left the bathroom, Kathleen tried to walk past me.

I stepped in her way. "Please," I said, "fry now and pee later!"

She elbowed me in the ribs and pushed me aside.

After I finished the testing at Mercywood, I let myself out of the ward and went over to the elevator. When the doors opened I saw Dr. Meyer, one of Mercywood's owners inside.

"How is the research going?" he asked as the doors closed behind me.

"We're getting significant results. I did some rough calculations. The data support the unilateral technique. There's no brain damage and the depressions are lifting. Have you asked the nurses and aides for their reactions? They're amazed at the difference. And when I go in to do my memory test, some of the bilateral patients plead with me to be allowed to have the 'good kind.'"

"I've seen all that," he said. "But frankly..." He looked around even though we were alone in the elevator. He leaned close and whispered, "...I make some of my patients brain damaged on purpose. They aren't so resistant to directions that way. They follow my orders better when they're confused and dependent."

Adrenaline surged through my body.

This is outrageous!

Take it easy. There isn't anything you can do right now. Calm down and let it process.

Back at the hospital I went into the main office to get my mail. Laura walked up to the mail boxes at the same time. She looked at me and stood with challenging eyes waiting for me to say something.

"Are you unhappy?" I asked.

My question startled her. Then she nodded a little. "Yes, I am some."

I remained silent and waited. She grew serious. "My younger brother was just married. My birthday last week made me feel older than I felt before." She raised her chin. "How did you know? I'm very good at hiding my feelings."

Don't tell her about the dream.

"Just a feeling."

I got into the elevator.

I feel oo hungry for that woman. I want to know her, learn her, touch her.

I need to talk to someone about what just happened. Maybe she will listen.

I phoned Laura from my office. "Will you go to coffee with me. Right now?"

"Yes, I will," she said.

In the cafeteria she reached into her pocket for money to pay for her coffee, then looked at me and asked, "Did the invitation include buying my coffee?"

"Of course," I laughed.

Fantastic. She didn't assume I would pay.

When we sat down she said, "I have the feeling something's bothering you. Are you all right?"

"No, I'm not. I'm upset by what a psychiatrist at Mercywood told me this morning. He said he uses ECT to make some patients cooperate with him. He said he brain damages them on purpose."

Laura touched my arm to comfort me.

"I feel so naive," I said. "I keep learning all these things that aren't taught in the courses."

"Some psychiatrists use medications that way too," she said.

"This isn't news to you?"

"No. Hospital psychiatrists do many things to patients that the public never hears about."

"I know if I tried to tell anyone about Meyers, he'd deny what he said. I never knew these things went on."

"I like how concerned you are, Al," she said, touching me. "You really care about people."

"I do. I feel what people feel and keep wanting to find ways for them to be happy. I'm curious about you."

"Oh?"

"You're such a loner. Why did you get married?"

"He was the first man to ask me. I did it to get away from home. It was a mistake, though." She laughed. "I could always outsmart him."

"There's a lot of gossip about you. The word is that you once dated a former patient. I also heard that you dated a biker and wore black leathers and all. How do you put up with the negative talk?"

"It's my opinion that counts."

"What do you think of yourself?"

"I'm number one."

"That's wonderful!"

"You like to hear me say that?"

"Yes! Let me tell you about Molly..." I went through the whole story.

"This is fascinating," Laura said. "We were amazed at the sudden change in her. And it all happened because you validated her feelings."

"Evidently. The key is to understand the automatic way the need for self-esteem operates. My problem is how to get the mental health experts to understand it."

"They don't know?"

"No, they don't."

"It's so obvious. I thought everyone knew that." She sipped her coffee.

We walked back to NPI. I rode up the elevator with her to the sixth floor. Instead of entering her ward, though, she unlocked a door to a stairway leading up to the seventh floor.

"Where are you going?" I asked.

"To check on one of Dr. Waggoner's private patients."

"I didn't know there were patients up there. There's no one listed on the patient census."

"It's a psychiatrist from Indiana. Dr. Waggoner keeps everything confidential. It's done to protect the doctor's reputation."

"Really?"

"Al, you *are* naive! Many psychiatric hospitals have confidential ways to treat psychiatrists when they have breakdowns. Patients get upset when they hear that their doctors have emotional problems."

"Jesus! What a cover up!"

"It's just real life, Al."

I reached out and touched her shoulder. "I'd like to talk to you some more."

She smiled. "I'd like that. I like talking about ideas and about me without the usual games. Most men don't care about me. They only want people to see them with a beautiful blonde on their arm." As she turned to go she added with a saucy smile, "You'll find I'm not bound by the usual traditions of society."

I returned to my office and tried to calm the crossfire of insights, emotions, and experiences coming at me.

I feel angry about the discrepancy between what I was taught in school and what I'm learning from first hand experience.

My experience with Molly is at odds with everything taught to me.

I feel dismayed and shocked about Dr. Meyers' disclosure.

I feel excited about getting first hand knowledge.

Laura stirs feelings in me I've never felt before.

The phone rang. It was Kathleen. "That was funny," she said. "I got it about an hour after you left. I've been laughing all morning. That was very funny."

"Thank you. I thought it was, too."

At rounds the next morning I heard that a newly admitted patient was diagnosed as "schizophrenic with paranoid ideation." I was assigned to test the patient so I brought him down to my office immediately. He was 26 years old and unemployed. He said he wanted to become an artist. The testing took about two hours. At the end of the session I asked, "What did you do and say that caused people to hospitalize you?"

"I told my parents," he said, "that their trying to keep me from sleeping around and taking drugs was not for *my* good. The way I live embarrasses them. They both have masters degrees and want me to go to college to become an intellectual. I told them they aren't good people. They are hurting and destroying my mind by trying to mold me into what they want me to be."

"So you've been shoving it to them and they can't handle the truth about themselves?"

"That's right."

"And you got to them so good that they reacted by having you locked up in here?"

"You got that right."

"Well, congratulations. You did a good job."

He smiled.

I asked what plans he had now that he had proved his point. We talked about whether or not what he was going through was worth the satisfaction he felt.

When we parted he shook my hand warmly and said, "You're good. I like you. I've talked to a lot of shrinks, but you're different."

"Thanks."

Waggoner called me up to his office to check my progress with the ECT project. I showed him that we had enough cases to establish highly significant differences between the unilateral and bilateral groups.

He was concerned that we only had a total of 24 patients in the study. He told me to get more. It didn't carry any weight with him that we already had enough cases to prove what we set out to do at beyond the chance level of one in a thousand.

Mercywood was closest, so I continued out there. I arrived early and let myself into the locked adult female ward. As I walked down the hall, a somewhat frantic woman rushed up. She was about 50, dark complexion, black hair with some gray, medium height, matronly figure, round shouldered, and about 170 pounds.

"Are you a doctor?" she said with desperation in her voice. "Can you help me get out of here?"

"Yes, I'm a doctor but not a medical one. I'm a psychologist."

"Please help me. I'm not supposed to be here!" She clutched my arm. Several aides came over to take her away. I motioned them away. "My husband and son put me here! Please help me."

"I have no authority to do anything here," I told her. "Why are you here in the mental hospital?"

"My husband put me here. I'm not crazy! I'm not supposed to be here!"

"Why did your husband put you here?"

We sat down at a table. She grabbed my hand.

"I said I would divorce him. I warned him before to stop being bossy. He always bossed me around. He came home from work Friday and was bossy again. I got mad. The last straw. I yelled and screamed at him. I said, 'Get out! Leave me alone. I divorce you!' He yelled at my oldest son to get the car out. He grabbed me and said I am crazy to divorce him. He wrestled me to the car. He threw me on the floor and held me down. He ordered my son to drive me to this place. Please help me! I'm not crazy. My husband, he's crazy. They won't let me telephone. I can't call friends or my sister. Please help."

"Are you Italian?"

"Yes."

"Catholic?"

"Yes. I pray to Jesus to get me out."

"Have you seen a doctor yet?"

"No. No one."

"You'll be able to talk to someone today. They will talk to your husband too. Everything will be all right."

Two aides came over. "Come on Mrs. Donnelli." They took hold of her arms and led her into a small lounge with a curtained door where all the patients were held during shock treatments.

Another aide walked over to me. "She's a bad one," he said. "Tried to escape twice this weekend. Made it out to the lawn once. Nothing but trouble. Saying she's not crazy. Stirring up the patients."

I went into the lounge. The two research patients I was testing learned their respective sets of words quickly. As I stood up to leave the "shock team" arrived in the ward dayroom. A nurse opened the door and called out, "Mrs. Donnelli."

What? Shock for her?

Mrs. Donnelli got up and walked out ahead of me.

She doesn't know what is waiting for her!

Try to help her!

I walked over to Kroll. "Dr. Kroll, if this patient is going to receive ECT, I can use her as a unilateral subject."

"No. She is a special patient. You can't include her. Please step back."

The aides led her toward the treatment table. She began to struggle. "No! What are you doing to me?"

"You need treatment for your illness Mrs. Donnelli."

"I'm not crazy! I don't want treatment!"

The aides closed in on her. Two men and three women. All husky.

"You are mentally ill Mrs. Donnelli," insisted Dr. Kroll.

Mrs. Donnelli struggled. "No! Someone help me! I don't want treatment!" They wrestled her onto the table and held her down. Dr. Kroll injected the muscle relaxant into her arm.

"No! I don't want treatment!"

The nurse pressed the rubber strip with the two electrodes down tight over her forehead.

"You need this treatment Mrs. Donnelli," Dr. Kroll said. "You are mentally ill."

"No! I'm not crazy!"

I saw Dr. Kroll turn the dials to increase the voltage and the duration of the shock. He turned back to her and smiled. The last thing she heard before he pressed the button was his voice insisting, "You *are* mentally ill, Mrs. Donnelli."

As I watched the convulsions rack her body, I felt enraged.

I've got to stop them!

I took a step forward.

Control yourself! Waggoner said to not interfere!

Get out!

No! I'm going to…

Get out! Get yourself out!

Now!

As Mrs. Donnelli's convulsions subsided the aides backed away from the table. I walked toward the ward door and gestured for one of the aides to come with me.

That's it. Stay silent.

I took the hospital pass key off my key ring. I unlocked the door and pushed it open. I turned and handed my key to the aide. The door shut behind me. I walked out of the hospital and got into my car.

I walked out of Mercywood with my mind and feelings reeling. I almost backed my car into another car.

Watch it! Relax. Be alert…Take it easy now…That's it…Drive slowly…Be aware…Okay…What in the hell is with these people? That was brutal!

But they don't see it that way.

No, they don't. They have it intellectualized. No emotional contact.

What is their perception?

The aides are nice, friendly people, but their jobs are to work with the "nuts," with the "crazies."

They don't see patients as people.

Their minds distort what they look at. They are blind to the harm being done.

The doctors?

The aides and nurses accept the doctors' perceptions. The doctors speak with great authority. They have the salaries, clothes, cars, homes, titles, free time, coats…The long white coats…It all combines to communicate, "We have the power. We know the truth. Accept what we say. You can believe us."

And they believe that the goal of eliminating mental illness is so compelling any means is justified. The perception of mental illness automatically justifies any action taken to remove it. Even if...

Even if patients disagree they are mentally ill.

Resistance is a sign...

It is an indication of <u>how</u> severely mentally ill the person is. The person's own view is dismissed because they are so sick they can't see they are sick.

Right, and that's why a patient is not present when the staff discusses his or her case. The patient would protest and be disruptive.

No! Remember what Giora said. The rationalization is that it would be too upsetting for patients to hear about their psychopathology. It is for the patients' own good that they are not allowed to attend conferences on their cases and are not allowed to read what is written about them.

Christ, I wish there was someone I could talk to. Everything I've been told is backwards!

Watch yourself. This is very dangerous.

Chapter Ten

Struggle and Turmoil

"It is dismaying to hear about Mrs. Donnelli, Al, and very angering to me. I had no idea that such things happened."

"Far too often, Sam. Even now, after all this time, reexperiencing that incident upsets me."

"I can understand why."

"And of everything that happened that summer, trying to stop them or get help for her is the only thing I wished I would have done differently."

"Like what?

"I've been through it a dozen times in my mind. I could have asked Dr. Kroll, 'If this patient hasn't been to court, doesn't she have the right to refuse medical treatment?' I could have called the district attorney's office to tell them what I witnessed. I've asked myself many times why I didn't do more to try to help her."

"Why do you think?"

"Part of the reason, I know, is that I was scared. I was afraid of what might happen to me if I wasn't careful. Psychiatrists back then had the power to lock up anyone who upset them. They could drug and brain damage a person with no risk of legal repercussions. Also, my disillusionment was still only partial. I was still enmeshed in the world of diagnostic labeling, testing mentally ill people, status, and titles. I was taught that psychiatrists knew more about these matters than anyone else and I was trained to not challenge psychiatrists. By the way, I was pleased to discover a few years ago that a Michigan housewife who went through an incident similar to Mrs. Donnelli won a $40,000 judgment in a suit for assault and battery and false imprisonment."

I went back to my office. It was time to start cleaning out my desk and bookcase. I opened the drawer of file folders with my reports of psychological testing and folders from my graduate courses.

I took out a folder with my notes and papers from a course on the psychoses.

This is worthless! The required courses on mental disorders train students to maintain an ineffective system! I refuse to allow this garbage in my mind!

I threw the folder in the wastebasket.

They can't cure any of these conditions, but they talk and write as if they know what they are talking about.

I took file after file out of the drawer and slammed each one into the trash. I grabbed handfuls of psychiatric journals left in the bookcase by the previous occupant and heaped them on top of the pile until the wastebasket couldn't hold any more.

There. That's where mental garbage should be.

I looked at the overflowing wastebasket and chuckled.

That will be a load for the janitor.

Over at the psych department I heard that Gerald Blum, one of my professors, was in the university hospital for minor surgery. His area was personality theory. He'd done a lot of research on defense mechanisms.

There must be someone who can follow my thinking.

Blum should be able to understand.

I wrote out a description of the two defense mechanisms, charity and tax collecting, and gave supporting evidence. The next day at the hospital I went up to professor Blum's room.

"Hi Doctor Blum," I said. "Would you look this over? I think I might be on to some defense mechanisms that have been overlooked."

As he read my short paper he frowned. "What is this?"

"There seem to be several previously unrecognized defense mechanisms operating in human behavior. I still don't have it all sorted out yet. What do you think?"

He shook his head. "This doesn't make sense to me. No. We know what all the defense mechanisms are. My work..."

Shit! I had hoped so much...

Maybe if I told him about Molly.

Forget it. Terminate the conversation.

"I'm sorry I bothered you. I was just kicking around a few new ideas and thought I'd try them out on you. I've got to get back to NPI. Thanks for your time. I hope you recover soon."

Saturday afternoon Nate Caplan telephoned. "Al baby!" How are you doing!"

"Great!"

"Hey, I'm working on my basement, remodeling it. Why don't you come over this evening and talk with me while I work? I want to find out what you've been doing."

"Sure. Sounds good."

"Good. Wait. We don't have anything in the house. How about bringing a six pack?"

"Sure. I'll be over in a while."

I sat on the basement stairs drinking beer. I looked at the pieces of plasterboard and wood scattered around. The old cement floor was littered with scrap. "This is quite a project," I said.

"How have you been?" Nate asked. "What's new?"

"I just had an amusing incident at the hospital. I don't know if you remember, but when I was at the court I went to the Cleveland Clinic to get my eyes checked. They prescribed glasses for me, but I had to take them off when I did really close work, like building my Heathkit stereo."

"They prescribed glasses you can't wear if you need to see clearly?"

"That's the way it was. I just had my eyes checked again at the hospital and learned that the glasses corrected my eyesight from 20/15 to 20/20.

"Remind me..."

"Without glasses I can see from 20 feet what most other people can see at 15 feet. The glasses corrected my eyes to 20/20 by making my visual acuity worse! No wonder I rarely wore them."

Caplan laughed. "They were just trying to help you be normal, Al."

I chuckled. "A losing effort." I took another drink of beer.

"Tell me what you've been doing this summer," he said.

Hey! Here's the opportunity I was hoping for. Caplan can be outrageous. Can I communicate these ideas in a way that he can be

*open to? Self-esteem attached to current beliefs shuts people's minds
to new ideas.*

Give it a try.

"Just messing around. Did some research on a new kind of
electroshock treatment this summer. Finally had some free
time to do some reading. Have you read *Atlas Shrugged*?"

"No."

"It was thought provoking. Rand shows how people act for
selfish reasons without knowing it. The gain in most cases, as I
see it, is esteem. The gain is indirect. It has to be kept hidden.
That is why someone like Cassius Clay..."

"Muhammad Ali..."

"...with extremely high self-esteem upsets so many people
when he claims to be the greatest boxer in the world. The inner
dynamics operate in a way that has even the mental health
professionals compelled to remove high self-esteem from a
person while claiming they are doing it for the person's own
good. I talked with a girl who was diagnosed as paranoid
schizophrenic because she claimed that God talked to her..."

Caplan measured an area of the wall and cut a piece of
plasterboard while I told him about Molly.

"One day," I said, "I talked with a resident who felt frustrated because a patient would not accept he was acting entirely for her own good, and yet he had a dozen selfish reasons
underlying his actions...

"There are two unconscious mechanisms that distort the
perception of people compelled to help others for their own
good. I call them 'charity' and..."

I kept talking. Caplan cut more pieces of plasterboard. I
helped him hold several of the larger pieces in place while he
nailed them to the studs.

"I've traced the problem down into our subconscious minds.
An infant cannot comprehend that the horrible, frightening
person that upsets it is the same loving, powerful, comforting
being that it loves and clings to. It splits the bad person away
as a separate being."

Caplan wiped his sweaty, dust-covered face with a towel
and took a long drink of beer.

"Freud was right about the symbolism in dreams and myths. A dream or story that everyone relates to can reveal a lot about common childhood experiences. I wondered about the story of Adam and Eve in the Garden of Eden. I discovered it is a metaphor for an infant's weaning experience. Adam is in Eden with two beings. God, the all powerful, all knowing good mother who created Adam, protects him and provides for him. There is only one rule. Don't bite the nipple. But when Adam bites the nipple and is weaned from paradise, who gets blamed? Eve a second, different, bad being..."

Caplan looked around the basement. "I'll tape the seams and joints tomorrow," he said. He took a broom and started sweeping up.

We are not on the same wave length. He is not excited. He is asking no questions. He's not checking to see if he understands.

"The infant identifies with the good mother, but our culture forces feelings of high self-esteem to be repressed. The way to bring your need for esteem to consciousness and remove control of it from others is to allow yourself to think, "As far as I am concerned I am the most valuable person who will ever exist."

Caplan paused and looked at me with no expression on his face. "I've heard that high self-esteem is correlated with success," he said.

I opened another bottle of beer.

Siebert, you aren't getting through to him.

What's the problem?

Well, either it isn't a good idea or I haven't presented it well.

Are these ideas no good?

I've tested and checked them. All the evidence supports them.

Then that means you don't know how to teach them well.

How can it be done? People have their esteem rooted in their belief of their old ideas.

"Do you see the possibilities?" I said. "Psychotherapists could respond to patients in ways that will *really* be healthy for them rather than breaking them down. It works! I've interviewed more patients now who were supposed to be paranoid. One guy, a young salesman, had a diagnosis of 'acute paranoia.' His main symptom was that he claimed people were trying to force thoughts into his mind. He told his boss, his wife, and his parents that they are selfish, that they are trying to rework his mind and brain so he'll work at doing what's good for them. So what do they do? Force him into a mental hospital. They tell him it is for his own good. And then the staff starts telling him he must believe he is mentally ill!"

You're pushing again. Back off.

"Don't you see? People really *are* trying to force thoughts into his mind!"

Just like you are doing to Nate. You are trying to make him accept into his mind some thoughts you believe are true.

Try something else.

"Have you read *The Myth of Mental Illness* by Dr. Thomas Szasz?"

Nate shook his head, "No."

"I looked through it last week. He explains that the term 'mental illness' was originally just a metaphor. When a person talked or acted in weird ways some physicians decided to say it was 'as if' the person had an illness of the mind. But in recent decades they dropped the 'as if' part, the 'let's pretend' game. Don't you see? 'Mental illness' is just a metaphor. It is something they made up

He's not relating to any of this. Damn. Might as well back off.

I looked at my watch. "Hey, It's late. I have to be up early tomorrow."

He looked at a clock. "It is late. I'll start taping tomorrow."

I stood up. "I'll see you later."

"Take care," he said, as I walked up the stairs with my unopened bottles of beer.

The third week in August was my last week at NPI. At rounds Molly's doctor announced, "I've transferred Molly to the open ward. She seems fully recovered, but I'll keep her under observation for a few days before I discharge her."

Laura and I looked at each other and smiled.

My softball team played a semifinal game on Tuesday. I was up to bat in the fourth inning. The other team had a good fastball pitcher, but we were ahead by one run. I felt very relaxed, very much in harmony with everything happening in my life and in the world. Standing at the plate I did not get into my usual intense, hyper-vigilant stance ready to smack any ball in the strike zone. This time I stood in my batting stance feeling an easy calm. The pitcher threw a chest high fast ball in the middle of the strike zone. In an effortless stroke that felt like a golf swing, my arms and body swung the bat. It connected with the ball in a way that made a pure, solid, perfect sound. The hit was a line drive home run that soared high over the center fielder. The ball landed and rolled across the railroad tracks far out in center field. It was the longest ball and the easiest home run I ever hit.

My teammates shook my hand as I trotted across home plate. "That looked effortless," Al Storey said. "How did it feel?"

I shook my head. "I don't know what happened. I didn't do it. My body did it."

At the end of the game McKeachie shook my hand. "I'll miss you Al," he said. "You are one of the best athletes and one of the best teaching fellows we ever had here at Michigan."

"Thanks. I appreciate all the help you gave me. I just regret having to miss the championship game next week."

"Good luck, and let me know how you do in their program."

"I will."

I gave the equipment bag to Dick Schmuck. "I'm keeping my favorite bat and a ball to take with me," I said.

"You deserve it," he said.

We shook hands.

"Let's keep in touch," I said. "Be sure to let me know how the game goes next week. You can write to me care of the psychology department at the Menninger Foundation."

"I'll do that."

At rounds on Wednesday we heard of one admission the previous afternoon, a 33-year-old housewife. Dr. Bostian asked the resident assigned to the patient, "What are your initial impressions?"

"The symptoms are withdrawal, loss of appetite, speaks reluctantly, avoids eye contact, laughs nervously when questioned. She is a schizophrenic."

Shit!

Leaning forward I asked, "Is she a schizophrenic or is it that when a person acts and speaks in a certain way, the idea 'schizophrenia' pops into our minds?"

Cool it Siebert.

I sat back and became absorbed in my cup of tea.

Later, just as we were ready to end the meeting, someone made a very funny remark. Everyone burst out laughing. At the moment we all laughed I looked at Laura. Her eyes had automatically turned to mine at the same moment. Our contact was deep. I savored it.

As we left the room Lois Jackson said, "That was a good question you asked."

When I got back to my office I called Laura.

"Would you be free to talk to me this evening?"

"I could arrange it."

"Good. About seven o'clock?"

"Yes. I'll be home by then." She told me her address.

I spent most of the day working up the ECT research results and writing a draft of my report. I never went back to Mercywood. The 24 cases I had completed established highly significant differences. The unilateral was less harmful to patients than the old bilateral method. I had taken my calculations over to John Milholland, my former statistics instructor, to make certain they were accurate. After dinner I gave it to Kathleen to type.

"Al, were you ever questioned about not going back to Mercywood or not testing more patients?"

"No, Sam. Our research with their patients was an inconvenience to them. They had little interest in our results. They would not have called Waggoner. My being questioned wasn't part of the dynamic at that time. Everything was happening and not happening as it should. Besides, if Waggoner had called me in I would have told him about Dr. Kroll and Dr. Meyers. My conversation with Laura made me suspect he did not want to officially know what they were doing."

Laura wore a yellow sleeveless cotton dress, no stockings, white leather sandals—the kind with one thin thong between the toes. Her skin was a golden tan, her hair bleached light gold by the sun.

It was a nice evening for a drive. She had me drive to her parents' place so she could see her dog. Her parents weren't home. The dog barked joyfully when it saw her coming. It was a small black Cocker Spaniel. She picked it up and held it close. She said, "Sometimes I feel that my dog is the only creature on earth who loves me."

How sad.

We walked her dog around the block. We left afterwards. I can't remember exactly where we went because we talked so intently. We drove some. Stopped and walked around several times. We may have played miniature golf. My new ideas were so exciting! And I had a person who could listen without getting turned off. I asked her about her feelings. "Do you think you will ever be really happy?"

She looked at me for many moments. "No."

I feel so sad for her. This isn't right.

I touched her cheek.

We drove back to her apartment. She showed me a desk she had designed. She said her father built it for her.

"You are very bright," I said.

She smiled. "I know. I wasn't behind the door when brains were passed out."

I pulled her close and held her for awhile. We sat down on the couch. I was hungry to be close to her. Totally close. I admired her so much. A capable, intelligent woman. Entirely in control of her own self and her own life. Not asking or demanding anything from anyone. Yet also lonely. It was exciting to learn that a person like her existed.

I stroked her shoulder and arm. She didn't resist. I brushed my fingers across her breast. I kissed her cheek.

"Please stop," she said. "I don't feel right about this right now."

I nodded. I knew what she meant. I felt like an awkward teenager.

Leave now.

I got up and went to the door.

She hugged me. "Thank you for a nice evening," she said.

Driving home I felt dazed.

Why am I so hungry to be with her? Why are my feelings so out of control?

Thursday afternoon Dr. Bostian telephoned me. "Al, I'd like to talk to you before you go. Would you have time right now?"

"Sure. I'll come up."

I put on my long white coat. I went down the hall and stepped into the elevator. It stopped at the fourth floor. Just as the doors were starting to shut, a resident came running up. I could have punched the "open" button but I stuck out my hand and let the doors hit it. The safety mechanism popped the doors back open and the resident stepped in.

"Be careful!" he warned. "You could lose a hand that way."

16 out of 20.

"Al, I notice you were counting how many times people said you could hurt your hand."

Al smiles. "I was beginning to appreciate Freud's insights. I was conducting a private experiment about the 'castration anxiety' he wrote about. Almost every time I stuck my hand in the elevator door when psychiatrists were near, one of them would say, 'You'll hurt yourself!' 'Don't do that!' or some such expression. The most frequently stated warning was, 'You could lose your hand!' The exception was Dr. Holmes. He was non-Freudian and he knew how elevator doors worked."

Bostian greeted me and I sat on the chair by his desk.

"Al, you are going to be leaving in a few days. Are you looking forward to the move?"

"Yes and no. It is an exciting opportunity, but I am becoming disenchanted with psychiatry."

"In what way?"

"Some of the things I'm seeing sicken me." I told him what Dr. Kroll did to Mrs. Donnelli.

"It is hard to watch when you are sensitive isn't it?" he said.

"Yes. Especially after having one of the doctors at Mercywood tell me he brain damages some patients on purpose."

"How long has this been going on?"

I was right. He isn't surprised. He's not bothered.

"About two months."

"What bothers you the most?"

"How blind so many doctors are to their selfish motives. How their unconscious need to feed their egos makes them do harmful things while being convinced they are doing something good. They are driven by a blind hunger for esteem and it's deadly."

"What are you going to do, Al?"

"Frankly, I've been thinking of walking away from the whole mess and becoming a professional bowler."

He laughed. "A bowler?"

"Sure. Right now this world of psychiatry and clinical psychology disgusts me pretty much."

"Would you throw away all you have worked for?"

"A Ph.D. is just a fancy union card. And, frankly, I admire the real workers more than most of the people with Ph.D.s and M.D.s."

"I see."

"At least real workers accomplish something useful. In the service station the other afternoon I watched a professor waiting for the mechanic to fix his generator. The professor walked around with his nose in the air. He talked down to the mechanic. He saw himself as superior to the mechanic. But what I saw was a big ass who was helpless. He didn't know shit about how to keep his car running. Without the mechanic he was helpless."

Bostian laughed. "Do you think you could succeed being a bowler?"

"I will succeed at anything I commit myself to."

"You would be giving up a lot."

"Perhaps."

"Tell me more of your thoughts about esteem. Your psychological reports recently have touched on this a lot."

This is going pretty well. Maybe you've found a good listener.

"Sure. I believe I've spotted several defense mechanisms that compel people to attack someone with high esteem. They blindly protect and feed their repressed need for high esteem by trying to eliminate consciously high esteem from others."

Bostian frowned.

"The solution to this, as I see it now, is for each person to acquire a consciously high level of esteem in a way which allows others to do the same. A phrase I think will work is, 'As far as I am concerned I am the most valuable person who will ever exist.'"

"That sounds like a Christ fantasy."

"See what I mean? You just did it."

"What?"

"Your anxiety triggered a defensive reaction. You couldn't handle the possibility of allowing yourself to think that about yourself."

"It is a Christ fantasy."

"What's wrong about anyone…"

Forget it. Look at his eyes. You've lost him.

Terminate.

"Is there anything else you wanted to ask me about?" I said.

"Wow!" he said. "I just felt a curtain go down."

"I felt like we were done. I haven't had a chance to think all this through, so I know I'm not communicating it well."

"My concern is about you. Are you going to be all right?"

I stood up. He stood up.

"Yes. I'll come out on top of it okay."

He grinned. We shook hands firmly. He said, "I wish you the best of luck."

"See. There it is again."

"What is?"

"Your feeling that my chances of success can be increased by your wishing me good luck."

He laughed. "Whatever it is, I do wish you the best of luck."

I knew what he meant. "Thanks," I said and left.

Bostian didn't get what I was saying. Then he projected a Christ fantasy onto me.

His version of being the most valuable person who will ever exist. But not knowing it's in his subconscious.

Should I go to the Menninger Foundation? It's going to be rough work. And dangerous.

Sure, but what better place for a breakthrough in the elimination of mental illness? They are the best minds in the country. They'll be able to grasp these ideas and see the value.

Still...

Back down in my office I took out a piece of stationary.

8/19/65
Dear Ranger:
Hey buddy, I'm getting into something that could become dangerous. I might need you for backup.

The Menninger foundation has awarded me a post-doctoral fellowship. This is big league stuff. Here I was thinking of trying to be a good minor league player and suddenly I'm the number one draft choice in the nation.

I'm also onto something big about the mental illness game the shrinks have going. I'm going down there to try to accomplish something no one else has ever done before. The poor bastards don't know what they've let themselves in for!

If I need help, I'll let you know.

    Agile

I stopped at a jewelry store on the way home. I found what I wanted and bought it.

After rounds on Friday, my last day at NPI, one of the residents walked toward the elevator with me. "Al, I hate to see you go," he said. "You ask questions that make me think a lot about what we are doing here."

Lois Jackson heard him. "I agree," she said. "The question you asked the other morning made me look at patients differently."

"I'm glad. To me it is bewildering to see how a person's main symptom is withdrawal and how this is supposed to be 'sick.' The person's mind and emotions are being assaulted. What is sick about withdrawing from that?"

"I see your point, Lois said. "I will miss your ideas. They were always useful."

"Thank you. Thank you very much."

Laura got into the elevator. I tried to say something that would impress her. She just smiled. I felt stupid.

Stop trying so hard.

With her it isn't what you do or say, it is the person you are that counts.

I've got a lot of growing to do before I'm equal to her.

Downstairs in my office I called Laura. I asked if she would please come down to see me. She said she would in about half an hour.

When she arrived I shut the door. I handed her a piece of paper. She looked puzzled.

"This is a map of the lower parking lot," I said. "It shows where there is a parking meter that gives you an hour's worth of time for a nickel instead of a quarter. I won't be using it any more."

She smiled, amused at me.

"Here," I said. "I bought this for you." I opened a small jewelry case and took out a gold necklace with a pearl on it. "Will you accept it?"

"Yes, I will. Thank you."

I started to hand it to her but she said, "Will you please put it on for me?" I opened the clasp and put it around her neck. Then I stepped back.

She looked at me, amused. "Aren't you going to kiss me?"

Our kiss was nice, but I felt awkward. Like a teenage boy. She started out the door.

"May I write you?" I asked.

"Yes. I'd like that."

Why do you get so awkward around her? You want her so much you can't resist trying to possess her.

And she can't be possessed. You are not yet equal to her.

I took the elevator up to the seventh floor and gave my research report to Waggoner's secretary. From there I went to the main office on the fifth floor. "Hi Katy. Here's my pass key." I handed her a small sheet of paper. "Here is a forwarding address for me."

"Just a second, Al." She rang an extension and said, "He's here."

Mrs. Martin came out of the records room and walked over to me.

"Dr. Siebert," she said, "the secretaries and I have been talking about you leaving and we don't know what we'll do now." She paused and laughed. "You were the only sane one on the staff!"

I laughed. "Thanks, but I'm sure you'll manage!"

She handed me a card signed by about a dozen people.

"This is a surprise," I said.

"You were our favorite. The girls used to fight over who would get to do your dictation. The things you'd say about relaxing and thanking them for doing the typing lifted their spirits. Usually the only time we hear from doctors is when they complain about a mistake. We'll miss you."

I felt myself blushing. "Aw shucks, ma'am. Just trying to make things more pleasant."

She smiled and shook my hand. "We wish you well wherever you go."

"Thank you."

Katy handed me my 50 cent key deposit. "Are you happy about going to Menninger's?"

"Yes, except I won't be able to play in the championship softball game next week. I'm looking forward to Menninger's. It will be an exciting challenge!"

"That's good."

"Are you coming to my going away party at Noni's house after work?"

"No. I have other plans."

"In that case I'll tell you now how impressed I've been with how good you are at your job. You handle so much so easily. It's amazing."

"Thank you."

"And you seem happier since you've been seeing your attorney friend."

She smiled. "I am. I'm much happier."

I stopped at the stock broker's office on the way home and had them sell my stock and transfer my account to their Topeka office. Kathleen wouldn't go to the party with me. The gathering was more of a chance for the NPI staff to get together on a Friday after work than it was a party for me. So many people came and left NPI such gatherings were held every one or two months. As usual, Don Holmes had most of the people surrounding him in the kitchen while he told amusing stories. I said my good-byes to the few people I knew best.

Laura had changed from her uniform into a tight orange dress that displayed the pearl above her cleavage. She walked outside with me when I left and gave me a hug. "I'll think of you when I wear this," she said.

"Good. I'll think of you wearing it."

Saturday morning I took the car to my service station for thorough servicing. While the mechanic had the hood up I checked to make certain my spare ignition key was firmly wired in its hidden place.

Chapter Eleven

Entering A New World

On Sunday we worked all day packing our belongings. The movers were supposed to come Monday, but they didn't show up. I called their office. They promised to be there the next day. We couldn't wait an extra day, so I arranged with the apartment manager to have someone let the movers in when they showed up.

We got up at dawn on Tuesday morning, August 24th, and packed our car. We took our sleeping bags and air mattresses, a basic supply of clothes, some dishes and cooking utensils. Everything *Consumer Reports* said we would need in case the movers were late delivering our things.

I added my tool kit, bowling ball, softball gear, portable TV set, important books and papers, stereo equipment, and two aluminum lawn chairs. At the last moment Kathleen brought out the box with her glass hurricane lamp. She didn't trust the movers with it. We placed the picnic cooler with our food and drinks where it would be easy to reach.

We took one last look at our apartment building. I looked at our old Rambler Ambassador, heavily weighted down.

As Kathleen opened her door I said, "Our car is going to look right at home in the Menninger parking lot!"

She gave me a small smile.

On the freeway I got the car up to speed. "Here we go! Off to the future!" I smacked Kathleen on the leg. "Isn't this exciting?"

She smiled politely and took out her knitting.

I have a major job ahead, but I'm going to the best place for new ways of thinking about mental patients.

I haven't communicated well so far. There must be a lot more to understand. I'll have to be tactful.

What is my plan?

I'll go through their seminars and classes looking for opportunities to ask naive questions.

Smith would be the one to ask about why psychotherapy research articles do not indicate if any patients were told they must accept that they are mentally ill.

Shevrin, "What is schizophrenia?"

Rosen about defense mechanisms. And self-esteem must come up in therapy. Perhaps I could write about Molly in an assigned paper.

Look for an opportunity with an analyst to ask about Melanie Klein and the story of Adam and Eve.

I have two years. I'll have to be patient, use good timing.

God, this is exciting! What an adventure!

I drove along with the window open, humming to myself. In the afternoon Kathleen drove while I took a nap.

Our trip went as planned. We arrived at the outskirts of Topeka about noon on Wednesday. I stopped for gas and obtained a city map. We went to a cafe, bought a newspaper, and looked for new apartment listings in our price range. I telephoned places that needed an appointment. I plotted our apartment hunting route on the map while we ate lunch.

We went to a few places and soon learned that good housing was going to be difficult to find. We didn't find anything decent by evening, so we checked into a motel. The next morning I went out for a newspaper while Kathleen made tea with a coil that heats water in a cup.

I made several phone calls and we started out again. Later that morning we arrived for an appointment to see one of the newly advertised places. It was the entire second floor of an old house.

We followed Mr. Wilson, the owner, up a narrow, creaky stairway. Upstairs the smell of fresh paint was so strong Mr. Wilson had to open some windows for ventilation. Kathleen and I liked what we saw—glistening hardwood floors in a huge living room with glass doors at one end that opened onto a large covered front porch. A large master bedroom, a big bathroom with old ceramic fixtures, a small bedroom that I could use for a den, walk-in closets, a sun porch off the kitchen with hooks up for clothes lines, a back stairway leading down to a locked garage, and a kitchen with lots of cupboards. It had a new refrigerator but no stove.

"Would you consider putting in a stove?" I asked.

"I might for the right couple. How long do you plan to stay?"

"Two years."

Wilson and I talked for about twenty minutes. He owned the insurance business located in the two-story building on the other half of the block. He purchased this house to get more parking space for his business and to acquire income property. He was a self-made man. I knew he was skillful in dealing with people from the way he questioned me. He said he had over thirty associates working for him. "You and Kathleen can rent the apartment if you want it," he said.

I took Kathleen aside and asked her what she thought. We decided to take it.

Wilson led us down the back stairs and over to his office. He handed me a receipt and the keys.

"We feel lucky to find such a nice place," I said. "Good apartments are scarce here."

"I know. This is the fifth time I've showed it today."

"None of the others wanted it?"

"They all wanted it, but I put them off."

"Then why did you rent to me?"

"I like the way you handle yourself."

He drove us downtown to an appliance store to let Kathleen pick out the stove she wanted. I could see from the flush of her cheeks that she felt thrilled, especially since it would be a gas stove.

"A gas stove," she had whispered, "is much better to cook on. That's what we had at home."

"Do you know anything about motivating insurance salesmen?" Wilson asked.

"Have you heard about professor David McClelland's research an achievement motivation?"

"No."

"He found that the way people day dream influences how successful they are."

"I want to know more about that."

"All right, but let me get settled in before we talk. Where's the nearest shopping center? Kathleen needs to buy some household supplies."

While Kathleen shopped I called Smith's office from a pay phone.

Mrs. Falley answered. "Hello, Dr. Siebert. Did you find an apartment yet?"

"Yes we did, a very nice one. Kathleen likes it a lot."

"Did she get my letter?"

"She did. That was nice of you to write."

"Is there any help she needs?"

"Nothing right now, thanks. I'll tell her to call you if she needs anything. Is Smith in?"

"Yes he is. He returned from vacation yesterday. I'll connect you."

"Hello, Al."

"Hi. I wanted to let you know I'm here and ready to go."

"I'm delighted. If you'll come out to my office tomorrow morning about ten o'clock, I'll show you where your office will be."

Friday morning Smith drove me out to the West campus. We climbed up the stairs to a small office in the attic. "This is a temporary assignment," he said, "until we can find a better office for you."

"No problem. It's a step up from my sub-basement office at NPI."

"You've been assigned to my team in the hospital."

"Good! I hoped I could work with you."

"There's a team meeting Monday afternoon if you'd like to attend," he said, pushing his glasses up. "It's a week before your fellowship is scheduled to start, but you can get involved now."

"Excellent. What's the meeting about?"

"We'll discuss a patient assigned to our team, a teenage girl in the hospital."

"Would it be possible for me to talk to her before the meeting?"

He frowned. "No. Dr. Cashman is the case supervisor. He'll present her case at the meeting."

Our apartment was only a few blocks from downtown. Kathleen wanted to stay home to put paper in the kitchen shelves, so I went by myself Friday afternoon to arrange for the utilities. I walked past a park with a small statue of Lincoln seated. It was similar to the one in the Lincoln Memorial in Washington, D.C. I arranged for telephone service, electricity, gas, and obtained signature cards for opening a joint bank account. At a hardware store I bought an aluminum rocking chair on sale for $10.

I went to the post office to rent a private mail box. When I gave the card and my money to the clerk, I started to explain, "I'm a professional person, I need to have a box…"

The clerk ignored me. He didn't care what my motives were.

Siebert. What are you doing?

You don't have to explain your motives or reasons to anyone.

Besides, you know that when a person starts explaining their motives without being asked, then they are trying to hide their real motives.

Right.

And your real motive is…to have an address so Laura can write if she wants to.

The heat and humidity of the day lingered at night. I sat out on the porch in my new rocker. Occasional thunder showers brought some relief.

Mmmm, the heavy rain invigorates me.

I spent much of the weekend in my rocker on the porch with a yellow legal pad nearby on the railing. On the top pages I wrote out my ideas. On the back pages I composed letters to Laura. After reading them over I wadded them up and stuffed them into the garbage. I could see that I was playing games with her that I didn't want to play. I could see my mind and emotions were going through some sequences that fascinated me. I was learning. I was author, actor, audience, and critic. I knew that my desire to try to get her to like me was causing me to feel and think things that, when analyzed, led me to the bigger question.

Where do these manipulative patterns start?

My mind and emotions are hungry for Laura. I wish she could be here to talk with. I'll ask her to come and see me.

I finally produced a letter that satisfied me and walked downtown to mail it.

Monday morning I drove downtown to buy new window shades. The old ones were in such bad shape we didn't want to put them back up. Wilson said we could deduct the cost of new ones from our rent. I stood and watched the lady cut the shades to the sizes we needed. She asked, "Why did you move here?"

"I'll be working at Menninger's for several years."

"Are you a psychiatrist?"

"No. I have fellowship in psychology."

"My son's in college, but he doesn't know what he wants to do. Why did you choose psychology?"

"At first I chose it to prepare me for a medical career, but then I discovered I liked psychology better. I'm fascinated by how the human mind works."

We talked while she cut and wrapped my order. She handed me my receipt. "You're a nice man," she said. "Would you talk to my son? He's interested in psychology. Will you call him?"

"I'll talk to him but I won't call him. They're supposed to install our phone this morning. You can get my number from the operator. If your son calls me, I'll be glad to invite him over to talk."

I saw a sale sign at a furniture store. Inside I saw a long, soft couch for only $125. I stretched out on it.

This feels good. And my head and feet don't even touch the arm rests.

I can sleep here instead of on the floor.

I bought the couch and arranged to have it delivered that afternoon.

When I got home Kathleen said, "The phone is in. Dr. Smith called. He wants you to call him."

"Did he say what he wanted?"

"No."

I dialed Smith's number.

"Al, are you doing anything important this noon?" he said.

"Not especially."

"How would you feel about coming out early to have lunch with me? I can show you around some more and we can talk before the team meeting."

Alert. Something in his voice. Reading: He wants me to come out so he can talk to me. Go ahead, see what's up.

"Sure. I can come out early."

"Good. Come to my office at twelve o'clock."

Shortly after I hung up the phone rang again.

"This is Karen Falley, Dr. Siebert. Dr. Mayman asked me to ask if you would participate as a control group subject in his research project."

"What does it involve?"

"The research is on perception. It is comparing perceptions of schizophrenics with a control group on a simple perceptual test. It takes about 30 minutes."

"I'd be glad to. When do they want me?"

"Please be at the research building at 10:00 a.m. Thursday. The secretary there will take care of you."

Smith was cordial when I arrived at his office. "Here is your first staff memo," he said. He handed me several pages stapled together. "Please read this carefully. Dr. Will has explained what to we are to say to anyone who asks about the tax assessor's effort to collect property taxes on Foundation property. We are a non-profit organization and intend to maintain our tax exempt status."

Non-profit? At the salaries these people pull down?

At lunch Smith introduced me to various people in the cafeteria. A psychologist asked if I wanted to play in the annual softball game against the psychiatrists. I said, "Yes! I've got my glove, ball, bat, and cleats with me. When is it?"

"On Labor Day."

"Good. I'll be there. I need the exercise."

And won't the psychiatrists be surprised! They'll think Mayman and Smith brought in a ringer.

Dr. Smith walked me back to his office after lunch.

"How do you feel about starting the program, Al?"

"Great. I'm looking forward to it."

"Do you think it might be stressful for you?"

"No."

He's fishing for something.

"Are you worried about any part of the program?"

He's trying to lead the conversation some place.

"No."

"Do you feel that you can meet all of the demands it will place on you?"

"Definitely. One of my personal goals is to do better in the program than anyone expects."

He said, "Good!" and broke into a big grin.

He seems relieved about something.

At ten minutes to one we walked over to the hospital for the team meeting. The conference room was nicely furnished with a very large, rectangular, dark wood table in the center. Smith introduced me to a few people, and we sat at the end of the table. When the meeting started there were about fifteen of us at the table. A few more people sat on chairs along the walls.

As the senior psychiatrist started the meeting, Smith took out a pad of paper and made a seating chart for me with the names of the people in the room. I looked at the names.

Wow! There's a Menninger sitting just three feet away from me!

As I sat memorizing everyone's name, various people gave their reports. The patient was the daughter of wealthy Texas parents. They flew her up to Topeka and put her into the Menninger hospital because she refused to obey them and kept running away.

Dr. Cashman, her psychiatrist, gave his report. "She is a management problem. She refuses to cooperate with me. She refuses to obey hospital rules, and she refuses to participate in the therapy programs."

The senior psychiatrist asked a nurse sitting by the wall to give her report.

"She's trouble," the nurse said. "She could be nice if she wanted, but she likes to start trouble. She doesn't want to get along."

"Thank you," the senior psychiatrist said.

This is a Menninger psychiatric nurse?

Our nurses at NPI are much better than this one.

As the people in the room discussed the case, I realized that only doctors were sitting around the big table. The people along the walls were nurses, case workers, and other "paraprofessionals." It also became apparent that only several doctors had seen her or talked to her.

As they discussed the girl's rebelliousness, I thought to myself:

Good for her! She's got spirit.

It takes a lot of self-confidence to stand up to these pressures. She is refusing to let her life be run by her parents or her psychiatrist.

The senior psychiatrist asked, "What is the purpose of her behavior?"

Several answers were offered cautiously, but he rejected them. "It's obvious," he declared. "She is trying to castrate her therapist!"

I smiled.

Ha ha! That is…

Hold it! Don't laugh.

Look. Most of the doctors are nodding in agreement. No one is disagreeing. Are they serious?

The meeting ended. A few humorous remarks were whispered about Cashman and the girl. I had the impression that everyone felt they had done a good afternoon's work.

Is that all there is to a staff conference at Menninger's?

This is disappointing.

When I got home Kathleen said, "Larry MacDonald just called. He will be here in a little while."

"Larry is coming by to visit? How did he know we were here?"

"I wrote him we were coming. He is on his way to a conference for student leaders."

"Very good!"

Larry was in good spirits. He talked about his plans for his senior year and about the student leaders' conference he would be attending. After dinner Larry and I sat on the front porch while Kathleen washed the dishes.

"I've got a major challenge ahead of me," I told him. "Psychiatrists are really blind to the selfish motivations underneath their efforts to cure people of illnesses many people don't agree they have. A hidden need for self-esteem is at the root of the incredible distortion in the minds of people trying to cure others of extreme feelings of self-esteem. Let me tell you about an 18-year-old girl I interviewed. She said that God spoke to her and told her..."

As I told Larry about my new ideas and experiences, a dark car stopped in front of the house. The driver sat in his seat for about five minutes, not moving. I looked closer. I saw a box-like object in the left rear window of his car and the outline of some equipment on the dashboard.

That's an unmarked police car!

This is a radar trap!

A few minutes later I got up and went inside. I picked up the phone and motioned for Larry and Kathleen to listen. I dialed the police department. I said to the officer who answered, "A car stopped in front of our house a while ago and the driver is just sitting there. He isn't doing anything, but it seems suspicious and my wife is getting nervous about it. Will you please have someone check into this?" The officer took my name and address.

We went back outside and watched. The man in the car turned on a flashlight and looked at a map. He bent over and flashed his light on our house number. Then he put on his policeman's hat, got out of the car, and walked over to the house. He yelled up to us, "It's all right."

"Oh! You *are* the police!" I said with innocent surprise. Kathleen and Larry were laughing so hard they had to hold their sides to keep from laughing out loud. Tears streamed down Kathleen's face. She had to go in the house.

The policeman walked back to his car and got inside. Just then a police cruiser with red lights flashing came speeding down the street and braked to a stop behind the unmarked car. As the second policeman hopped out, another police car came speeding up from the other direction with its lights flashing. Our sides hurt so much from laughing we were all in pain.

Larry and I went inside. "Well," I said, "I guess we added some excitement to their boring evening." We laughed and laughed.

Larry left for his conference later in the evening. I sat outside late into the night. My mind was silent as I enjoyed the breeze, the stars, the planet. I felt in peaceful harmony with all life, with all that existed, with all eternity.

Everything is so perfect.

I went running and walking Tuesday morning. Just before lunch Smith called. "Will you come out to my office to see me?"

"Sure."

I went to his office after lunch and walked in. He said, "Dr. Siebert, your wife is starting into psychotherapy here at the Foundation. How do you feel about that?"

His warmth for me is gone.

I shrugged. "She can do anything she wants."

That's funny. She hasn't mentioned anything about this to me. This isn't like her.

"Good." Watching my face closely he went on, "When a person starts into therapy here at the Foundation, we also interview the spouse. How do you feel about that?"

"It's okay with me."

Therapists don't do that.

They don't meet with family members this way.

"Good. You and Kathleen have an appointment to see Dr. Dennis Farrell at one o'clock Wednesday. Will you go?"

"Sure."

When I got home Kathleen didn't want to talk about the appointment, so I left her alone. I took my bowling ball and drove around until I found a bowling alley. After I came home I went for a walk around the neighborhood.

The poor kid has really been under a lot of pressure. It's reasonable that she might be doing this. I know she's been to see a priest here. Maybe he recommended it.

Things could get hairy here. I'd better consolidate my resources and protect myself.

I walked along feeling excited and very alive.

This is thrilling.

On Wednesday we drove to the outpatient clinic and parked in the lot. As we walked toward the entrance, I saw Mrs. Falley returning from lunch. I grabbed Kathleen by the hand and hurried her up the sidewalk. "Kathleen, this is Karen Falley. Karen, this is my wife, Kathleen."

They murmured quiet hellos. They looked at the ground instead of at each other. They were uncomfortable. Tense.

Something is wrong. These are warm, friendly women. At this moment they should be smiling and talkative, happy to meet each other.

I am being set up! Kathleen isn't starting into psychotherapy. She and Smith have been lying to me and Mrs. Falley knows it. These people are poor actors.

Okay. Let's play along with them and see what develops.

Kathleen and I checked in with the receptionist and sat down in the waiting room. In a few minutes the receptionist sent us upstairs to Farrell's office.

About 48, short light brown fine hair, thinning. Average height, weight. Pale skin. Not a happy person. Looks weak, stressed.

After several minutes of superficial talk he suddenly said, "Mrs. Siebert, will you please go down to the waiting room? I want to speak to Dr. Siebert privately."

Confirmation. The spouse is never interviewed first before their partner starts therapy.

After Kathleen left Farrell said, "We would like some help from you. What do you think is upsetting your wife?"

Choice point.

Should I be honest with him or should I only tell him what I think he can handle?

It will be very tough trying to last out two years doing it the slow way. Look, he must be good. They picked him to question you.

But what if he can't handle these ideas either? I could lose the fellowship.

True, but if you have to be deceptive to keep the fellowship, then it isn't worth having.

"It could be some of my ideas."

He glanced at me. This was going to be easier than he expected. "Tell me about these ideas," he said.

You've only got about 20 minutes so make it good.

"I've been trying to figure out why human beings continually attack and hurt each other's minds and egos while believing they are doing something good. This has been going on for centuries, and no one seems to understand it. Not well enough to know how to stop it. I figured that the answer must lie in common experiences that every human being has no matter what century or country he was raised in."

Farrell tilted back in his swivel chair and looked at the wall.

"There is only one experience that every human being has. He was once an infant who was nursed and then weaned. And there's the answer. Melanie Klein is close in her writings about the infant's 'good-mother' and 'bad-mother' perceptions. Look at the story of Adam and Eve, a story which millions of people find easy to remember. A story which people have accepted for centuries as an accounting of the beginning of man's struggle in the world.

"God—the good mother—created—gave birth to—Adam— the infant. Then God gave paradise—the breasts—to Adam. Adam could eat freely—with one restriction. He could not eat the fruit from one tree. From within Adam came Eve—the evil mother. Eve got Adam to bite into the apple—the nipple— with his teeth. After he did this God—the good mother removed—weaned—Adam—the infant—from paradise—the breasts. Adam could never return again. He had to wear clothes. He had to start working for a living. And men have blamed Eve—the evil mother—in the world for their difficulties ever since."

Farrell sat rigidly in his chair. No emotion showed on his face or his eyes.

That was pretty heavy.

"You know that when a child loses the object of his love," I said, "he may try to handle the loss by becoming like the lost object. And that's what happens. Many adults unconsciously act like the breast they lost. That's why psychoanalysts have such poor cure rates. They treat other human beings like infants who need to be rescued and nurtured. They attack a person whose conscious self-image is too high. Look at how psychiatrists act when a person says he is God or Jesus or Napoleon. The psychiatrists declare that he is no longer sane. He is turned over to them to be cared for. They put him in a place where he is treated like an infant. They try to eliminate such thoughts from his mind. The rationalization for this is that this is all for his own good. But the facts show hospitalization usually hurts a person more than it helps him."

Still no reaction. No questions.

"The way to really be effective with people is to consciously have such high self-esteem you aren't threatened by what another person thinks about himself. One way to do this is to think, 'As far as I am concerned I am the most valuable person who will ever exist.' This allows a person to free himself from the defense mechanisms of charity and tax collecting, especially in the way he uses ideas."

"What do you mean?"

At last.

"The world is filled with people whose minds are out of control. They try to build up their self-esteem by forcing their ideas and opinions into other people's minds. They think it's an act of charity, but it isn't. It is a highly defensive, selfish act. The target person is given no choice. He must accept the ideas and perceptions offered or the donor becomes desperate.

"And if a person goes to a psychiatrist complaining that people are trying to force thoughts into his mind, look what happens. The psychiatrist, in effect, says to him, 'That isn't true, and you must accept into your mind the thought that you are mentally ill because you believe people are trying to force thoughts into your mind.' It's a double-bind. It breaks a person down. It causes withdrawal.

"Tax collecting is when we demand compliments or appreciation from others. They must produce or else we will think and say bad things about them. We revert to the infant mode. Perhaps blackmail would be a better term. Whatever you call it, the threat is that we will regard the source of what is wanted as an 'evil mother' unless they give us what we need."

No response.

This guy is not relating.

Try a softer approach.

Loosen him up some.

"We had a good laugh last night. We were sitting on the porch when this car pulled up in front...

"Our sides ached from laughing!" I smiled and laughed as I relived the experience.

He's not reacting. He has no emotions.

I feel anxious.

Why?

I expected him to laugh. Predicted it.

"I feel anxious," I said, "because you didn't react as I expected. I must have had self-esteem attached to predicting your behavior. Then when it didn't happen, I got anxious."

Try something else. Tell him about Molly...

"What I am trying to understand is how the mind acts to protect a person's self-esteem. If a therapist can relax and allow it to operate naturally in others, then you can understand how it works and really be helpful to them.

"Before I left the university hospital I interviewed a girl who said that God told her she was going to give birth to the second savior. I refused to let my mind think of her as mentally ill and did not try to eliminate that thought from her mind. Instead, I questioned her so that she saw that her experience raised her self-esteem at a time when she was extremely lonely and depressed. She immediately opened up to people and within two weeks was headed toward discharge instead of the state hospital. You see? It works like a homeostatic mechanism.

"What this means is the problem is in the viewer, not in the patient. Mental illness is an illusion. The problem is right where the professionals can best work on it—in their own minds!"

"I've tried to explain all this to Kathleen, but she can't handle it."

Tone: We professionals can delve into areas the average person can't handle.

"She is disturbed and depressed."

"I know."

"What are your feelings about her calling us up and asking for this consultation?"

"I appreciate that fact that she saved me a lot of time. I had been wondering how to bring these ideas to the attention of the senior staff."

He was slightly startled and leaned forward. "You *wanted* us to know about your ideas?"

So, he isn't completely emotionally blunt.

"Of course. I figured that the best place to begin a new breakthrough in the field of mental health was from the leading psychiatric facility in the world."

He glanced at the clock on his desk. "We are going to have to stop now. I have other appointments to keep."

He picked up his phone and asked the receptionist to send Kathleen up. As she seated herself next to me he said to her, "You were right Mrs. Siebert, he is mentally ill."

"What!" I blurted out. I was halfway expecting it, but wanted so much for him to understand my ideas that the words came as a shock.

"You are the one who is mentally ill, Dr. Siebert, not your wife."

"I am not mentally ill."

"Your thought processes are loose."

"I'm going through a developmental crisis. It's healthy. I just don't have things straightened out well enough to present them well."

"Your first wife felt that you were mentally ill and she is a clinical psychologist."

"She did?"

"That's what Mrs. Siebert reports."

He and I looked at Kathleen.

"Yes," she said. "When I called people to find out what to do I found out she told people he was mentally ill."

Aha! That explains why some of my professors and old friends were unexpectedly cool to me when I returned to the University! That's funny.

I turned back to Farrell. "So?"

He responded, "Doesn't that prove to you that you were mentally ill before?"

"No. What my first wife chose to tell people why her marriage broke up is her business."

"The letters you've been writing to the nurse at the hospital show thought disturbance."

"What?!" I turned and looked at Kathleen. She lowered her head.

She dug the throw-aways out of the garbage!

"Did you dig things out of the garbage?"

"Yes. I wanted to see what you were writing about."

I turned to Farrell. "But I never mailed those. I thought better of it."

"What about the incident with the police Monday night?"

"What about it?"

"You must recognize that something like that is a sign of mental illness. That isn't something you would ordinarily do."

"Yes, it is! My college friends could write a book about all the things I've done. I was arrested for climbing a church steeple my first week at college."

"I am not going to argue. You *are* mentally ill and need to be in a mental institution."

"I do not need to be in an institution! I will appear any place you name to defend the accuracy of my ideas. I have a legitimate thesis."

"You must go in immediately. You are quite sick."

"Well, you are going to have to…"

Stop! Don't finish that sentence!

A person who goes in voluntarily can get out ten times more easily than a person who is committed. These people are desperate. They will commit you if you don't handle them right. Give them hope. Buy some time.

"This is quite a shock," I said. "Let me think about it."

Divert.

"Say, am I going to be charged for this time with you?"

His eyes brightened. "That's a very good question, Dr. Siebert, very good indeed. No. We'll just write this off as professional courtesy."

"Professional courtesy?"

"Yes," he said with a warm smile.

Chapter Twelve

A Whole New Ball Game

Driving home I said to Kathleen, "Back at the university, Caplan and Bostian called me because of your calls?"

"You talked so crazy. I had to talk to someone. I went to the priest. He said to find out what people who knew you thought."

"What did they say about me?"

"Nate said you needed psychiatric treatment. He said you were mentally ill. He told me what your first wife said."

"And Bostian?"

"He said to leave you alone, that you would be all right."

Good for him!

"But you called Smith anyway?"

"Yes."

"Did you plan this before we left?"

"You spoke highly of the psychologists here. I thought they could help you."

Damn. A total violation of being free to say what you want in your own home.

I parked the car in our garage. Upstairs Kathleen went to the kitchen to put water on the stove for tea. I paced around the living room.

Damn. She completely undercut me. Took this out of my hands.

From deep within me I felt a surge of anger. I strode into the kitchen.

"You're a Judas!" I yelled.

"No, I'm not!" She started crying. "I only wanted to help you. I promised God in our wedding vows to stay with you if you got sick."

"You also promised to obey me," I yelled, "and I'm telling you if you don't stop making phone calls telling people I'm sick and need help, I'm going to turn you across my knee and give you a spanking you'll never forget! Do you understand!?"

She hid her face in her hands.

"I am trying to handle the biggest challenge of my life and you are not helping me! You are sabotaging me! Go talk to a priest about me all you want but not to anyone else!"

I took a deep breath and regained some calmness. "I will also admit that I'm impressed. The job you've done wrecking my career, my fellowship, and my reputation has been one of the best handled, most well organized things you've ever done. But you will stop making phone calls about me! Do you understand me!?"

She sobbed, "Yes."

I left and went for a walk.

I hated doing that. She feels overwhelmed, helpless. Damn. This sure confirms the way people act for selfish reasons while claiming they just want to help the person upsetting them.

God, the human mind is so fragile.

I have to regroup.

I looked through the stockbroker's section in the Yellow Pages and saw that my brokerage firm had a branch in Kansas City, Missouri.

Good! If you have to make a run for it, you can get across the river and get your funds quickly. Safer this way than in a local office.

I called their number and made arrangements for my funds to be transferred. I wrote a letter to the government insurance office requesting all the cash from my GI life insurance policy.

I hate to cash this in, but I have a hunch we're going to need money in the weeks ahead.

I walked downtown to mail the letter and check my mailbox. Nothing there. I strolled around town thinking.

There has got to be a way to reach people! I know I have something because of the strength of their reactions. It fits. It's all there. But there must be more.

Okay. Go get it.

God this is exciting. I'm onto something really big. I feel so fantastic.

I experienced a sense of power and force in me that I'd never felt before, a strong power.

Contact.

My eyes briefly caught the eyes of an attractive woman about 20 years old at the end of the block. She was walking my way.

Peripheral scan...

Nice walk. Trim figure.

Don't let your eyes go back to hers yet.

Tease her.

Look off to her left.

Bring your eyes slowly toward her.

Look above her head. She's looking at me. Good.

Look off to the right.

Back slowly toward her eyes. Above her head. She's still looking. Left of her. Back over—right—back—over—left.

She's getting closer. She's still looking.

She's fascinated.

Hold your eyes at her eye level slightly to the left.

Hold it. Smile a little.

A lazy blink and with full power...flick 'em in.

Now!

In all my life I have never seen such a reaction like hers. Not on TV or in the movies. With my peripheral vision I knew she was watching me and enjoying my teasing her. The moment I looked fully into her eyes her eyes widened, her mouth parted, I heard a sharp intake of her breath, her steps faltered, and her back arched as a shiver swept through her body. The several moments we looked into each other's eyes seemed to last for minutes. Our contact was intense. I felt a powerful, loving connection. She stopped, turned, and watched me as I walked on. It was a beautiful moment.

After sunset on Wednesday the temperature cooled down enough for me to go jogging. I stayed out for several hours.

What do you want to do? Take off? Leave?

No. I got myself into this by deciding I need to change, not others. Something very important is happening here. I'll see it through.

Early Thursday morning Smith called. "I want you to come to my office this afternoon," he said. "Come about two o'clock."

"Okay."

Maybe Smith will understand. I sure wish Mayman was here though. He seemed to have the best mind.

At ten o'clock I showed up for my appointment at the research building. The receptionist telephoned someone. Soon a slender young woman came out to get me. She introduced herself as a graduate student in psychology working as a research assistant for the summer. I followed her down a hall to a windowless, empty room with a wooden chair and a small wooden table. A tripod with a small black box on it stood about five feet away from the table. A cardboard box turned upside down in the corner looked out of place.

That is an autokinetic apparatus on the tripod.

There is probably a tape recorder under the box.

"Dr. Siebert, have you ever participated as a subject in an autokinetic experiment?"

"No."

She has good eyes. Nice energy.

She had me sit at the table. A freshly sharpened pencil lay on the large white sheet of butcher paper that covered the top.

"Here are the instructions," she said, reading from a card. "In a moment I will turn out the lights and leave the room. You will see a small point of light coming from this black box. Using the pencil on the table, you are to draw on that large piece of paper any movement you see the light make. Trace its path on the paper to record what you see. Do you have any questions?"

"No."

"Fine. Let's begin."

She turned out the lights and left.

The pin point of light was about six feet ahead of me. The natural movement of the eye muscles can cause such a light to appear to move. That's why it's called *autokinetic*. It means "self-movement."

I moved my head slowly from side to side while watching the light to avoid spontaneous eye movements.

My eyes are getting tired of remaining focused on one spot.

Okay. Relax them.

Hey! The dot split into two dots.

It's like looking past my finger at a distant place. The image of my finger splits and my eyes register seeing two fingers.

Might as well play with this.

Together. Apart. Together. Apart.

Use your left index finger as a reference point on the paper for drawing the back and forth movement from two dots to one.

See how far apart you can make them go. Look past the light as though you are on a mountain top trying to look 50 miles or more.

Hey! What happened?

The right dot went out and disappeared!

What? It wasn't the apparatus.

The image hit the blind spot!

The blind spot is where the nerve fibers from the sensory cells collect and leave the eye. Since there are no cells at that point, visual images hitting there seem to disappear. The blind spot in each eye is toward the nose. With practice a person can cover one eye and, while keeping the open eye steady, hold a dime up and move it around until it disappears. Since the blind spot is in different parts of the visual field in the right and left eyes, few people ever know about it. Only psychology students, eye doctors, and one-eyed persons.

Problem: using one pencil, how do I draw a dot of light splitting into two dots, moving apart, and then have one dot disappear?

Does Mayman know about this? Does he have a faulty research design?

I was twisting my head around trying to map the shape of the blind spot in my right eye when the researcher came back in. She turned the lights on. She walked over to the cardboard box and picked it up. She switched on the tape recorder. "What did you see?" she asked.

I told her.

She asked me several questions about ever feeling disconnected or dissociated from the world. I said I hadn't.

When we were finished she said, "Thank you for taking time to be a control subject in our research."

"You're welcome. I'd like to receive a copy of your findings when you have them written up."

"I'll tell Dr. Mayman."

At two o'clock I walked into Smith's office and sat down.

"We have decided that to protect our program," he said, "we have to let you go. We cannot trust you with our patients."

"Okay."

"How do you feel about that?"

"I believe that you have the right and the responsibility to do what you think is best for your program. I'll go figure out another way to present my ideas to people."

He stared at me. "We don't want you to do that. You need to stay here and go into the hospital. You are quite mentally ill."

"My ideas make sense if you'd listen. Look, I've been trying to analyze why psychiatrists can't stand a person speaking metaphorically about having high self-esteem when they say they are Napoleon or Jesus or Cleopatra. Have you ever realized that when a person says people are trying to force thoughts into his mind, psychiatrists try to force him to believe he is mentally ill? The key is to not listen to the words but to observe the behavior and its consequences. Psychiatrists are acting out an infant's personality theory. The story of Adam and Eve is about the good person/bad person split that Klein wrote about. There's a developmental stage that Freud overlooked. The way to break free is to think..."

Smith shook his head. "Dr. Farrell went into that with you yesterday, and he decided that these ideas are symptoms of illness."

"He listened to me less than 20 minutes. What is sick about my ideas?"

"You are mentally ill, and we have a reputation for knowing what we are talking about."

"That may be, but please give me a logical explanation."

"Your ideas make me feel uncomfortable. You should be in a mental hospital."

"My ideas make *you* feel uncomfortable so *I* am the one who needs to be in a hospital?!"

He laughed. "Well, you are mentally ill and in·need of help."

"I don't need anyone's help. I know exactly what is going on and will take care of myself as I always have."

He leaned forward. Smiling, he said, "If you stay here and work on your illness, you can reapply to the program when you are well."

What a bunch of crap.

He's trying to give me an incentive.

"I do not have mental illness. I can logically explain and support everything I have been saying. Why won't anyone make an effort to listen to my ideas?"

"We recognize mental illness when we see it."

"But no one seems to be able to give me any logical reasons. Look, I'm a reasonable person. I'm open to consider that I have become mentally ill. What are the signs?"

"You recognize that you are more excited now that you usually are."

"Yes, I'm excited! I'm getting insights into human behavior that I've been searching for all my life."

"Hypomanic excitement is a sign of mental illness."

"I'm going through a developmental crisis. It's happened before."

"So you've had emotional breakdowns before."

"No. I've been through developmental crises before and have always emerged with more insight and competence."

"You were married once before, and you are not getting along well with your present wife."

"True. It is a strain to have someone you love and respect calling up your friends and colleagues telling them you are mentally ill."

"She seems to believe you are mentally ill."

"I told her she wouldn't understand my ideas."

"Well, instability in marriage is a sign of mental illness."

"I outgrow people."

"What do you think will happen to this marriage?"

"I believe it is beyond repair."

"Why is that?"

"I cannot live with a woman I cannot trust with my private thoughts and feelings. I don't believe I could ever fully open myself up to her again."

"But she has been doing all these things to help you."

"I do not question her motives or intentions. But that does not excuse a person from being responsible for the pain they cause others."

"How do you feel about her calling us?"

"I feel angry. I told her to stop calling people and telling them I need psychiatric help."

"She is quite upset and needs your support."

"I understand why she is upset. I also complemented her on the job she has done wrecking my career. If I had known people were inquiring because of her phone calls, however, rather than out of natural curiosity, I could have told them they would be frightened."

"We aren't frightened," he said.

"Don't you recognize defensive behavior when you see it? When people asked me what I was thinking I answered their questions honestly. I didn't come to you, you came to me. And look at everyone's reaction. No one says they disagree with me or that I should go away. Everyone gets extremely upset. They insist that I need to be locked up."

"You do need to be in an institution."

"I will remain in town living at my own place and will meet anyone any time any place to defend the accuracy of my ideas."

"No, that won't do. You need to be in a mental hospital."

"But no one seems to be able to give me a logical reason why."

"You'll just have to take our word for it."

"I do not understand how you can expect a person to accept your diagnosis without being prepared to back it up with facts or evidence."

"Your asking to see Dr. Cashman's patient was inappropriate."

"What's wrong with wanting to talk with a person when I am going to participate in a decision about their life?"

"We don't do that here. Your request was inappropriate. You *are* mentally ill."

I shook my head.

This guy is hopeless.

He grew thoughtful. "When I called you to come out for lunch the other day," he said, "what did you think about that?"

"I sensed that you had a reason for wanting me to come out so I came."

"But you controlled the conversation we had."

"Did I control it or was it merely that I refused to allow you to control it?"

"There's no difference," he said with irritation. "Your wife says you aren't sleeping well at night and have been getting up early in the morning."

"Our furniture hasn't arrived. I am sleeping on an air mattress with a hole in it. By three o'clock I'm sleeping on the hard floor. I prefer to get up and watch the sunrise. I enjoy the quiet. Then I take a long nap in the afternoon."

"A disturbance in sleep pattern is a sign of mental illness. She says you aren't eating well and have lost weight."

"This is partly true. She claims that she is cooking for me and doing all these things entirely because she loves me and that she is not trying to hang on to me or control my emotions. I find both her love and her food a bit hard to stomach at this time."

"Eating disturbance and weight loss are symptoms of mental illness. You look like you have lost some weight."

"I bought some shirts on sale that are a half-size too big."

"Well, you *are* mentally ill and need very much to be in an intensive care hospital."

"What I need is to be left alone. Throughout all this my only request is for people to get off my back."

"But we don't want you to do anything that might ruin your career. You do seem to have some good skills."

"I must go into a mental hospital in order to *not* have my career ruined?"

"Yes. I myself was in serious trouble once, and my colleagues recognized that I was not able to do my job and was not in any condition to work with patients. You are mentally ill and need long-term psychotherapy."

Oh, oh. They got him.

Verify.

"And you're only doing this for my own good?"

"Yes."

"No selfish reasons motivate you?"

"Assuredly not."

These people are so blind.

And they think they are the most enlightened.

"I can see we've reached a dead end," I said. I stood up and walked out of his office. I went home. Larry was at the apartment talking with Kathleen. The temperature was over 80 degrees and humid outside. I changed into my shorts and T-shirt. I went for a walk around the capitol grounds trying to problem solve my situation.

How can I reach these people? Get them to see what I'm talking about?

Present your ideas in an attractive way. Ask questions. Use intelligent reasoning, logic they can't resist. I'll make them listen. Force them. I'll ram it right down their throats! I'll...

No. No force. Get away from here. Drop out. Make them come to you. Make them plead *for the answer they need. Make them beg. Yah! But what if no one comes to me? How will anyone know I have anything valuable? Hmmm.*

Okay. So I won't do that. What I'll do is write out all the answers into a big beautiful thesis and dump it on them. They won't want it, but I'll bury them with my ideas!

Forget it.

Why?

It won't work that way. Be kind. Just be available to help them. Why get mad at them? They're doing what they were trained to do. They're doing their best. Make your mind available to them. No games. No force. They'll eventually see how valuable your ideas are.

Bullshit. They are so incompetent they are beyond hope. I'm going to chew them up and spit them out.

I'm going to...

Sure you are.

I'm...

I'm what?

I'm scared. I'm scared by how scared they are. Their distress makes them unconsciously perceive me as dangerous. That I must be destroyed. That's possible.

Even the best are doing what humans have always done. Destroy someone who comes up with upsetting ideas. Its a blind, unthinking, animal response. If you destroy the person with the ideas, then the ideas will be destroyed. But "good" people don't try to destroy people who upset them, they try to "cure" them.

Christ. This is still the dark ages. I feel like a man from the future who has awakened in a barbarian world. Is it possible to try to improve this world and to survive?

The chances seem slim.

Wait a sec. Look at the sequence your mind and emotions just went through.

Larry stayed over. He slept on the couch. On Friday he and I spent much of the morning on the porch talking. Kathleen made ice tea for us.

Larry was mostly quiet while I talked. He worked hard trying to fathom what I was saying and feeling.

"Do you realize how egocentric it is," I said, "for humans to believe they are the only intelligent life in the universe? There must be civilizations far more advanced than ours. And what if our earth is just a speck of dust in another world? Sometimes I imagine that this is all just an experiment. That we are some college sophomore's term project."

Larry laughed.

"Now I feel like there are other worlds identical to this one where everything is happening just the same. Each one is vastly bigger than the next. Like there is a whole series of worlds. I can feel all the others. Close your eyes and try to pick up what I'm feeling."

Larry closed his eyes. I tried to project what I was feeling into him.

"Did you pick up anything?"

He shook his head.

"Did you know there's no such thing as a non-profit institution?"

"No."

"The profit is esteem, praise, the feeling that one is helping unfortunate people. And they can never succeed because of the need for perceptual contrast. Good people must have bad, sick, miserable people around them to establish perceptual contrast for their identity. It is a powerful, unconscious need."

"Oh."

"I'm dismayed about how these Menninger people can't understand me. These guys are the best. They should know about developmental crises. I know what I'm going through is healthy and I'll come out of it much stronger and have more depth of understanding than before. But they don't comprehend. They don't even listen well. They should be curious about this, but they aren't. They're panicked out. I've tried to see things from their view. You know how I am. In our T-group you saw how good I was at seeing things from the other person's view."

"That's right. I liked you better than the trainer." Larry leaned over and gave my arm a light jab with his fist. I smiled. It was a little joke between us that came from a Peanuts cartoon. Linus tells Charlie Brown he liked a girl so much he hit her. One evening in Bethel I was sitting on a wall when Larry walked up and hit me on the arm. I knew what he meant.

"I have carefully examined how things look from their point of view," I said, "but it just doesn't compute." I let out a deep sigh. "Man, I sure am tired of this. It's tough enough going through this without having them and Kathleen thinking I am a sick person who needs curing. Oh well, 'Sticks and stones.'"

"What?"

"When I was a boy I'd go home crying sometimes because someone called me a name. My mother told me to just say back to them, 'Sticks and stones can break my bones but words will never harm me.' She raised me to not get upset about words other people might say to me." I stood up. "Want to go for a walk? We'll be back in time for lunch."

Larry and I walked downtown to the post office.

I unlocked the box and took out a letter from Laura.

Aha! Here's the letter I've been waiting for.

"Come on," I said to Larry. "I want to read this letter by the river."

We climbed up the dike. I sat down on a rock. "Now to find out if it's the lady or the tiger."

Larry prowled around a pumping station while I read the letter.

When I finished I walked over to him. I smiled. "It's neither," I said. "She has surprised me again with an unpredictable response. She wrote some things about herself she wanted me to know. It was a thoughtful, sincere reply. The more I know about her the more I like her."

"Kathleen is afraid you're going to leave her for the nurse," he said.

"Hmm."

That would be possible but...

"Even if I wanted to, Laura says she will not play any part in breaking up a marriage. She has affairs with married men, but she won't break up a marriage."

We walked back to the apartment. Kathleen had iced tea and tuna fish sandwiches with crispy lettuce and sliced tomatoes ready for us.

In the afternoon I drove Larry out to the Menninger museum. "I don't understand," I said, "why I am having to work so hard to get these people to comprehend what I'm saying to them. They are supposed to be the best listeners in the world, able to understand anything a human might say to them. But it's like they have walls around their minds. God, it is frustrating."

Larry smiled sympathetically. "I don't understand a lot of what you are saying either," he said.

"I know. Some of the thoughts I get sound weird to me too, but I'm bottom fishing in the unconscious of the human race. I dredge something up, try it out, and keep what seems to have value. The discards go back.

"You're doing it on purpose then."

"Right! Mental illness is when a person can't keep crazy ideas from bubbling up. I'm pulling stuff up on purpose. Like I said your first day here, if the world isn't working well, then it is up to me to change myself, not try to change others. This is where my path is taking me."

I drove up past the fountain and parked in front of the museum. Inside I showed Larry the relics from old insane asylums. "The Menningers," I said, "worked all their professional lives to make the treatment of inmates more humane. Largely through their efforts 'asylums' were turned into 'hospitals' and 'inmates' became 'patients.'"

I showed Larry the chains and shackles once used to restrain the insane. "Hosings and wet tubs were stopped," I said. "Lobotomies done less frequently. The human snake pits gradually disappeared. Rooms filled with groveling human animals were eliminated. The long dark basement corridors with living zombies slumped down against the walls were cleared out. The dedicated work of the Menningers and the people they attracted to work with them led to a revolution that significantly improved what had been barbaric practices."

I showed Larry the Freud exhibit. We looked at the patient art. As Larry and I strolled around I recognized the museum curator. He was standing at the bottom of a narrow back stairway talking to an assistant. He didn't look at Larry or me. He said to the assistant, "We must put a gate across this stairway with a sign that says, 'Private. Visitors Stay Out.' People are coming upstairs and…"

I walked up behind him. I said, "Excuse me, please," and touched him lightly on the back to move him aside.

Without looking at me or breaking his train of thought he moved out of my way and continued saying to his assistant "…walking into offices. Dr. Roger doesn't like it. Get a ruler and measure the width here."

I walked up several steps waiting for him to realize what I was doing. He didn't. Larry grinned and had to turn away to keep from laughing out loud. I stopped on the stairs. When Larry looked at me again, I shrugged. Then I walked back down the stairs. As we walked away the curator continued. "It has to be a quiet gate. It mustn't squeak."

Back at the apartment we got some ice tea and went outside to cool off. We took off our shirts and sat down.

"Larry, I'm trying to decide if I should take off or stay here and do what they want."

He looked at me for a moment. "I don't think you have a choice," he said.

Alert.

This is useful information. He's been talking to Kathleen. He knows what she and the doctors are saying.

They are hoping I will go in voluntarily but are getting close to forcing an involuntary commitment. They are that desperate.

"Thanks for telling me."

"I have to leave," he said, standing up. He grasped my hand hard. "Good luck, Al."

"Thanks. You too."

After Larry left I told Kathleen, "I'm going for a walk to think things over. Maybe I should sign myself in."

It started to rain, but since it was early September in Kansas it was very warm out. I changed into shorts and a white T-shirt, took my umbrella, and walked over to the capitol grounds.

Flashes of lightening zipped across the sky followed by loud cracks of thunder.

I feel so <u>many</u> feelings...

Anger at Kathleen for acting behind my back.

Pity for her because she is alone and doesn't understand what is happening.

Anger at the Menninger staff for being so closed-minded.

Waves of rain came pounding down.

Fascination with my mind.

Joy because I'm getting answers to questions that have puzzled me.

Frustration because I don't understand these new ideas well enough to know how to present them in a way that others can hear...

And I feel very alone.

I walked over to the Lincoln statue. I looked up at him sitting in his chair.

Why can't they hear what I'm saying?

Why is everyone so upset? So desperate?

These ideas work! Why are the Menninger people so blind?

Rain came down harder. I turned around and leaned back against a narrow, sloping ledge under Lincoln's feet. I propped my umbrella over my head and shoulders. I leaned forward and put my face in my hands. I broke into heavy sobs. Thunder cracked overhead. The rain pounded down. Tears streamed down my cheeks.

This is very dramatic.

Hey.

What's happening?

The back of my pants felt wet. I looked around and saw water running off the statue down across the ledge where I was sitting.

Hell. Here is one of the most dramatic moments of my life and I get rain water running down the crack of my ass.

Oh well.

I got up and started walking again.

Saturday morning I decided to try again. I called Smith at home. "Will you and some staff members please meet with me to talk?"

"Why?"

"Look. I have a thesis. A *doctoral* thesis. I have done research on it. I have developed my case for it. I will meet you any place, any time to defend it. This is the Menninger Foundation. *Someone* here should be able to understand what I'm talking about. Please take time to listen to me."

"We don't have to," he said. "We recognize illness when we see it."

"It is not illness. I'll stay here in Topeka and be available."

"You can't do that. You must go into the hospital."

"Why? I'm not dangerous."

"We have to protect our program and the reputation of the Foundation."

Shit!

"Smith! You can take your Foundation and stick it up your ass!"

He chuckled and said, "Now that's appropriate."

What! He's seen my tolerance, understanding, and empathy as inappropriate?

Did he really say that?

"What did you say?"

"I said that's appropriate."

Man. It's hard to believe this is really happening. Terminate.

Wait.

"Tell me, Smith, how are you going to explain to people why it was that when a guy like me came here, you clutched up so fast all you could do is throw me into a mental hospital?"

"That's my problem."

"Okay," I said and chuckled to myself as I hung up. After that I got angry.

I told these people on my application what I was like. Didn't they read it? These stupid bastards are starting to piss me off.

After I calmed down I thought to myself.

I sure wish Mayman was here. Things probably would not have developed this way.

Could try Rosen.

He seemed to be an intelligent guy.

I'll call him.

"Dr. Rosen?"

"Yes?"

"This is Al Siebert. Could I talk to you for a moment?"

"Yes. What is it?"

"Well, I'm having difficulty trying to find anyone around here with the capacity to handle some new ideas I've come up with. They make a lot of sense to me, but they seem to make other people extremely anxious. Will you listen?"

"Go ahead."

Good!

He's heavy into psychoanalytic theory so start there.

"One key insight came when I started comparing the story of Adam and Eve with what all infants experience..." I outlined my interpretation to him.

"I've also discovered that what people do with their minds follows all the stages Freud outlined. Except there are two defense mechanisms he didn't discover. I call them "charity and tax collecting."

Rosen listened without comment.

"The key emotion underlying all this is the unconscious feeling, 'I am the most valuable person who will ever exist.' If a person can allow himself to be consciously aware, to have absolute high self-esteem, then we can see how it exists in others. Everything falls into place."

He isn't asking questions or showing any positive responses.

Stop. Ask what he thinks.

"What do you think about some of these ideas?"

"Do you want my frank opinion?"

"Yes."

"They sound like sickness to me."

"But I know these ideas are correct."

"What makes you think your ideas are correct?"

"Because I've tested them out. And I did like Freud. I traced everything out in my own mind."

"Without going through psychoanalysis?"

"Sure. I've always been able to do anything anyone else could do. I don't know why Freud should be an exception."

"Al, this sounds like sickness."

Damn.

"It's discouraging to hear you say that but thank you for listening. I appreciate your frankness."

"You're welcome."

I hung up.

Isn't that something. Freud achieved valuable insights by doing a self-analysis. But years later his followers believe that deep self-insight can be reached only by going through analysis with them. This is a peculiar kind of progress.

Well. That was the last hope I had. What the hell. Here is another person I respect saying I'm sick. Maybe it's true.

I said to Kathleen, "My life insurance check will be arriving soon. I want to make sure you have money, so I'm going downtown to find someone who can tell me how to handle this."

I walked downtown to a professional building with many law office signs on the outside. I saw a man in casual clothes unlocking a door. He looked like he could be an attorney.

"Are you an attorney?"

"Yes, I am," he said, looking at me with caution.

"I'd like to ask you a question."

He nodded.

"How can I arrange for my wife to cash a check that will be arriving while I am out of town?"

"Do you have a joint bank account?"

"Yes."

"Tell her to take the check to the bank. Write 'for deposit only' on the back. The bank will accept it for deposit. After the amount is recorded, then she can withdraw the funds."

"Thank you! Thank you very much."

"You're welcome."

Back at the apartment I told Kathleen what to do with the check.

"I knew you wouldn't leave me without any money," she said with great relief. "When I called about you, he said to put all our money in a bank account in my name only."

"Smith did?"

"Yes."

"I'm not surprised."

A short time later the phone rang.

"Dr. Siebert?"

"Yes."

"This is Dr. Farrell. How are you feeling?"

"Okay. A little tired."

"You are very sick Dr. Siebert. You need to go into a hospital."

I wonder why he called now?

Probably Rosen and Smith.

"Maybe you're right."

At least this way I can get them to all relax a little.

I could use the rest. It would give me a chance to think.

"Yes, it would be best. You are a veteran aren't you?"

"Yes."

"Will you stay there for awhile until I call back?"

"Yes."

Watch it. Could be a play to keep you here until the police arrive.

"What is your reason for asking that?"

"We have an excellent Veterans' Administration hospital nearby. If we can get you into it, all your hospitalization will be free."

"I see."

A few minutes later he called back.

"Dr. Siebert, I have talked to the director of the hospital. They have a six-month waiting list, but he is a friend of mine. He has authorized your immediate admission. If I drive over and pick you up, will you let me take you over?"

Choice point.

Should I take off or go along with them?

Scan it…

Nothing negative.

"Okay."

"Fine. I'll be there in a few minutes. Pack a few things in a bag and bring a change of clothes."

I went into the bedroom and emptied out my athletic bag.

Take casual clothes, extra underwear, socks, sweat shirt, gym clothes.

Take your address book.

I saw a dusty old Cadillac with oxidized paint pull up in front of our apartment. I knew it had to be Farrell. I said good-bye to Kathleen and asked her to come and visit me as soon as she could. Then I went downstairs and got into Farrell's car.

"You have made a wise decision," he said. "You will be better off now."

And by going in voluntarily it will be ten times easier to get out.

"We have a fine VA hospital. There are many Foundation trainees placed there. They have a six-month waiting list, but the director is one of my friends. He is admitting you today as a favor to me."

"You told me that already."

Amazing. He has this twisted around to see this as an act of kindness and charity.

He drove along with an artificial smile frozen on his face. His face glistened with sweat. His hands gripped the wheel so tightly his knuckles were white.

Jesus, this guy is tense.

Try to get him relaxed a little.

"You know, this will be an interesting experience for me," I said.

He looked at me.

"Any time I go into a new situation I learn a great deal from it. This should prove to be the same. I know I'll learn a lot."

A look of pity swept over his face as he stared at me. He seemed to be thinking, "You poor deluded soul. So out of contact with reality you are happy and optimistic about your plight."

Try something else.

"I'm sorry we didn't have longer to talk. I didn't have a good chance to tell you all about my ideas."

"Would you like to tell me more?"

"Yes. No one has given me a full chance yet. Would you be willing to come over and talk with me?"

He turned and smiled at me. "Yes, I'd like that."

Tilt!

I don't believe him. He is probably following S.O.P. with a mental case.

Lies and deceptions are okay if it will get the person locked up without force. The end justifies the means.

I'd like to see an article in a psychiatric journal justifying their habit of lying to people.

It's like trying to open a savings account by writing a bad check.

Chapter Thirteen

My Menninger Post-Doctoral Education

Our drive was short. The VA hospital was located in a residential area only about a mile from our apartment. The grounds were well kept. Large areas of flat, manicured lawns surrounded a sprawling network of buildings. It looked something like an airport terminal—a large central administration building connected by long brick and glass corridors to the surrounding two-story buildings.

I sat waiting in the reception area for about 20 minutes while Farrell was off some place. I shut my eyes and leaned back. The cool air from the air conditioning felt good. Farrell came back with a clerk. They handed me a clip board with the Voluntary Admission form. I signed it. The clerk left. Farrell stayed with me. We were waiting for the doctor on duty to come and admit me.

I hadn't eaten any lunch and was getting very hungry. I told Farrell. He gave me a quarter to buy some candy bars from a vending machine.

A doctor finally arrived. Dr. French. He took me into an examining room. Farrell left. It was the last time I saw him.

Dr. French asked for my wallet, watch, and keys. He sealed them in a large heavy envelope and wrote my name on it. He showed me where he was acknowledging receipt on the form he had.

"Your valuables will be held for you by the security office until you leave," he said. Looking over to another part of the form he asked, "What is today's date?"

I smiled. "September fourth." I almost laughed.

He smiled. We both knew that the usual way a psychiatrist checks a person's "orientation to time and place" is to ask the person what the date is.

"Military serial number?" he asked.

"RA19479788."

"Branch of service?"

"Airborne. Army Airborne."

"Rank at discharge?"

"E-5."

"Any military injuries?"

"Tinnitus, left ear."

"How did it happen?"

"Machine gun range."

He gave me a quick physical.

He seems bright, capable, competent. About 30 years old. Black hair. Solid build. Healthy looking. He's friendly and pleasant.

When he finished the exam, he asked, "How do you feel?"

"Tired but okay. This is quite an adventure."

He smiled. We had good eye contact.

"What provisional diagnosis are you admitting me under?" I asked.

"What do you think?"

"I'm not sure."

"Take a guess."

"Probably acute schizophrenia."

He grinned.

"That's great!" I said.

"Why do you say that?" he asked, still smiling.

"Because I'm going through a developmental crisis. This means that what is viewed as schizophrenia is a healthy transformation!"

He led me out of the examining room and down a long corridor.

It never occurred to me.

But of course! I can see it now.

This is fantastic!

Schizophrenia is a developmental crisis.

"Remember the old term dementia praecox," I said, "the mental disease that mysteriously struck young people?"

Look! He's thinking!

He's listening.

Fantastic. Maybe I've finally found someone who can follow my thinking!

"What if it has been something healthy that the rest of us haven't understood well? Something that causes us to attack and interfere when we should be facilitating?"

Dr. French said, "I'm assigning you to my ward."

"Good. I'm looking forward to talking with you. By the way, I have a request."

"What?"

"That no staff member calls me doctor. Please have them call me Al. I'd prefer to not have the patients know."

He nodded his head. "Of course." He introduced me to the nurse on duty and left. I looked around the ward room as the nurse did the paper work on me.

Observation: Good feeling here. About 30 men, ages 18 to 50.

Most of them alert, focused outward. Some reading. Some writing letters. Card game going with several onlookers. Checkers game. A few watching TV. Several pairs talking. A few sitting or standing alone. Only a few asleep. Only one man shuffling slowly along the hallway. The men here are more physically healthy than I've ever seen on a locked ward. Looks like no ECT patients here. Probably few drugs used. Feels good.

The nurse finished filling out the forms. She looked up and asked, "Do you have any change on you?"

"Yes."

"You'll have to let us keep it here. The doctor has to authorize patients to have any money."

I handed her the coins from my pocket. She counted it. "Eighty-six cents." She put it in an envelope and placed it in a cupboard. Please go with Mr. Stennis now. He will show you where your bed is."

"Certainly. When will we eat?"

She looked at the big clock on the wall. "In about an hour."

Stennis led me down a short hallway to a sleeping area.

He's about 45. Strong. 220 pounds. Looks like cattle rancher. I don't want to tangle with him.

There were about 16 beds in the room, all made up nicely with white bed covers. Dark brown night stands stood next to each one. A slender man about 27 was lying on a bed with his hands behind his head and his legs crossed. He stared at the ceiling, lost in thought.

Stennis walked over to the next bed. "Here is your bed. Store your things in here. When you want a towel and wash cloth, get them from the linen closet in the hallway."

He reached for a pack of cigarettes. "Want a smoke?"

"No thanks. I don't smoke."

"Listen for chow call. We go to the dining room in the main building as a group. Got any questions?"

"Not now."

Stennis left. I put my shaving kit in the drawer. I opened the doors underneath, put my clothing on the top shelf, and stuffed my empty athletic bag underneath. Then I laid down on my bed to rest and to think.

This is unbelievable. How can a person get a Ph.D. in psych from one of the best schools in the country, win a fellowship to the Menninger Foundation, and then, when people discover what thoughts he has in his mind, end up locked up in a V.A. psychiatric hospital?

Can this really be happening?

"Have you been in a hospital like this before?" said the man across the aisle.

Yes. But not as a patient.

"No."

"It isn't a bad place," he said, sitting up. "They treat you nice. The aides take it easy on us. They're friendly."

I studied his face.

What an unusual face. His skin is dark black, but his facial structure is Caucasian.

He asked, "Why are you in here?"

"My wife got unhappy about what I was thinking. She started telephoning people and here I am."

He nodded. "My wife too. I told her if she didn't lay off bugging me all the time, I'd divorce her. That set her off. She screamed and yelled at me. She said I had to support her. Said I was crazy if I thought I could divorce her. The next night the police came. She had me committed here."

"How did she do that?"

"One time when she was getting on my nerves I told her I had thought about suicide several times. She went down to the court with a friend and signed a form saying I was threatening to kill myself. The court psychiatrist only talked to me for three minutes. He just walked into my cell and asked if I'd ever thought of killing myself. I said 'yes' and that was all it took." He paused and looked at me intently. "It's a tough trip," he said.

I nodded. We looked at each other with complete empathy.

Isn't this something.

The first sincere caring I've experienced in weeks is coming from a person who is supposed to be a mental case. This whole thing is backwards!

His name was Leroy. He had been a radio operator in the Air Force and now worked as a TV repairman. We walked together to the cafeteria. He told me about the hospital routines, the patient organization, and recreation facilities.

"What about Dr. French?" I asked.

"Frenchy? Most of us like him. He's the best in the place. He listens good and helps a lot of people get out."

That's encouraging. Maybe I'll finally get some time with someone with the capacity to listen.

After dinner a patient walked up to me and shook hands. "I'm Hal Davis. I'm the president of the patients' group on this ward."

Probably 32 or 33. Dark brown hair, prematurely balding. My height. Paunchy stomach. Looks like a hefty, beer-drinking truck driver.

"If you want to know anything just ask," he said.

"Thanks. Leroy has filled me in pretty well."

That evening the nurse called me over to the nurses' station.

"Mr. Siebert. Here is a sleeping pill for you."

"I don't want it."

"Please take it. It will help you sleep tonight. The doctor ordered it for you."

"Thank you, but I don't want it."

She looked at me a few seconds. Then she said, "I understand. It will be here if you change your mind."

I went to bed. My mind was churning. It wouldn't stop.

How could this have happened?

Why can't I reach them? Get them to understand what they are doing?

Why are they so blind?

Everything seems too obvious to me. What am I doing wrong? What don't I understand yet?

Are the ideas wrong?

Maybe so, but I've gotten so much confirmation. And why can't they explain where my thinking is off if they understand me so well? How can I approach them better?

This is bewildering. They are the experts, the top pros.

They can't be this weak, this dense, this defensive. They can't be. I just don't know.

Well, Frenchy seems pretty sharp. If I organize my thoughts and evidence carefully, maybe he will take time to listen.

And so it went. About 1:00 a.m. I went out to the nurses' station and asked for the sleeping pill.

Sunday was a dull day. I read the newspaper. I read magazines for awhile.

Hal Davis came over and sat next to me. "How did you get in here?" he asked.

"People got scared about what I was thinking."

"You committed?"

"No. I'm voluntary."

"Yah? Why did you come in?"

"To get them off my back. They're less nervous now with me locked up. It won't be for long. It's easier to get out if you go in voluntarily. How about you?"

He got a disgusted look. "Committed…for the third time. My folks did it."

"What caused them to do it?"

"They're square. So I go shack up, get boozed. What the hell, it's my life."

"Where's the problem?"

"The cops take me home. My mother cries about her corrupt son. The old man preaches to me. He calls the minister and our doctor. They decided I'm a mental case, but they're the ones who need help."

"I know what you mean. How about Frenchy? What does he say?"

"He's all right. He doesn't talk like the other doctors I've had."

"Why do you stay around your folks?"

He looked at me and smiled. "I won't next time."

I was restless being confined with little to do. I asked an aide, "Is there any recreation planned today? Any chance of getting to the gym?"

"No. We're a light staff because of the holiday."

"What about tomorrow?"

"Not tomorrow either. That's Labor Day."

Jesus, I need some exercise.

I need a workout bad.

During the afternoon I circulated around, talking to anyone available. I spoke to Leroy, Hal, several patients, the nurse and the other aide on duty. In each conversation I said, "I feel restless without any exercise. What are the chances of us going to the gym?" Each person's answer was negative.

About eight o'clock I was sitting at a small table playing solitaire. The evening duty nurse came over to me.

About 40. Skinny. Thin dark brown hair. Hatchet faced. Tired. Anemic.

"May I sit down?" she asked.

"Sure."

She sat watching me play cards for awhile. Then she asked, "Why did you come into the hospital?"

"Everyone tells me I am mentally ill. I don't believe I am, but I'm a reasonable person. I decided to give them a chance to explain their views to me."

Her eyes clouded over. With pity in her voice, talking more to herself than to me, she said, "It is such a tragedy so many people in here do not know they are mentally ill."

It's a tragedy you don't know the patients are right.

"Yes, it is," I said, nodding, and continuing my card game.

"Is everything all right?" she asked.

"Sure, except I need exercise. Any chance of us getting to the gym tomorrow?"

"No. We won't have enough staff on duty."

Sure lady. There's always a reason.

She sat there for about a minute. She stood up and asked, "Is there anything you'd like? Any nourishments?"

"Do you have any milk?"

She smiled. "Yes. White or chocolate?"

"Chocolate, please."

She smiled. She was happy now. She could do something for me.

At bedtime she called me over to the nursing station. "Here's your sleeping pill," she said.

"I don't want it," I said. "I never take pills like that."

"The doctor ordered it for you."

"That may be, but I don't want it."

She looked at me thoughtfully for several seconds as though making a decision. "All right, but it is here if you want it later."

"Thank you."

I couldn't fall asleep because my mind started churning with questions again. I got up and walked out to the nurses' station. I asked the nurse, "May I have my sleeping pill, please?"

Monday morning, after breakfast, Hal Davis walked over to me. He said, "The ward president gives out the ward work assignments. I'll give you the linen closet. It's easy. Stack the fresh linen on the shelves after they bring the laundry cart in."

"Okay."

Stennis was back on duty. Later in the morning when he wasn't busy I asked him about taking us to the gym. He said, "The hospital is lightly staffed today, but I'll check."

About 2:00 p.m. Stennis came over to me. "I talked to the nursing supervisor. If a few of you want to go to the gym, I'll take you. They'll cover the ward for me."

Five of us went to the gym. I was bursting with energy. I did fifteen quick chin-ups. Then I grabbed a basketball and dribbled down the floor as hard as I could. I drove in for a lay-up, caught the ball and raced back to the basket at the other end at top speed. I kept up the racing, driving lay-ups for a long time. Man, I was built up. Exercise had never felt so good to me before.

When I got tired of running I shot free throws and set shots. Afterward Stennis took us to the canteen. Perspiration was dripping off me. I put on my sweat shirt so I wouldn't catch cold. I felt very thirsty.

The others had change on them for cold drinks, but I didn't. Stennis loaned me a quarter. The canteen prices were low. I bought a quart of Coke with a slice of lemon. I chugged it down, then filled the cup with ice water.

We stayed in the canteen about 30 minutes. Stennis was sincerely interested in all of us.

A good man.

When I got back to the ward an aide called me over to the nurses' station. He said, "Mr. Siebert, you are being transferred to another ward." He handed me the envelope with my coins. "This is Mr. Sims. He'll take you over."

About 55, short, heavily grayed, curly hair and balding. Good size belly.

He's sizing you up. He's had a lot of experience. He's street smart.

Sims stayed at the station while I went to get my things from my night stand. As we started for the door I said, "Just a minute." I tore open the envelope. I walked over to Stennis and gave him the quarter I owed him. He grasped my hand in both his hands and gripped it tightly. Looking very intently at me and with concern on his face he said, "Good luck, Siebert."

Sims walked next to me down a long glass and brick corridor.

Alert!

Stennis was telling you something.

What?

Don't know.

Okay…be open…cautious…scan…

We went through several doors and then along another long corridor.

Sims is pretty relaxed. He's alert but not nervous.

He opened a door for me and then took me up a flight of stairs. Then through another locked door. We entered a ward.

There were six men in the corridor.

Slowly walking. Thin, poor grooming, skin pallid.

Eyes down. They glance at me but don't study me.

We turned the corner. As we walked toward the nurses' station I scanned the ward dayroom.

About two dozen men. Half of them sprawled on chairs. Many asleep in awkward positions. Mouths open. Six-seven in front of an old black and white TV set. Only two watching. Five men standing or walking. Ill fitting clothes, sagging muscles, lethargic. Three men reading. Two patients talking to themselves. Two aides playing cards. Stale smell here.

Impression: Lifeless. Men heavily drugged. The dregs.

This is the back ward!

That's what Stennis...!

I threw back my head and laughed.

They've put me here to prove to me how mentally ill I am!

"Only the most severely mentally ill are on the back ward. Therefore, if you are on the back ward, Mr. Siebert, this must prove to you that you are severely mentally ill!"

It was a deep, long, full laugh.

Mr. Sims asked me for my change. He counted it and put it in an envelope. Then he went through my bag. He took two glass bottles out of my shaving kit, my aftershave lotion, and my hair cream. He said, "We have to keep these here." One of the aides placed a piece of white tape on each bottle and wrote my name on the tape.

"Why is that?"

"Standard suicide precaution." He winked. "Don't want you slashing your wrists. You can have them in the morning during hygiene period. Please give me your belt."

As I handed my belt to him I asked, "Why are you taking these now? I've been in the hospital three days already."

"It's the rules on new admissions." He turned to the others. "Manny, you and Bob get Siebert squared away. Give him the bed by the window."

Manny and Bob walked ahead of me down the hall. They stopped at the linen closet to get sheets, blankets, towel and wash cloth, and a bed cover.

Manny looks about 24. Medium height. Medium build. Walks easily. Could play guard on a basketball team. Bob looks about 20. Slightly shorter. Solid build. Tanned squarish head. Black hair. Looks strong. Could play half-back.

Any problems here?

Scan...

No. Feels okay.

The bed was standard military. Metal frame with wire mesh. Just like I spent three years on in the Army.

Several springs missing. I'll take care of that when I have a chance.

They started to make the bed.

"Hey. I'll do that. I'll make my own bed."

They looked up and smiled.

Bob said, "We usually have to make the beds for the ones they bring in here."

I took over. Bob left.

Manny said, "That's your night stand. Put your clothes in it for now. You'll have a locker later."

"Okay."

"How are ya doin', man?"

"Okay. Does this ward go to the gym often?"

"Every day. Some don't do nothin.'"

"Can I make a phone call?"

"Not 'til the doctor says."

"Manny, I'm curious about something."

"What?"

"You took my glass bottles and belt for suicide prevention."

"Yes?"

"Look at the fan near the ceiling on that little shelf. It has a long wire cord. A guy could hang himself. If a person really wanted to commit suicide, there are all kinds of ways."

"Right, man. I don't know why precautions aren't better. See the metal blades on the fan? A man climbed up and took the guard off and shoved his wrists into it. He splattered blood all over. Blood on the walls. Blood on the ceiling..."

"That must have been a mess."

"It was! Took us almost two days to clean up."

I nodded in sympathy as I pictured him cleaning up the mess. He walked away shaking his head.

Good rapport. Looks like these aides are good people.

After I finished making my bed I laid down and put my hands behind my head.

The suicide prevention is a farce. Typical psychiatric procedure. Go through the motions but don't accomplish the purpose. Especially if it takes extra effort.

So why is it done? Taking the glass could be to protect the aides and staff. A broken bottle could be used as a weapon.

There's more to it than that though.

What?

There's a message for the patient. "We are in complete control of you. You are like a child. And we are going to protect you from doing yourself harm."

It's funny. If a patient commits suicide, the psychiatrists believe he couldn't cope with his illness. Yet when a psychiatrist commits suicide the remaining ones tell the public that it was caused by stresses therapists are constantly subjected to.

An aide called "Chow time!" I got into line with the others by the ward door. One aide led the way while another one stood and counted. The second one locked the ward door and brought up the rear. I strode along with the group whistling and humming. I felt happy.

What a fantastic experience. This is much more interesting and educational than I expected!

Tuesday evening I started feeling sorry for myself. I sat in the day room looking at the heavily tranquilized men.

I feel abandoned.

When is someone going to realize that a mistake has been made? Why doesn't someone step forward and demand that I be released? All my life I've worked hard at helping other people. I was there for people who needed me.

Now that I need help, where are they? They walk away shaking their heads. "My, my, such a shame he became ill. Seemed like such a nice young man."

The Golden Rule is a lie. A big damn lie.

Chapter Fourteen

Survival in the Haven

The aides awakened the ward about 6:00 a.m. Tuesday morning. I got up quickly to get into the showers first. I shaved, dressed, made my bed, and went into the dayroom until breakfast time.

After breakfast I sat in the dayroom reading a magazine.

This is boring. I've got to find something to keep my mind occupied.

"Medications!" an aide yelled. The patients slowly lined up by the nurses' station. As each one stepped forward the nurse looked at her chart. Then she selected a cup from her tray and handed it to the man. As he swallowed the pill or pills the aide asked, "Juice or water?" The man would state his preference and be handed a cup. Then he would move away and the next patient would step up.

As the last one in line walked away, the nurse looked at her chart. "Siebert," she said to the aide. He yelled, "Siebert!"

I got up and walked over.

"Here are your medications."

What the hell!

"I haven't asked for any medications."

"It's on the chart. You have to take them. Doctor's orders."

"I haven't seen a doctor. I don't want any medication."

Two aides edged toward me. The nurse said, "If you don't want to take the pills, there are other ways you can take it."

Threat!

Problem—they are going to use force if necessary. That means shots—probably the isolation room—get a bad rep with staff.

"Who is the doctor who ordered it?"

"Dr. Baum, the ward doctor."

"What is the medication?"

"Thorazine."

Chances of successful resistance?

Zero.

Of persuading them differently?

Slight.
Best solution for long-term survival?
Go along with it for now.
I reached for the cup. The aides relaxed. "Juice or water?"
"Juice."
This pisses me off.
A doctor I haven't even seen forces me to take Thorazine.
Do I need this?
No.
I put the red capsule in my mouth and drank it down with the juice.
So why is this happening?
The message...
The message is, "We are so much in control of you we can force you to take into your body whatever we decide. You are powerless against us."
Anything else?
"Since only the most severely disturbed patients are on tranquilizers, and you are on tranquilizers, you must accept that..."

A few minutes later the Thorazine started taking effect. I felt groggy, sleepy. I went back to my bed and laid down. When I woke up, my throat felt very dry. I got up and drank a lot of water.

Our ward had an afternoon gym period. As we walked along I thought to myself,

I might be forced into making a break. I must stay in peak physical condition. I could run cross-country at night and hide during the day. At least until I get across the state line. States seldom bother chasing down mental patients and have almost no communication with other states about it. I need the gym period for a heavy work out.

When we got to the gym I grabbed a basketball. I dribbled it from one end of the court to the other and did lay-ups at top speed. An aide came over to one basket and started shooting. I played one-on-one basketball with him for awhile. When some aides and patients finished a volleyball game and started a new one I joined them. The aides, overall, were good athletes, well-coordinated, but the patients were so drugged their reaction times were slow. Their reflexes were very bad. During the game I ran around and jumped a lot just for the activity.

Between games I drank lots of water. When we left the gym to return to the ward I was dripping with sweat.

Back at the ward we all showered under the supervision of the aides. After I dressed and returned to the dayroom a balding aide with a fringe of blond-gray hair walked up to me. His name was Thompson.

Solid build. Strong. About 52 or 53. Looks Scandinavian. Good tan.

He said, "Your wife brought more clothes for you."

"That's great. I need them."

Thompson took me to the nurses station to get the clothing Kathleen had brought. Then he led me to a room next to the showers. He assigned me a locker and I stored my clothing inside.

On the ward I alternated back and forth from falling asleep and being restless for something to do.

This is getting to me. Little activity.

Nothing for my mind. I'm used to much more.

I'm experiencing sensory deprivation.

That's it! I'm adapted to much higher level of stimulus input and activity.

Jesus, I'm learning a lot about what mental patients go through. No wonder they act weird. Sensory deprivation does that to anyone.

Find ways to counteract it.

I went to the nurses station and asked an aide, "Do you have any stationary here?"

"We should." He poked around and located some plain white sheets of paper, a pen, and several envelopes.

I went over to a table and started writing.

9/7/65

Dear Dr. Mayman:

(Why do grown men call each other "dear"?)

I want to thank you for the unusual fellowship you arranged for me. I thought I was going to have to spend two years sitting through dull seminars, lectures, reading, doing papers, and conducting testing. Now it turns out that I've got a full-time, real-life practicum. I am getting a first-hand observation of how psychiatry deals with mental patients. I am learning far more than I expected.

Not only that, but you've provided some good strong men for me to test my athletic skills against. Thank you. Most clinical types are too flabby to do anything. This experience is certainly much more exciting and educational than I thought it was going to be.

By now you have probably heard that some people here picked a fight with me. They will have their own view, but that's how I describe it. As to the outcome—well, you've seen the trophies in McKeachie's office. Do you know why the trophy for the faculty intramural championship is there? Because when I fully commit myself to something, there are then only two states of existence for me. Either I have won or I haven't won <u>yet</u>.

It's too bad you weren't here. You probably would have handled things differently. I have some ideas I've discovered that you might be interested in.

Al

p.s. How have you classified me in your autokinetic test? As a control subject or a schizophrenic?

Now for a letter to Mom.
Should I tell her about this?
No!
If she gets wind of this, she'll fly out here and take this place apart brick by brick if she has to in order to get me out. She would lay Kathleen and the Menninger people out flat. I don't want out yet. I have important things to try to accomplish.

9/7/65
Dear Mom:
My fellowship isn't exactly what I expected, but <u>highly</u> educational...

I addressed the envelopes, sealed the letters, and handed them to a nurse.

She handed them back. "Don't seal the envelopes when you write letters," she said.

"Why not?"

"The doctor has to read and approve them before they are mailed."

"What! Why...?"

"It's to protect the public," she explained, "from the wild letters some inmates write."

I addressed new envelopes. When I gave them to the nurse I said firmly, "This is my fourth day in this hospital and I am being forced to take medications I don't want by a doctor who has never seen me. When am I going to see the doctor?"

"I'll find out for you."

This is ridiculous. What kind of place is this?

I walked around the ward, as I'd been doing more frequently, rehearsing what I wanted to tell the ward psychiatrist.

Early Tuesday evening an aide called, "Medications!"

Oh no!

Wait.

I noticed that only a few men walked over to the nurse's station. I remained seated at my table. When the last man left they put the tray away and stared filling out the paperwork.

Whew! I guess I'm only scheduled for once a day.

Wednesday morning I took the medications they gave me without protest. I drank lots of water and walked up and down the halls to try to stave off the impact, but my efforts didn't succeed. I felt lethargic. My body felt weak and fatigued. I sat down in a chair and was soon asleep. When I awoke my mouth and tongue felt thick.

After lunch an aide had me get my clothing from my locker. He took me to a store room where he inked up a press to stamp my name on all my clothes. He said, "All your clothing has to have your name in it with indelible ink."

"Why?"

"They need it in the laundry."

"That makes sense. It's nice to be in a place where they let you wear your own clothes."

I helped him with the stamping so I wouldn't miss going to the gym.

Late Wednesday afternoon Mr. Biggs, one of the aides, called me over. "Dr. Baum wants you in his office."

At last.

I followed Mr. Biggs around to the ward doctor's office.

"Hello, Dr. Siebert," Baum said, extending his hand.

An old 28. Badly overweight. Fleshly. About 6 feet tall. Brown hair. Strong cigarette smell.

Weak grip.

"Please sit down," he said. "I apologize for not seeing you sooner. I went home for the Labor Day weekend. I was gone four days. My home is in New York. I'm sorry no one could see you..."

He paused waiting for me to excuse him.

Don't tell him it's okay. It isn't.

His professional laxity is his responsibility.

He lit a cigarette.

I remained silent.

"You understand," he continued, "Labor Day weekend no one stays except emergency staff. I'm sorry you went so long without seeing anyone."

I waited.

"You must be feeling depressed about being in here."

"No, I'm not. I'm happy."

"What?" His eyes widened. He stared at me.

I leaned back and put my foot up on one of the other chairs near his desk. I smiled and said, "What I am doing is in the best of American traditions. In our country the way to get to the top is to start at the bottom. I figure that being locked in the back ward of a Veterans' hospital, diagnosed as psychotic is about as bottom as a psychologist can get."

He stared at me as though he could not believe what he was hearing.

"What I *am* feeling is sensory deprivation. I need something to occupy my mind. Will you arrange for me to go to the hospital library?"

"I can't do that yet. I can bring you some books of my own."

"Wonderful."

Maybe this guy will be okay.

"This drug you're making me take. It's knocking me on my ass. I don't want it. Will you please take me off it?"

"Not yet." He gave me a paternalistic smile. "It's good for you. It will help keep your illness under control."

"What illness?"

"You are quite mentally ill, Dr. Siebert. You must recognize that."

Oh no. Not again.

"You haven't ever talked to me, and you..."

Don't argue with him.

"How long will I have to take the Thorazine?"

"We'll see."

"When can my wife visit? I haven't seen her for days."

"How do you feel about her?"

"I still feel a little anger about her going behind my back, but I can understand why she did it. You don't have to be concerned about any trouble when we see each other."

"We'll talk about visitations later."

"Could I have permission to telephone her?"

"Not yet."

"When will you and I have a chance to talk?"

"I have to give you a physical tomorrow. We can talk then."

"I have a request. I'd like to have the staff call me Al. It would be better if the patients don't know about me having a Ph.D. in psychology."

"I'll tell the staff."

"Thanks."

I went back to the day room and sat in a chair. I stared out the window and recalled the story of Ignaz Semmelweis.

Poor guy.

"Who was Semmelweis, Al?"

"He was a Viennese physician in the 1850s. He saw that physicians' dirty hands and bloody instruments were spreading the dreaded childbirth fever that killed so many women in hospitals. He discovered he could eliminate the problem by frequently washing his hands and his instruments. But when he tried to explain to his colleagues that they were the cause of the problem, they laughed at such a ridiculous notion. They ostracized him. Their rejection of this valuable discovery broke his spirit. He became depressed and committed suicide.

"Knowing of his story helped me resolve that I didn't have to suffer just because the medical profession doesn't learn from such experiences. I'm no martyr. I decided to keep on playing with the situation and be ready to cut out if it got too tough."

"You're saying you did not feel depressed or unhappy?"

"At times I felt frustrated, discouraged, or bewildered, Sam, but not depressed. Most of the time I felt elated about the fantastic, real world education I was getting. I felt energized. Something wonderful was happening. I was getting knowledge, insights, understanding, and practical information about how things really work. I remember walking by the head nurse's office one day and looking in at a nurses meeting. The nurses looked out at me. I looked at them and just smiled. They had no idea what my perception was. None of them ever asked."

Sometimes several wards would be in the dining room at the same time. The aides would stand together and talk while they watched us. The food wasn't too bad. We usually had choices about what we ate.

At dinner time I went through the line and, as I'd been doing, took two glasses of milk. Manny walked over and said, "Only one glass to a patient, Siebert."

"I always drink lots of milk."

"Cafeteria rules. Only one to a patient. If you want more, talk to your doctor." He made me put one glass back.

I woke up Thursday morning with a dry throat. After medications I sat down in a chair. The Thorazine knocked me out again. Sometime later...

How long have I been asleep?

My body feels funny. Lifeless.

But my mind is awake.

My mouth and tongue are dry. Thick.

What is wrong with my body?

It's the medication!

Now I know how they were able to get rid of straight jackets. They turn your body into a straight jacket with drugs. Those rotten sons-of-bitches.

I must have my mind fully alert. Have to get off the drugs.

"Barber!" someone yelled. I got up and looked in the bathroom. A barber had set up shop in front of the wash bowls. Bob and Manny herded in the patients who needed haircuts. Manny stayed to supervise.

I stood in the hall watching.

Mine is getting shaggy. Check to see if he can do a good crew cut.

I asked the barber, "You any good at crew cuts?"

He hardly glanced at me. "Yup."

"Manny. How can I get some money to pay him?"

"He's paid for by a Veterans' group. It's a contribution they make."

I decided to go ahead and got in line. When the barber finished with me I looked in the mirror.

Just as I suspected. Fairly flat but lots of long hairs sticking up. He didn't get them all. This won't do.

I asked the barber, "Can I use your scissors to trim off these long ones sticking up?"

The barber looked at Manny. Manny looked at me. I stood waiting. Manny slowly nodded his head. "Thanks," I said. I took the scissors the barber held out to me. I looked in the mirror and trimmed off the long hairs sticking up.

Thursday afternoon after gym period Baum gave me a physical examination. He asked the usual questions.

I gave my usual answers: "No allergies. Tonsils removed when I was a child. Small birthmark left groin, scar on outside of right foot from stepping on a broken bottle. Father had diabetes. He died of an infection when I was eleven..."

Why do I feel uncomfortable? I've had many physicals.

He seems to be <u>enjoying</u> it.

"Stand up," he said. "Extend your arms. Close your eyes. Touch the end of your nose with your index finger. Alternate one hand with the other. Good. Drop your arms to your sides.

Stand still. Keep your eyes closed and jump up and down on your right foot. Now your left. Fine. You may stop."

I looked at him.

His pupils are slightly dilated. Smiling. He must not be used to giving a physical to someone in good condition.

"Sit on the table," he said.

He struck the tendon below my right knee with a reflex hammer. My foot kicked way out.

"Wow!" he said.

"Do you have anything for athletes foot?" I asked. "It's getting pretty bad."

He looked between my toes. "I'll prescribe a potassium permanganate foot soak for you," he said.

When the physical was over he sat in his swivel chair and signed a number of forms.

I sat down next to his desk. "Did you bring the books?"

"No," he said. "I'll wait for awhile."

Damn. I bet his supervisor squelched it.

"Will you authorize a pass for me to go to the hospital library?"

"No, I want you to rest. You shouldn't read any psychology books for awhile."

"Other kinds?"

"Perhaps later. I'll think about it."

That means, "I'll have to ask my supervisor."

He pulled an envelope out of his desk. "This letter to Dr. Mayman is extremely sarcastic. You don't want it mailed do you?"

"I thought it was mailed."

"I read all mail before it goes out. We want to protect you from writing anything that could hurt your career."

Saved again. I'm living in a world of saviors.

"What's sarcastic about it?"

"It seems sarcastic to me."

"Not to me. I'd like it mailed please. He has a right to hear from me.

"Yesterday," he said, "you indicated you don't believe you are mentally ill. Why do you think your wife and others believe that you are?"

Should I be honest with him?

What the Hell...

I leaned back in my chair and crossed one leg over the other. "The most upsetting thing for others has been when I answer their questions honestly and reveal that I've been experimenting with a way for people to bring repressed feelings of self-esteem into consciousness. A statement I've been testing is, 'As far as I am concerned I am the most valuable person who will ever live.' People can't handle hearing me say that."

Baum stared at me.

Another strike out? I'm throwing him fat pitches.

Tell him about Molly.

"People not being able to listen well is why a patient I interviewed at NPI at the University of Michigan hospital was diagnosed as paranoid schizophrenic when she revealed that God spoke to her. She had been depressed but felt elated when she heard she was going to give birth to the second savior. Her problem was not from hearing the voice but from everyone being so intolerant of her experiencing such high self-esteem. When I talked with her as a friend and validated her feelings, she recovered in a few days."

Look at his eyes. He's not hearing you. Stop trying.

He shook his head. "You must accept that you are mentally ill before we can do anything for you."

Shit.

He sounds like Frank.

"I'm willing to listen, but so far no one has shown an ability to comprehend what I've been trying to say. I find that very puzzling from people who claim to be experts at listening."

He's not comprehending.

Get practical.

When can Kathleen visit? I'd like to see her."

"Not right away. I'll think about it."

"Something else. I was told at the cafeteria that if I wanted two glasses of milk at a meal, I need permission from you. Will you please authorize that for me?"

He tilted back in his chair. "You shouldn't drink too much milk, Mr. Siebert. It isn't good for your health."

"I've always drunk a lot of milk. I have averaged from a quart to a half gallon a day for years. This change in my diet makes me feel edgy. The milk seems to help relax me."

"The medications will relax you. Milk contains saturated fats. Our medical research has related saturated fats with circulatory and heart..."

I tuned him out. I sat looking at him while he talked. I could hardly stop myself from bursting out laughing.

Look at him. Fat. Face sweaty. Hair greasy. Needs a haircut. Dingy shirt, the collar so tight the ends curl up in the air. Shirt stretched so tight across his stomach the buttons look ready to pop. Belt hidden between folds of fat. Cheap, wrinkled, wash and wear suit. Pants so tight across his fat abdomen the zipper on his fly is worked one-third down. Scuffed, worn-out shoes. Fingers on right hand and teeth badly stained from cigarettes. Slouched in his chair.

Here I am, tan, lean, sinewy. Crew cut. Fresh from shower. Clean white T-shirt and shorts, white socks and tennis shoes.

And he is giving me a lecture on how to take care of my body!?

Careful. Don't let yourself laugh. Just cool it.

"...the hospital dietitians prepare a nutritious, balanced diet."

"How about authorizing a pass for me so I can go to the canteen and buy my own milk?"

"Not yet. Be patient. After you've rested here a few days I will transfer you to an open ward where you'll have more privileges." He looked at his watch. "I have other appointments. Do you have any concerns?"

Use reverse psychology.

"Yes, I do. Everyone is desperately trying to prove to me I'm mentally ill. You'll probably order me to take shock treatments next."

He smiled. "We don't do that here. We don't use shock treatments here."

"I'm not convinced. Look at where the Menninger people put me. They are desperate. The next step is to use electroshock on me."

"Don't worry about that. This hospital doesn't use ECT."

"You may not want to but if your supervisor orders you..."

"Now, now, don't worry."

If they don't use it here, that will be fortunate. Let him think I'm paranoid. Therapists like to prove to patients they are wrong about their "misperceptions."

I've got to use every means I can to survive.

Better check out what he says.

September in Topeka is very hot and muggy. A huge, old, air conditioner in some distant part of the building droned on all day and all night. It kept the temperature down, but it recirculated stale air being breathed by hundreds of men not in the best of health. Whenever possible I had an aide crack open a window on the shady side of the day room. They had to use a special handle that fit through a hole in the steel mesh gratings. I'd sit on the arm of a chair and lean near the window to get whiffs of fresh air.

The aides and nurses listened to patient requests and acted on them when possible. The staff had sincere concern for patients. They were pleasant, active people. They handled difficult patients in a professional manner with gentle firmness. I saw no patient abuse.

In the dinner line that evening I thought to myself:

Looks like Baum is a loser.

Provided through courtesy of the Menninger Foundation.

He's in training. He's not able to deal with me. Not his fault. Just doesn't know what's happening. Covers up with "I will decide" or "I'll think about that." Reassuring himself he is in control.

His actions aren't for my good. They're for the good of his ego. No wonder psychiatrists are afraid to be alone on the wards. They're aware of the bottled up rage in the patients.

But...

But they perceive the rage as a symptom of illness. How could anyone in his right mind hate such kind, loving, self-sacrificing saviors?

At the beverage counter I took one glass of milk. Then I reached over and took a second glass. Manny left the group of aides and walked over to me.

"Hey Siebert. Did you talk to your doctor about the milk?"

Yes! The doctor said "No" but...

I looked at him and nodded my head. "Yes I did talk to him." Then I turned and continued down the line.

Sorry Manny, but I need my milk.

I sat next to a patient who had been in for awhile. When the time was right I asked, "Do they give shock treatment in this hospital?"

"Sometimes."

"Do you know anyone here who has gotten shock treatments?"

"No."

"How do you know then?"

"Heard about it."

"Who was it?"

"I don't know."

Maybe the risk of shock treatments is low here. Better keep asking though. Why isn't there an official group of professionals I can appeal to?

Some people who will sincerely look at my side?

Right. Especially for psychologists or psychiatrists.

A.P.A. ought to have a special, on-call, crisis team.

Yeah! Available to people who question and think themselves into developmental crisis.

Thursday evening several men wheeled a homemade craps table into the day room. I walked over to Mr. Sims. "What is this?" I asked.

"The V.F.W. brings this around to entertain patients," he said. "Come on."

The aides and visitors encouraged the more alert patients to participate. Some patients came over and we all received an issue of play money. Mr. Sims and Carver, a night duty aide, became very involved in throwing dice.

This is a good change of pace for them. This ward is boring as hell.

The game didn't appeal to me. I'm not a gambler. I bet my play money and lost it all. Mr. Sims was hot with the dice. I was amazed at his run of hits. He and the other aides had a great time.

About 2:00 a.m. I got up to get a drink of water. I walked past Carver and the other night duty aide sleeping on the ward chairs they had pulled into the hallway. They positioned the chairs to block the hallway between the two sleeping rooms and the ward door.

Look how sound asleep they are. Heads back. Throats exposed. Keys hanging from their belts.

Friday morning I made a decision.

"Medication" Manny yelled. "Time for big red!"

When it was my turn I stepped up. "Juice please."

Okay.

Head back. Tilt the cup.

Catch the pill under your tongue.

Good.

Take the juice cup. Big swallow.

Gulp your throat.

Good. Step away.

Stand and watch the others. Now saunter across the room.

Sit near the bathroom door for awhile.

What if it melts and I swallow some?

It isn't melting yet. Only the coating.

Okay now, into the bathroom.

Urinate in a toilet.

Good. Now flush the toilet and spit the pill into it.

Good.

About ten o'clock Manny told me I had to have a dental examination. I walked with him over to the main building and up a stairway to a dental clinic. The waiting room had eight other patients with one aide in charge. Manny said to him, "I have to go back to the ward." Moving his head in my direction, he said to the other aide, "He's okay." Then he left.

The aides know what the shrinks don't.

After the dental exams were finished the aide had to get all of us back to our respective wards. He led us outside and put us in a small hospital bus. It drove around the outside of the hospital complex to a ward. The aide got out with several men, walked over to a door, unlocked it, and put them inside.

We drove to another building. The other patients climbed down out of the bus leaving me alone. The aide looked at me sitting alone in the bus. He hesitated for a few seconds. Then he called me out. "See that gate over there," he said. "That goes into your exercise yard. They have some patients outside right now. You can get back to your ward by going in there."

"Okay," I said. I walked across the open lawn toward an iron gate in a six foot high brick wall.

Here's a good chance to take off if you want to go.

You can outrun any man in this place—either short or long distance.

Sure and with my survival training...

Why stay?

It's possible I may eventually get through to someone. Besides, I've got lots of thinking to do. Here I've got time to think, free room and board, a good gym.

There's Thompson with some patients. Get some mileage out of this.

I peered over the iron gate. "Hi, Thompson."

He's surprised...Smiling now.

"It's a nice day to be outdoors, isn't it? How about letting me in?"

He walked over and unlocked the gate.

You're such a smart ass.

He smiled at me as I walked inside. "Where were you?" He asked.

"Dental exam."

Baum interviewed me in his office after lunch. He asked many questions about my childhood and my relationship with my parents.

I asked him my usual questions. "Will you stop the medications? Will you authorize Kathleen to visit? How about a phone call? Can I have a pass to the library? A pass to the canteen?"

He gave his standard answers: "I'll think about your requests. You need to rest and think about your illness." He did authorize my going with a supervised group to the weekend movie in the auditorium.

My interview with Baum was disappointing. I'd spent a lot of time carefully rehearsing how to present my ideas to him, but he tuned me out when I tried to get him to understand.

During the afternoon I walked by the nurses' station. Leaning up against the window I saw a large brown envelope addressed to "Al Siebert, Ph.D." and two letters addressed to "Dr. Al Siebert."

What?

They had been forwarded to me from the Menninger Psychology Department.

Oh no! How long have these been here? How many patients have seen these? Why did they do this? God that was stupid.

I asked the aide for my mail. I asked him how long the envelopes had been in the window, but he didn't know. I looked around the room.

No one seems to be looking at me any differently. Maybe no one noticed

One letter was from the Ranger. Several phrases stood out. "I've been behind the locked door. No problem opening the gate...Whistle if you need help...Keep in touch old buddy."

Very good. I knew I could count on him for deep backup.

The other letter was from Dick Schmuck. He wrote, "We won the championship game against Math by a score of 2 to 1. I played second base. We got some lucky breaks. They had man on first who tried to steal second. I ran toward second to take the throw from Norman, but the batter hit a line drive straight to me and I tagged out the runner for a double play."

Yeah!

The large envelope was from McConnell. It contained several chapters from James G. Miller's manuscript on *Living Systems.*

Great! I finally have something interesting to read.

Late in the afternoon I watched Manny and Thompson play cards with two patients. I'd never seen the game before. They used a standard bridge deck. Hearts seemed to be trump. The black Queen was important. When the game was over, one of the patients left. The other three seemed to want to continue. I said, "I'd like to play if you'll show me how the game is played."

Manny and Thompson smiled at me. I sat at the fourth chair at the table. I said, "Will you guys do me a favor? The next time I get mail just keep it for me. Don't let anyone put it in the window."

They agreed. They explained how the game of Hearts is played.

The next morning, Saturday, I put on a short sleeve shirt with a pocket.

Manny looked at me closely after medications yesterday. Probably because I went into the bathroom so soon afterward.

I went out and sat in the ward room. Duane, a short, stocky man with brown hair, paced around the room talking to himself. One of the nurses walked onto the ward.

She's an attractive woman. Good figure. Fairly tall. Easy smile. Nice to have around.

She stood near my table surveying the room. Feet apart. Hands in her sweater pockets.

Duane rushed over to her. He looked up at her with a big grin. "I fucked you all night!" he said.

She looked at him with an amused look on her face. "Well then," she said. "You aren't doing too badly for yourself."

I burst out laughing.

What a beautiful, healthy ego! Women are so great! And they say women are the weaker sex.

Hah!

Before medications I sat down at a small table near the nurses' station. I opened a magazine and started reading.

"Time for big red! Come and get it!"

When Manny and the other aide and nurse were busiest, I stepped up for my medication.

"Juice please."

Okay, be natural.

Sit back down now. Right under their noses. Become engrossed in the article. Cross your arms. Lean on the table, read.

They aren't paying any attention to you.
Now, right hand up, cough.
Good. Hold the pill in your hand.
Read more.
It's getting my hand sticky.
It will dry. Read...
They're gone now.
Hand over your pocket.
All clear. Drop the pill in.
Good. Stay here for awhile. Flush it later.

Saturday was a much better day without the Thorazine in my body. I walked in the ward hallway. I hummed and whistled to myself while we walked to and from the cafeteria.

Not being drugged I felt restless. After dinner I asked for writing paper.

Writing to friends will help keep my mind occupied.

9/11/65
Dear Dick:
Thanks for telling me about the championship game against Math. I'm delighted to hear that we won. Your catch of that line drive over second base sounds sensational.

My fellowship at Menninger's is much different than I expected. It is more educational than I imagined and I've had some fascinating insights into the workings of the human mind. Especially about the reasons why psychiatrists see mental illness all around them. The whole thing starts when bright people with weak self-esteem convert themselves into impressive nouns. You know how perception is always a function of contrast...

I chuckled to myself.
Baum will be challenged trying to follow this.
Hey! That's it! It's obvious he isn't going to spend much time talking with me. But he will read my letters.
So...I'll write to lots of people. I'll use Caplan's "loud talk" technique! I'll indirectly teach Baum how the human mind works. That's it! That's how I'll reach him.

9/11/65

Dear Elton:

I hope all is well with you and that your physical exam turned out okay. I'm having a great learning experience in Topeka.

I remember when I was your TA for the Developmental Psych course how you used to joke about Freud's oral, anal, and genital stages. Now I believe that you were more correct than I gave you credit for at the time. I've been thinking about Freud's developmental stages and believe he missed one, the one where a person gains control of his or her brain. I'm calling it the cerebral stage.

A person in a cerebral crisis sees inconsistencies between the words people say to him and their actions toward him. His reactions to their mixed messages upsets others because their inconsistencies and hypocrisies are repressed. They can't handle what they hear him tell them, declare that he is crazy, and try to cure him of this strange malady.

What I'm seeing is that schizophrenia is not a disease or illness. It is something that should be validated, not interfered with.

More later.

Al

Saturday evening an aide took six of us over to the auditorium in the main building to see the movie. When Hal Davis and Leroy saw me, they came over. We sat together and talked. The movie was an old western.

Sunday was another slow, boring, hot day. After breakfast I sat down at a card table with the newspaper. It kept me occupied for awhile. I checked the stock market reports and read the editorials. An aide turned off the TV set, went back into the nurse's station, and turned on some music. It came through overhead speakers. The ward felt nicer with the music on.

I walked over and asked him, "How did you do that?"

He showed me how the speaker system had a radio in it and how to dial any station.

I got some stationary from him and wrote more letters.

9/12/65
Dear Jim:
This Menninger fellowship is a fantastic learning experience. I'm getting a first hand look at how psychiatry really operates. It is fascinating to see how psychiatrists react to ideas they can't handle. They don't know their own minds have been overwhelmed and they view the person speaking as sick. They try to force their belief that he is mentally ill into his mind. Then they take action to try to cure him of an illness he never agreed he had. That they may ruin his life, his mind, and his body in their efforts is no deterrent. Sound weird? It is.

What puzzles me is the blindness psychiatrists and clinical psychologists have to the contradictions between what they say and what they do. They are unable to observe their own behavior and the consequences of their behavior.

Fortunately, what I'm learning is not a total surprise to me. The irrational rejection of your memory transfer findings prepared me for the closed-minded reactions of experts who pride themselves in being open minded.
With appreciation,
    Al

9/12/65
Dear Stephen:
I finally figured it out. Remember in our psychopathology course how we would ask Adelson, "How do you cure this type of neurosis?" He would laugh embarrassedly each time and say "there isn't any cure." Do you know why? We were asking the wrong question. The right question is, "Is there such a thing as mental illness?..."

While I sat writing my letters I noticed one of the patients talking to himself in an animated way.

Just like so many patients. How is Hank different from you? You've been pacing around rehearsing what you want to say to Baum. You've been talking heatedly to yourself.

Maybe that's what he's doing. Find out.

I walked over to the fountain and took a drink of water. Then I walked by the man. "Do you think it will do any good?" I asked. "Do you think Baum will listen to you?"

His eyes slowly focused on me. He shook his head in a resigned way. "He won't believe me about the Judge and Mayor. The Police Chief sent police out when I wrote to them..."

Poor guy. Frustrated.

Rehearsing the story he wants to tell the doctor. Where else can he do it? This is his home. He's just like anyone who's worked up and wants to be heard.

An older nurse came on to the ward after we returned from the noon meal She stood watching awhile. She looked as if she had a lot of experience. The younger nurses were okay, but they spent most of their time in meetings. They tended to be "therapeutic" in their interactions. They talked to us like mental cases. They didn't see the men as people as much as the aides did. But this nurse made good eye contact with me. She was different. She walked over to me and asked, "Why are you on this ward?"

"The Menninger people are trying to prove to me how mentally ill I am."

She laughed. "There must be other reasons."

"Yes. They got scared when they found out what I think. It all started with a nurse I knew. I asked her if she would ever be happy and she said, 'No.'"

"I wonder why she said that?"

Hell. She went therapeutic on me. Terminate.

"She believed it. If you don't mind, I'd like to finish my letter."

"Of course."

Late Sunday afternoon I was walking up and down the ward hallway. I was deep in thought. The ward was quiet. No nurses were on duty. One of two aides was off the floor with a small group of patients. My back was to the main ward as I walked slowly down the corridor toward the ward door.

How can I teach others about a developmental transformation I don't fully understand myself?

"Now we got you Siebert!"

I turned.

"You're all alone now!"

I looked up.

Observation: Two of the strongest, most alert patients. Rapid strides toward me. Fists clenched. Fierce grins. Eyes fiery.

"You're one of them doctors that keeps us in here. You ain't no patient."

Okay smart guy. Let's see you handle this.

"They put you in here to spy on us!"

Time estimate: three seconds.

"We been waiting to get you!"

Place right hand on wall, left on hip.

Into a non-fighting stance. Put right foot across left, toe on floor.

Reverse it. Sneer.

"You guys can't fool me," I declared. "You're in here to spy on me."

Good! They're faltering!

Get mad. Stand up straight.

"Everyone in here is a spy! You tell the doctor everything I do! You know I spotted you so you come down here to try to trick me!"

It's working! They're puzzled, looking at each other.

Drive it home! Yell at them!

"You stupid sons-of-bitches need a better story than that to fool me."

Walk off!

They stared at me as I stepped past them and walked down the hall.

One said to the other, "Maybe he is crazy."

I went into the sleeping area and laid down on my bed.

That does it. I am pissed.

Here I am, showing maximum toleration for these blind, stupid, clutched up psychiatrists and now what does it get me? Their victims come after me!

That's it. I am through trying to be nice. No more. This is war.

Those rotten god damn no good cock sucking mother fucking pissy assed…no good slimy yellow bellied sons-of-bitches have had it. They are mine! They belong to me! I am going to get them. Somehow, some way, I am going to get them!

They have had it.

They are through.

No more playing around. They are finished.

Those dirty bastards!

So everyone is selling Siebert short?

Well, Siebert is buying Siebert!

They want to abandon me as a lost ship? That's fine. Now I have complete salvage rights!

I own me. No one has a claim on me any more.

They are in trouble. Trouble with a capital T and that means me.

Wait a minute. Do you realize you are taking on thousands of the most intelligent men in the world?

I chortled.

Yeaah...They don't have a chance. Heh, Heh.

Later, Manny touched my arm gently. "Siebert? Are you asleep?"

"No. Just lying here."

"Want to play Hearts?"

"No. Thanks Manny. I don't feel like it."

"Please? We need you. You're the only one who can pay attention to the cards."

"Not now. Thanks for asking, but I've got some important thinking to do."

He walked away sadly.

Sorry, man. I've got work to do...

The bastards overlooked one small detail. I've got me on my side and there's no one I'd rather have on my side than me. Now then, should I escape?

What would that accomplish?

Not a whole lot right now.

I'll keep it as an option. Have got to get Kathleen visiting regularly to get the car here.

Why stay?

One, free room and board with much thinking time available.

Two, it's a nice place. Aides, nurses, gym, good atmosphere.

Three, this is so unbelievable it would be useful to stay until they have the admissions conference on me.

Right. That will establish firmly in the V.A. records that I was here. Good thing this is a VA hospital. Years from now the Menninger people could destroy the records if I was in their hospital.

I laughed.

I've got them right where I want them!

... said Jonah to the whale.

Why not? It was the safest place for him.

What about the patients?

Jesus, I've been stupid about that.

Here I am so preoccupied with my own situation I've been completely ignoring them.

What should I do?

"Let me get this straight, Al. You'd been locked up a little over a week when something bizarre and frightening happened. What is amazing to me is that on the one hand the Menninger psychiatrists saw you as so sick they locked you up in the back ward of a hospital and forced you to take tranquilizers against your will. On the other hand the patients saw you as so healthy they decided you were one of the doctors they hated so much and came after you. Both groups saw you as one of the 'others' and you were trapped between them. What a frightening dilemma!"

"It was like the old Red Skelton civil war movie, Sam. Red is trapped in a stone building between the advancing armies. He tries to escape by marching up a road with Confederate soldiers lined up on one side and Union soldiers on the other. He walks along carrying a flag. At first both sides stop firing. They wave and cheer as Red marches up the road. He had sewn a Confederate flag and a Union flag together so that each army saw its own flag. But then the wind changes, reverses the flag, and both sides start firing at him. I felt like that."

"Did you tell Dr. Baum or ask for protection or ask to be transferred?"

"Hell no. He would have decided I had developed paranoid fears. No, I knew I had to handle it by myself."

"Besides acting paranoid to turn the tables on the two patients who accosted you, did you start acting crazy with the other patients?"

"No. I scanned my memory for useful guidelines. Two frames of reference came to me. I remembered that when I returned to college after the service, I didn't know many students in my class, the Junior class. Since this was going to be my graduating class, I wanted to know them. I studied the photographs in the yearbook and memorized each person's name. About 200 all together. Then on campus I would introduce myself and find out something about each one. An unexpected result was that the next year I was elected Senior class president.

"I also recalled from Professor Ted Newcomb's lectures in graduate school that feelings of friendship develop from frequency of contact more than any other variable. One study, for example, revealed that in apartment houses the people living closest to the garbage cans were named as friends most often by others in the building. That was because they were seen by their neighbors most frequently. The farther apart people live, the less they feel like friends because of infrequent contact."

I worked out a survival strategy very quickly.

A patient walked in and sat down on his bed. I walked over to him. "Hi, I'm Al. What's your name?"

"Barry."

"How long have you been here?"

"Six months."

"What branch of the service were you in?..."

That night I fell asleep thinking,

Why do psychiatrists think I'm psychotic when I try to tell them how to be successful? What is with them?

I've got to push my mind. I've got to make my mind bigger than the psychiatric profession. I've got to understand them better than they understand themselves.

How?

Get distance—visualize sitting up on the moon looking down on all this. Look at them.

Baum is only a pawn. He doesn't know what's happening. I'll keep trying to teach him with letters and questions.

Kathleen is a victim. She was raised to trust what authorities tell her, that a good person follows their instructions. But with what result? It's tearing her apart.

The "experts"—they are reacting blindly to eliminate the source of ideas they can't handle. Yet as individuals they are nice people. I like them.

So the question I must answer is...

How can such nice people be so blind about how destructive they are?

Good. That's enough for now.

Chapter Fifteen

Mental Health

Monday morning Baum spoke to me in the hallway. "I'm giving you normal ward privileges," he said.

"Does that mean I can call Kathleen now?"

He paused to think. "I can arrange for it."

"When can she visit?"

"How do you feel about her?"

"I want to see her. A visit will be good for both of us."

"I'll think about it."

"How about a library pass? I need something to occupy my mind."

"I'll think about that."

Thompson brought my belt, my aftershave lotion, and hair cream. I put the bottles in my shaving kit in my night stand.

I walked back to the ward room.

Ward privileges. I wonder what they are. No one has told me.

I caught a glimpse of a fast movement coming toward me. It was Duane.

Danger?

Stay relaxed. Face him.

Duane stopped abruptly and looked up at me. He yelled, "Siebert, the next time you spend the night fucking my wife you ask me first!"

What?

He may have decided you have thoughts like he does.

"Well, what did you expect me to do?"

Good. A puzzled look is registering on his face.

"You spent the night fucking my wife," I said, "so yours was the only one I knew for sure would be available."

Good. He's thinking...Now a grin coming.

He grabbed my hand and shook it. "Siebert you're okay! I like you!"

"That's good news."

He turned and strode away.

Coming back from lunch on Monday I worked my way to the head of the line. When the aide unlocked the ward door I hurried into the dayroom and pulled the plug on the TV set. Then I asked an aide to turn on the music. He tried several stations. One was a fast-talking disc-jockey station. I said, "That's it. That's what we want."

One of the more deteriorated men went over to the TV and pulled the power switch on. It saddened me to watch as he stood there for almost 15 minutes waiting for the set to warm up.

"What were you doing?" Sam asked.

"I liked the music better, but more importantly I'd noticed something happening with the patients on the ward. They seemed to want to be near me. They liked my happy sounds. Especially the chronic mental patients.

"When I noticed what was happening I remembered research done by Jesse Gordon, one of my professors. Blind children are usually more psychologically healthy than deaf children. A hearing child can feel comforted by the pleasant sounds from its mother while she works around the house. A deaf child doesn't feel the same connection. It must be touched to be comforted. I figured they were being attracted by the happy sounds I made. I decided to experiment."

What would happen here if music was played frequently? Not the lulling kind. Rock, fast paced.

Later in the afternoon an aide I didn't recognize walked up to me. He asked, "Did you want to make a phone call?"

"Yes."

"Come with me please."

His name tag read "Miller." He took me off the ward down to the lobby. He pointed to a pay telephone on the wall.

"That's a pay phone," I said. "I'll need some of my money."

"The doctor didn't authorize us to give you any money."

"But I must have a dime to make a call."

"I'm sorry, but he only authorized the call. He didn't authorize any money."

Typical.

"Do you have a dime I could borrow?"

"We aren't allowed to loan money to patients. It's against the rules."

"What do you suggest I do?"

He was silent for a moment. He glanced around to see if anyone was watching. No one was. He brought a dime out of his pocket. "Here," he said. "Don't tell anyone about this." Then he stepped away so I could have some privacy.

I dialed our apartment. "Hello, Kathleen," I said.

"How are you?" she asked.

She's tense, cautious.

"I'm fine. I'd like to see you if you'll come out."

"Will it be all right with the doctor?"

"He hasn't approved yet, but I just wanted you to know I'd like to see you."

"I'd like to see you, too. I've been very worried."

"Everything will be okay. Well, I guess I'd better go."

"I'll come to visit when they let me."

"Fine," I said and hung up.

There's the door. You could outrun this guy easily. Want to break out?

Not yet.

I walked over to Miller. "That's it. Thanks for your help. By the way, I'm curious about something."

"What?"

"Why did you leave me alone at the phone? Why didn't you listen?"

"By allowing patients privacy it helps them maintain their self-respect."

Steve was a patient I made certain to be friends with. About 19, he was about 6'2" tall and 225 pounds. Big strapping kid. Looked like a Kansas farm boy. Probably played tackle or guard in high school. Baum had him on such a high dosage of Thorazine his lips were swollen and his tongue protruded. His speech, as a result, was slow and thick.

"What branch of the service were you in, Steve?"

"Marines."

"How did you get here?"

"They said I went crazy. I don't remember."

"Are you still in the Marines?"

"No. They gave me a psycho discharge and put me here. What were you?"

"A paratrooper. Eleventh Airborne."

"You do lots. Are you on medications?"

What should I say?

I hate to lie to him.

"Some. I exercise a lot and I drink lots of water."

"Will exercise help me?"

"It might. Come on, let's see if a Marine can do more push-ups than a paratrooper."

We got on the floor and started in. I kept count. At 25 he was so red in the face he looked as if he was going to pop a blood vessel.

I stopped. "Hey, that's enough this time."

At our next gym period I taught Steve how to set up the volleyball for me. I'd take the serve and tap the ball to Steve. While he was hitting it up in the air, I would run around to get into position to spike it.

Meanwhile I continued thinking…

This is something. The patients don't see me as mentally ill. Real people on the outside don't. How long is it going to take the doctors, the aides…

But wait, what if the aides don't see it either?

What if they…

The Last Time I Saw Archie!

Do it! Do what Mitchum did in the movie!

"Mr. Biggs. Are you busy?"

"No."

"May I ask you some questions?"

"Ask away."

I conducted my first staff interview. The questions included:

"How long have you worked here?"

"How well trained were you for your job?"

"Do you feel you have adequate supervision?"

"How do you feel about your work? Do you like it?"

"What is most difficult about your work?"

"If you could make any changes…"

From then on whenever I had an opportunity I would interview aides. There were a lot. I learned that this was a training hospital not only for doctors but for nurses and aides as well. I also learned that Bob had dropped out of college and wasn't sure he would go back.

Tuesday morning Mr. Biggs came over to my table where I was writing another letter. He said, "Mr. Siebert, you like to read, so I saved this for you. It came yesterday."

He handed me the latest issue of the *Reader's Digest*.

"Thank you. That was nice of you."

I flipped through the pages. On page 54 I saw an article titled, "How Good is Your Mental Health?"

Well, let's see.

Hey wait a minute! Who wrote it? Harry Levinson. A Menninger psychologist!

I read the article.

Major flaws! This description has big gaps in it. My undergraduates at Michigan did better than this.

I'll set him straight.

9/14/65

Dear Dr. Levinson:

The description of mental health presented in the current issue of the *Reader's Digest* is good as far as it goes, but you overlooked some essential elements. A truly mentally healthy person has a high level of self-confidence. He has the ability to stand up for what he believes even when subjected to pressures by co-workers, neighbors, or loved ones. He has the inner strength to stand by his convictions and refuse to be dominated by people who try to make him conform.

A mentally healthy person has an inner complexity that makes him or her a unique person—unlike anyone who has ever existed on earth or will ever exist again.

A mentally healthy person is able to listen with an open mind to feedback about self-defeating actions.

A mentally healthy person is curious, playful, asks questions like a child, and loves learning.

A mentally healthy person can commit himself to a challenge and persevere with amazing tenacity...

I wanted this letter to be mailed, so I saved it in my night stand.

The gym had an indoor swimming pool next to it. I had seen a few patients using it, so I inquired. Yes, it was available to me during our recreation period. Yes, they provided swimsuits and towels. I changed my routine. I worked out vigorously in the gym, then swam in the pool for the last few minutes. I liked this new routine because I could shower right away. I didn't have to wait to return to the ward to shower.

I kept the ward TV set turned off as much as I could except for some evening programs. I enjoyed watching a special broadcast by Reverend Billy Graham. I was impressed with his message. I wrote down the address they gave at the end of the program.

Tuesday evening I said to an aide, "Hey, there's got to be more around here for a person to do."

Carver, an aide who played in a band on the weekends, heard me. He said, "Let's dig out that ping pong table in the closet." He went over to a large door behind several chairs. He unlocked the door and pulled it open. He began to shove boxes and other clutter aside.

Several minutes later he rolled out an expensive, top quality, folding ping pong table. They set it up and dusted it off. It was almost new. Bob rummaged through the closet and found a complete set of new paddles and balls.

"This is great!" I said. "Come on, Carver. Play me a few games." Carver was a fair player. He was more practiced than I, but I had better reflexes. It felt good to have the activity. When Carver had to stop to do other work, I tried to get Duane to play. He didn't know how. I tried playing with Steve, but his reflexes were too slow. Before bedtime I helped Carver put the table away.

The vent over my bed pumped dry, stale air on me all night long. My throat felt dry and sore each morning.

Boredom was a serious problem. I asked a nurse to let me into the visitor's room so I could play the piano. I did some scales and played chords for awhile but didn't get much satisfaction from it. My parents made me take piano lessons for eight years when I was a child. They were determined that I would have, "the opportunity" they always wished they had. I hated taking piano lessons.

A few minutes before noon on Wednesday two nurses, Mr. Biggs, and another aide took about a dozen of us off the ward. We walked outside and got into a small bus. They were taking us for a picnic at a city park. Mr. Biggs sat next to me. He had a portable radio with him. He handed it to me saying, "I brought my radio for you. I noticed you listen to music a lot."

"Thanks, that was thoughtful of you."

It really was, but Jeeze, I don't want to listen to the radio when I'm out in a park. Maybe I've gone too far with this. Oh well...

I sat on a park table eating the sack lunch they gave me. I turned the radio on low.

Should I take off? Look at that open territory. I could be gone and they're a long way from any phones.

No. You've got to see this through until they hold the admissions conference. You must get this incident recorded in the permanent V.A. records.

We were near a play area, so I walked over and did some chin ups on a bar. Duane strode over to me. "Siebert, Do you believe in God?" he asked. Duane had been in seminary school before coming into the hospital.

"Do you believe in God?" I asked.

He looked startled. Then he said, "Yes."

I shrugged. "Then God exists."

Back at the hospital I happened to be in the hallway when Steve stopped Baum and asked, "When can I stop medications?"

Baum looked patronizingly at him. "The medications are good for you. They'll help you get well. You take them the way I say."

Rage flooded up in me.

That bastard! I want to choke him and pound his head against the wall to knock some sense into him. Can't he see...

Stop!

Do not do anything. Back off. Relax.

It won't accomplish anything for Steve and will only get you in trouble.

Baum walked away. Steve turned to me. He looked at me pleadingly.

"Why won't he stop my medications?"

"He needs to play doctor with you. It's all he's got."

"What?"

"Nothing. The medications will eventually be stopped. Remember in the service? Hurry up and wait? It's like that. Try to relax and wait."

"Will writing letters help? You write lots."

"Maybe it would..."

Maybe Baum would get to know him as a person better.

"Write to your mom and others in your family. Talk about things you used to do together, okay?"

No wonder so many psychiatrists commit suicide. Frustration and stress from acting this way and then if they become aware...the guilt...the distress would be overwhelming.

As I sat down to write another letter, I noticed that the ward had become more active. Other patients were asking for writing paper and pencils. Several played at ping pong. More played cards. Others read more.

9/15/65

Dear Jim:

The current issue of the *Reader's Digest* contains an article about mental health by a Menninger staff member. Reading it is like reading an essay on sex written by a ten-year-old child. These people have a weak and distorted view of what true mental health is like. It just hit me that the efforts of people in what is called the mental health field are not aimed toward understanding, seeing, and increasing mental health in others. They are mental illness fighters!

They are trying to reach a negative goal! That is why they are so ineffective. They are trying to eliminate mental illness instead of promoting mental health! The mental health experts don't know shit about mental health.

More later,

Al

"Al, could you clarify what you mean by a negative goal."

"Sure, Sam. A negative goal is to try to stop a person from doing a certain thing, such as stopping smoking or getting angry or gambling too much. B.F. Skinner proved that it is almost impossible to reach a negative goal. What works is to describe the behaviors you desire and then reward the pigeon, rat, child, or person for any small step in the desired direction."

"I see. You were telling McConnell..."

"And Dr. Baum."

"...that the effort to eliminate mental illness from others is much different from an effort to develop better mental health in them."

"That's exactly right, Sam. And this insight unfolded into a fascinating new undertaking for me a few hours later."

After our recreation period I took a nap. When I woke up I went out to the day room. I asked the aide to turn off the TV set and play the radio. He asked for a show of hands. Duane held up both hands and grinned. "They say I'm schizophrenic," he said, "so I get two votes!"

Another patient diagnosed as schizophrenic smiled and said, "I like the music the way it is. It sounds fine to me."

We all laughed at his joking about auditory hallucinations. The radio won.

Walking to dinner and back I noticed more men talking to each other.

They are walking faster, standing taller. They're more alert than before.

That evening I noticed an extra aide assigned to our ward.

I sat near the window thinking.

My response to Levinson's article was interesting. Then my letter to Jim. What would be a positive behavioral description of mental health?

Hmmm. And why is it that in all my readings about personality I've never run across a description that seemed to be talking about me?

I walked over to the nurse's station and got some pieces of blank paper from the aide. I sat at a table.

Okay. What is a fully mentally healthy person like?

Uuh. Uuh. If there is no such thing as mental illness, how can there be mental health?

Hmmm. Okay. No mental health either. So what can I use as a concept? Have to go to an operational definition. What works? What is the outcome? What is observable?

Successfully dealing with real life. Surviving unexpected difficulties. I'll pursue that.

I'll pretend like I'm writing the results of psychological testing of the paratroopers I trained with, the combat survivors. Include yourself, too. That way there will be at least one personality description you can relate to.

Right, and my mother, as well.

At the top of the page I wrote, "Qualities of the Survivor Type Personality." I began listing the traits.

"What irony, Al."

"I know, Sam. It is ironic. It suddenly came together—the many descriptions I'd read in the term papers from my class, my three years in the service with combat survivors, my self-description on the Menninger application, Maslow's writings about self-actualized people, my appreciation for my mother."

"All as a reaction to the blindness of mental health experts..."

"And their deafness, their inability to hear what I was saying. Their perception of my mental health as being extreme mental illness triggered in me an understanding of exceptional mental health. It felt thrilling. I sat at the table humming, smiling, and writing."

The aides gave me my foot soak in the evenings. My throat had gotten worse, so I stole salt from the dining room and began to gargle frequently with salt water. My brain felt physically tired from the many memories, associations, and questions that were churning through it. I sat looking at my feet soaking in the purple water in the steel bowl.

Do my cortical cells need extra sodium and potassium?

When I finally went to bed I couldn't sleep. After awhile I realized there was a full moon out.

I'm always restless when there is a full moon. It must stimulate my nervous system just as it causes tides in the ocean.

Oh, no! This means I am literally a lunatic!

Thursday morning I watched Cleo, one of the female aides, go around the day room with a basin of warm, soapy water. She washed all the vinyl cushions on the chairs. They were very dirty. It took her several hours.

"Why are you doing that?" I asked. "You don't have to."

"No, I don't. But I would if this was my home. This is home for these men."

I liked Cleo. She was warm and friendly. She had the best eye contact with me and always talked to me as a person. Cleo had fascinating skin. It was a patchwork of black and albino.

She's a bright woman. Self-confident. Capable.

"How much schooling have you had?" I asked.

"High school. And I finished computer school. My father lectured at us to get an education."

"So why are you working here? You could do much better."

"My husband's job is here in town. There isn't a job for me except this."

Dang.

The hospital gym was quite large. Usually more than one ward of male patients was in it at a time. When our gym period was over the aides called out our ward number. "Two A two!"

Totally lacking in imagination. Why don't they name the wards after Presidents or something? Give patients something easier to recognize?

But notice. Even though they are supposed to be severely deluded psychotic people, totally out of touch with reality, they always recognize their ward number.

Yes, and they always know where their own beds are. They aren't as disoriented as I was taught.

Right, and no homosexuality evident.

When we returned from the gym to the ward Thursday afternoon, the aides led us, as usual, into the locker room shower area. Thompson said, "Shower time." The men undressed and took turns stepping into the shower. I didn't because I'd just showered at the pool. "You too, Siebert," Thompson said.

"I just took a shower at the pool."

"That doesn't count. I have to see you take one here."

"Look, my hair is still wet. I have water behind my ears."

"The rules say I have to sign the page saying I watched you take a shower here."

What in the hell? Thompson is a nice guy. This isn't like him. Why?...

It's your undercover act! Nice going. If he believes you're turning in reports, then he must stick with the rules.

Damn rules!

I stripped down and took a shower.

A while later I heard an aide in the hallway yell, "Visitor for Siebert."

Kathleen is here! No one told me.

The aide who opened the ward door for Kathleen unlocked the door to the small visitor's room and left us alone.

Kathleen handed me a small paper sack. "I made some chocolate chip cookies for you," she said.

She's frightened of me.

"Thank you." I took the sack and set it on top of the piano. I opened my arms and reached for her. She came to me. We held each other close.

Mmmmmmmmmmmm, she feels good...and the SMELL of her. I've missed that.

I asked, "How are you doing?"

"I'm all right. The furniture arrived. I've been busy unpacking and putting things away."

"How have you been?"

"I'm fine. Sunday, Dr. Rosen and his wife invited me over for dinner. We had a nice talk. Mr. Wilson invited me to his farm on Labor Day." She smiled. "I went horseback riding for the first time. I liked it."

"Good."

That was thoughtful of Rosen. It's good to know they care about her...I knew they were nice people.

"How are you?" she asked.

"Fine. The nurses and aides here are really nice. This is a good hospital. Did the check come?"

"Yes. I deposited it like you said. I'm fine."

"Good. Do you have a dime?"

She opened her purse and looked.

"Yes."

"Good. Give it to me. Do you have more? Give me several. Thanks. I have a request."

"What?"

"I don't want to have all my clothes done by the laundry here. I've been washing out my socks and underwear in the wash basin, but that isn't so good. Will you take my dirty clothes each time you come and bring me back fresh ones?"

"Yes, I will if it's all right."

"It is. I've got a whole pile now. I'll get them before you leave. By the way, will you bring me my other pullover shirt with the pocket? The orange gunnysack one?"

"The burlap, yes."

We talked for awhile longer. When it was time for her to leave I went to my night stand and got my dirty laundry. I gave her the bundle and said, "I'd like for you to type this letter for me. Put our apartment address on it." I handed her the letter I wrote to Levinson.

We stood by the ward door until Miller came down the hall to let her out. There were other people nearby. As he walked back toward the day room, I called out, "Hey Miller."

He stopped and looked back at me.

"Did you drop this?"

I held out a dime. He looked puzzled. I walked up to him and put the dime in his hand.

"I thought you accidentally dropped this as you walked by," I said.

"Oh, oh yah. Yah! Thanks Siebert." He smiled.

I winked at him.

A healthy, all-American young man in a crisp white shirt and dark tie walked up to me. He smiled and said, "I'm Mr. Helser. I'm your social worker. I'm available to help you with your problems."

"What makes you think I have any problems?" I asked.

There is an expression about a person being "struck dumb." That's what happened to Helser. I stood waiting about five seconds for him to react. He was speechless, frozen in place. I turned and walked away.

After dinner Thompson, another aide, and a patient agreed to play Hearts with me. We played several hands. Finally the situation was right. Thompson's card would take the trick.

"Wham! Eat that black Queen! This is revenge for the shower you made me take!"

He laughed.

That evening when Mr. Sims came on duty I asked him, "Why is there an extra aide on duty now? How come the night supervisor keeps coming in?"

"The ward is stirred up," he said. "It's agitated. They're afraid there's going to be trouble."

Incredible! Patients start getting active, they want to do something about getting out, and the staff perception is that there's potential danger! Man, this place *is insane!*

I wrote a letter to Billy Graham.

9/16/65

Dear Rev. Graham:

Thank you for your inspirational message. I identify with your vision of a better world. Like you, I believe that people can live together in harmony and that everyone can live a happy, healthy life.

I find it unfortunate, however, that so many people with good intentions believe that the desired improvement will occur only when other humans change. "Good" people have a self-defeating flaw in their thinking. It is their perception that other people are bad nouns or mentally "sick." Efforts to change, "save," or "cure" others seen as defective can never succeed because the problem is in the mind of the beholder...

I wonder how Baum will react to this one.

Try questions with him instead of statements. Use McConnell's technique.

9/16/65

Dear Jim:

My fellowship continues to be a fascinating learning experience. I've developed several intriguing questions about schizophrenia.

How can ten different people be diagnosed as schizophrenic and yet all have different symptoms?

If schizophrenia is a disease, as psychiatrists claim, why doesn't it act like one?

If a person is emotionally withdrawn, what is sick about that? You are familiar with the work of T.C. Schneirla. He researched the principle of moderate stimulation. His data showed that all surviving creatures move toward moderately strong stimuli and away from extremely strong stimuli. This means that an emotionally withdrawn person has been subjected to extremely strong stimulation. If they couldn't physically leave, their emotions pulled back. Then we professionals assault their minds by trying to make them believe they are mentally ill because they have withdrawn from people who assault their minds. Are we looking at sickness or at the consequences of what we are doing?"

From talking with patients I have discovered that fewer than half of the people in the mental hospital agree that they are mentally ill. Did you know that? It's no wonder psychiatric cure rates are so low.

I'm curious about what questions you have about schizophrenia and about psychiatric treatments.

Best,

Al

On Friday afternoon Kathleen brought my clean clothes and orange shirt in a suitcase. I signed the letter to Levinson and asked her to mail it. She gave me several dollars for buying snacks in the canteen. Our visit was brief. She was doing what I requested but was not sure it was really okay.

After Kathleen left, Baum had me brought to his office. He asked questions about my college experiences, my military service, and my relationship with Kathleen. He was very thorough inquiring about the details of my life. It was just my thinking he couldn't follow, no matter how carefully I presented ideas to him.

When the interview ended he said, "I've decided to transfer you downstairs."

"To the open ward?"

"Yes. I'm the physician for both the locked and the open wards in this building."

"When will this happen?"

"Right now, this afternoon. I'm also stopping your medications now."

Super. I've been off for over a week and no one noticed!

"Thank you. How about a pass to go visit Kathleen?"

"No. Not yet."

"Look doc, I'm horny as hell. Jacking off just doesn't do it for me. By the way, I was thinking that the term 'jacking off' probably comes from 'ejaculation.'"

He stared at me.

"Anyway, it's been two weeks since I've had sex and I'm a healthy guy."

"Later perhaps."

"When will the admissions conference on me take place?"

"It isn't scheduled yet. We will have psychological testing first. I want to talk to you about the letters. Many of them are inappropriate..."

I'm still not reaching him.

I went to my bed and took all my things out of my night stand. An aide unlocked the locker room so I could get my other clothes.

Duane rushed up. "Are you leaving?" he asked.

"I've been transferred downstairs."

He hurried away. He returned shortly with a book in his hand. "Here," he said, handing it to me. "I want you to have this. You're my only friend."

He handed me his worn copy of the *New Testament*.

"Thank you," I said, and shook his hand.

Chapter Sixteen

Testing

Downstairs, the aide showed me my new bed and walked off.

Directly below an air vent. Dang.

I put my things away in the night stand.

With Kathleen coming every day I can keep my possessions at a minimum.

I walked around the ward.

Very few people here. One nurse. One aide.

I asked the aide, "Where is everyone?"

"Most of the patients are away at their work assignments," he said. "The doctor will choose one for you soon."

"Oh." I turned and left. In the hallway I noticed a patient leaning over a small table. He was signing his name in a loose leaf book. I walked over and looked.

"What's this?" I asked.

"The sign-out book. Sign your name here under the date. Write the time when you leave. Put down where you will be, and then write the time when you get back."

"You mean I can just sign myself out?"

"Yes. During the day. Not at night except to go to the movies. You have to be here to go to meals with the ward."

Fantastic. This has possibilities.

I think I'll try it out. I'll go to the library.

Levinson mentioned Einstein in his article. People say only three or four scientists can understand Einstein. Is it true?

Should I accept that? I seem to have a good mind. What if I read his theory of relativity for myself?

Why not? Go get his book from the hospital library to see how well you can follow him.

"Nurse, I'm not sure what your procedures are. I'd like to check a book out of the library. Can I sign out here and go by myself?"

She smiled. "Yes. But be back by dinner."

"Okay."

I signed myself out. I asked people for directions to the main building and found the library. I found Einstein's book on relativity and checked it out. I walked back to the ward and signed in.

Fantastic. It works. I'll try it with the movie tonight.

Hey. How did you know Einstein's book was there? This is a small library.

I don't know, but it was.

Look at how many times you wanted information and it showed up or you found it.

Hmmm. There is a connection of some kind. It sure is fun!

After breakfast Saturday morning, the start of my third week, I signed out.

"Siebert/9:10/Canteen."

I walked to the main building. I discovered a big recreation room with a few patients in it. In the center hallway of the main building I saw a letter depository.

Nice. I can mail letters here that I don't want Baum to see.

A door sign said, "Office of Veteran's Assistance." One corridor led off in the opposite direction from my ward. I walked past door signs that read, "Chaplain's Office" and "Chapel."

The door with a glass window at the end of the hall was unlocked. I stepped outside. The cement walk led to the corner of the hospital grounds. A store of some kind was across the street.

Rows of homes stretch out in all directions. Nice homes. Green lawns. Shade trees. Flowers.

I took a deep breath.

Oh, it feels good to be outside.

I let the door swing shut. Then I pulled it open to make sure it remained unlocked.

Great!

I walked around the main building on the outside. I found another door. It was unlocked. I went back to my ward and signed in.

After we returned from lunch most of the patients signed themselves out to various places. Only one aide was on duty.

He was doing paper work. It was a typical psychiatric hospital on a warm Saturday afternoon.

"Siebert/1:20/Recreation Room."

I walked through the hospital to the main building, down the corridor past the Chapel, and out the door.

Relax now, just stroll along. If anyone asks, I'm just going to the store.

I went into the small store across the street from the hospital grounds and bought a pack of gum.

Whoops. Forgot to get my change when I transferred downstairs.

I stepped outside and looked around.

No one is around. Everything is calm.

Fine.

Cross the street.

Good.

Down the block.

Cross over. Next block.

Cross over. Good.

Pick up your stride now.

Long rhythmical steps. They don't look like you're walking fast but they eat up distance.

I rang the doorbell to our apartment and waited. Footsteps came down the stairs. The door opened.

"Hi, Kathleen."

Her eyes opened wide. "What are you doing here?"

"I came to visit."

She led me upstairs. "Do you want anything to eat?" she asked.

"I just ate lunch, but if you have some milk and cookies..."

"I just made cookies to bring to you."

"Great."

It felt good to be away from the hospital. I turned on my stereo and flopped down on the couch.

Kathleen brought in a cup of tea and sat in a chair.

"The place looks nice." I said.

"Thank you. I've kept busy."

"How about coming over here," I said, sitting up.

Kathleen was tense, but she came and sat next to me. It didn't feel right to try to kiss her or be affectionate.

"Maybe there's a college game on," I said. I got up and turned the TV set on.

About an hour later I said, "Let me have your car keys. I need to get a better crew cut. The hospital barber can't do a good one."

I drove to a shopping center near the Foundation. The barber shop was crowded, but I went in anyway. About 10-12 men sat waiting. I saw an empty chair. As I walked toward it I scanned the group.

Dr. Lerner!

Our eyes caught. I nodded and said, "Hi."

He's puzzled. He's heard about me.

My walking in is inconsistent with what he's heard about me. He's seen you now. Might as well go ahead and get your hair cut.

What if he calls someone? Tells someone? I can't do anything about it. Play it cool and wait to see what happens.

When it was Lerner's turn, he walked by me and asked, "Would you like this magazine?"

"Yes. Thanks."

I read the magazine until Lerner was done. He smiled and nodded to me when he left.

Back at the apartment I said to Kathleen, "I was hoping we might make love, but I'd better get back now."

Kathleen drove me to the hospital. I got out near the main building and went back in the same door I came out of.

In the evening I signed out for the movie and walked over to the auditorium with a man from my ward. I saw Leroy and sat next to him. Steve came in with the group from upstairs and I called him over to sit with us. We talked until the film started. It was a good cowboy film. Lots of action. When it ended and the lights came on I felt a letdown in the auditorium as people looked around and realized they were patients in a mental hospital.

After lunch Sunday I went back to the ward, signed out, and walked home again. When I went upstairs Kathleen hugged me.

Good. She isn't as frightened.

"I love you," she said. "I only wanted to get help for you."

"I know." I patted her on the back.

I don't love her any more. This doesn't feel right.

I picked up the TV listings and saw that the Jets' game was starting. I turned on the TV set and laid down on the couch.

"I thought you wanted to make love," Kathleen said.

"I do, but Joe Namath is quarterback for the New York Jets. I read an article in a magazine where he said he dreams of playing a perfect game sometime. Maybe he'll do it today."

When the game was over Kathleen said, "Al, you better go back."

She's right.

"You're right."

Siebert, you're pushing your luck.

If she tells the doctor, they might put you back upstairs.

Kathleen drove me back to the hospital and let me out at the front entrance.

Einstein's book didn't take as long to read as I expected. Skipping all the math, it took about two hours.

Now I see why few people can understand his theory about the nature of the universe. He used his beautiful equations and mathematical logic to prove that Mach was wrong. In the book it is easy to see that Einstein disliked Mach. Mach believed that the universe is spherical, so Einstein brilliantly "proved" that the universe is shaped like an "S," open at both ends.

Although Einstein's mathematics may be flawless, it does not feel right to me that, while atoms, small drops of water, bubbles, most fruits, balloons, the earth, and the sun are all spherical, the universe should be "S" shaped and open at both ends.

Further, if the universe is spherical and is a self-contained unity and the electromagnetic waves traveling through it are traveling in curved lines, astronomers looking through their telescopes might be looking <u>around</u> the universe instead of through it.

What if astronomers are looking at earth through their telescopes?

That has possibilities.

Sure, perhaps as a small part of a science fiction story.

Miller saw me with Einstein's book. "What is that relativity theory?" he asked.

"Einstein says that time moves quickly or slowly depending on what you are doing."

"Is that all?"

"That's about it."

"Oh. I knew that."

"You're a smart man."

Einstein endorsed Edwin Hubble's theory that the outer edges of the universe are rapidly expanding.

Hubble came to his conclusion because light arriving from the most distant stars is shifted toward the red, the slower end of the light spectrum.

It doesn't make sense that the universe is exploding. What would be a different way of accounting for the red shift?

Hmm. Einstein developed his theory of relativity by conducting a thought experiment. He imagined himself as a particle of light traveling through the universe.

Okay. I'm a particle of light travelling toward earth from a far away galaxy.

Trying to reach earth made me feel tired. I fell asleep in my chair until dinner time. I woke up thinking...

Blum will schedule me for psychological testing.

That means what tests?

An IQ test, certainly the Rorschach.

I wonder what I might see on it?

Well, you know all the cards, why not get ready now?

Monday morning I went upstairs to my old ward and knocked on the door. An aide let me in. I walked around to the nurses' station. Mr. Sims was inside doing paper work. He looked up. "What are you doing back here?" he asked.

"I just couldn't make it on the open ward," I said. "Having that much freedom was more than I could handle."

He shook his head. "No," he said, smiling. "When men are brought back up here they don't act like you."

I laughed. "You're right. I came for my change in the cabinet there."

He unlocked the cabinet and took my envelope out.

"By the way, is the ward still worked up?" I asked.

"No. It's calmed down. Funny how that happens sometimes."

"Yes, it is."

I'm sure Baum and his supervisor will soon have the ward back the way they want it to be.

Mr. Sims walked down the hall with me and let me out. Back downstairs I signed myself out again. I walked over to the big recreation room. As I sauntered around the room I noticed a suggestion box.

Aha! If patient suggestions are read at a staff meeting, maybe I can get their attention this way.

I asked an aide at the desk for a piece of paper and a pencil. I sat down at a table and wrote: "Why is it that when a person goes to a psychiatrist and says, 'People are trying to force thoughts into my mind,' the psychiatrist reacts by saying, 'No they aren't, and you must now accept into your mind the thought that you are mentally ill because you believe people are trying to force thoughts into your mind.'" I dropped the paper in the box. Unsigned.

Maybe that will make a few people think.

Maybe.

Maybe it will make them think you are a <u>nut</u> for dropping mysterious anonymous messages around. It won't be hard for them to figure out who did it.

Back on the ward a man wearing a wrinkled suit and a bow tie came up to me. He said, "Hello. I'm Mr. Bowen, the ward psychologist. Will you please come with me?"

"Certainly."

"Mr." that means Master's level. No Ph.D.

Medium height. Slight build. Not athletic. Long, fine brown hair. He's alert. Intelligent.

We went to his office. I sat in the chair next to his desk.

"This won't take long. I have a meeting to go to in an hour."

Thanks a lot. It's my life and you can only squeeze in an hour for me. At the university we always reserved a half day.

"Your date of birth?"

"January 21, 1934."

"Place?"

"Portland, Oregon."

"Education?"

He doesn't know!
Pause. Wait until he looks up.
Tone: calm, casual, innocent.
Now.

"I have a Ph.D. in Clinical Psychology from the University of Michigan."

I have to give the guy credit. Even though the pupils of his eyes dilated and the blood drained out of his face, he hardly flinched.

After a very long pause he asked, "How well do you know the WAIS?"

"I can administer it from memory. That's the way they trained us. You can observe patients' reactions better that way."

"Are you familiar with the Bender-Gestalt?"

"I see you have the manual for the revised version on your desk. The author trained me. In fact, I sat through Professor Hutt's evening seminars covering his first draft of that book."

"Do you know the MMPI?"

"I was trained by James Lingoes, one of the best in the country. And, besides, when I took the test a while ago, I obtained as healthy a profile as one can get."

"And you won't take the Rorschach or T.A.T."

How's that for being a salesman.

"But I want to!" I exclaimed. "I've already worked out how I wish to describe the cards!"

Bowen looked puzzled. He reached for his Rorschach cards.

"I do not need to look at the cards," I said, holding out my hand to stop him from opening the packet. "I already know what I want to say."

Slightly bewildered, Bowen poised his pencil over a blank record sheet.

"Ready? All right. Card one. At first there was a black—no, scratch that—a dark, cloudy swirl, and then a child was born.

"Card two. The child grew up. He played and danced around. He felt anxiety and stress.

"Card three. Then one day he looked in a mirror. He asked, 'Who am I? What am I?' He looked at himself. He decided, 'I am a man.'

"Card four. He got a big hard on and went looking for his woman.

"Card five. He found his woman. She spreads her cunt open for him.

"Card six. And just at the moment when he is about to fuck her, along comes a snoopy psychologist who looks right up his asshole."

Bowen smiled. He glanced at me and almost laughed.

Good. Maybe he'll be a better listener than the others.

"Card seven. His woman is beautiful! She is happy. She dances around with her pony tail flying.

"Card eight. They experience love, happiness, and peace.

"Card nine. In the misty vastness of her womb a child takes form.

"Card ten. After the baby is born, they all visit Paris in the springtime!"

There. Organized primary process.
I wonder if he'll see that I have given him a projective test.
Probably not.

"Whew! Al, you played with him!"

"I sure did."

Sam laughs. "You didn't care what he thought, did you?"

"Not a whit. In my burst of insights I realized that clinical psychology graduate students are not forewarned that they may some day test a playful, complex, creative, and self-confident person who doesn't care about not appearing to be healthy to psychologists."

"Explain what you mean by 'organized primary process'."

"Primary process thinking is primitive, crude, unsocialized thinking. It is taken as a sign of ego disintegration, as a symptom of psychosis, like when Duane said to the nurse that he fucked her all night. The Rorschach perceptions I gave Bowen were integrated at a level that I suspect was beyond what he was trained to deal with. I was testing him, defying him, to see ego strength in my Rorschach responses. I did the same when he gave me the T.A.T."

"Fill me in."

"The Thematic Apperception Test, the T.A.T., is a set of over 30 photographs and scenes. It gets information about a person's needs, motivations, and social development. David McClelland, the famous Harvard psychologist, used it for his research in achievement motivation."

I picked up Bowen's set of T.A.T. cards. "I'll look through the cards," I said, "and tell you if anything comes to mind." I sorted through them. "Nothing here...nothing here...nothing here...okay. Here's one, 6GF." (Young woman seated in chair turning to look at a man with pipe in his mouth leaning down to her.)

"This young woman went to a party. She's a pleasant, sensitive, quiet person. Still unmarried. She continues to hope that some day, some place, she will meet the man of her dreams. She's been sitting here alone watching the people. Then a man arrives. He's tall, distinguished. Their eyes meet. She looks away. 'Could this be him?' She knows he's seen her. Out of the corner of her eye she sees him coming across the room. She breathes faster. He leans over and says to her, 'Excuse me Miss, do you have a match?'"

Bowen laughed.

I went through more cards.

"Nothing here...nothing here...okay, card 11." (A dark surrealistic scene.)

"This group of people has been trapped in a deep, dangerous valley. They have been frantically searching for a way out. There is much danger. Vicious monsters, steep cliffs, falling boulders. They are desperate. Suddenly a guy yells, 'Hey gang! Over here! I found a way out!' He leads them across a bridge to safety.'

"Next card. Let's see. Nothing here...nothing here...nothing here...nothing...nothing...okay, 17BM." (Muscular man hand-climbing up a rope.)

"This man was walking along. He saw a rope going up into the sky as far as he could see. He was curious. He started climbing it. And the funny thing was he didn't get tired. The higher he climbed the stronger he got! People gathered around and said he couldn't make it to the top. He ignored them and kept climbing. They tried to knock him off. They grabbed at him to pull him down, but he kept on climbing. The people threw things at him."

"Why would they do that?" Bowen asked.

"I don't know."

"There must be an explanation to this story."

I smiled. "That's your job."

"What do you see in the story?"

"McClelland would probably see a certain level of achievement motivation in it."

Bowen gave up trying to test me. He reached out and took the T.A.T. cards back. "How did your illness start?" he asked.

"You're assuming I have an illness."

He looked at me, puzzled.

"I am going through a developmental crisis."

"A developmental crisis?"

"Yes. I'm calling it the 'cerebral crisis' because it's the stage where you bring your mind under control. In the past, people going through it have been viewed as schizophrenics or having dementia praecox. Then, because the people around them are being exposed to something very powerful, they do things that interfere."

He's listening, but...

"What do you mean?" he asked.

"It's like the difference between a person taking a house apart for remodeling versus being trapped inside a house collapsing from decay or fundamental weakness. The problem is the so-called experts can't tell the difference. They see both ends of the normal distribution curve as being sick.

He's writing this down. Use him for a secretary! Get it written down while I am going through this. Too bad the Menninger people were so stupid.

"I have the whole sequence of steps figured out. I'd like to describe them to you."

Bowen glanced at his watch. He poised his pen over his pad of paper.

"The cerebral crisis comes about like this. Let's say a person has reached the adult stage of psychosexual development, at least according to current social norms. Like most people he has been raised without much conscious self-esteem. He is a good noun of some kind. He has a role that requires him to get others to accept the products of his mind into their minds. But he has an inner personal need as well. He must succeed at getting others to accept his thoughts into their minds or he experiences a loss of esteem.

"If the target person resists, his mind tries either to seduce or coerce the target person into accepting his thoughts. If the effort is unsuccessful, the pattern changes. The ego drops back to the prior modality. Here the basic behaviors are withholding or dumping. He does this with mental products—with ideas and words. Refuses to talk, gets obstinate, or unloads everything on them.

"If that doesn't work and he cannot stop making the effort without experiencing loss of esteem, the ego shifts back to an earlier modality—to crying for nurturance, or biting. The person's mind, serving unconscious needs, now tries to get the target person to do what he needs because he needs it so much. He acts hurt or becomes demanding."

Slow down. He can't write that fast. He's not getting it all.

"If the target still resists, if tricks to get help or the demands don't work, the ego shifts back again. This is the stage Freud overlooked. The ego regresses to the first stage, the God stage."

Hah! He does the same thing I do. Writes Frued instead of Freud.

"In this stage the infant identifies with the good mother—all powerful, all knowing, and all loving. Here, then, the person's mind functions without self-awareness along the lines of his infant images and experiences. He tries to use word magic. He acts like the 'Good Mother.' He tries to save target people from being in their awful state. And if a target person resists being saved, his mind sees them as even worse, as a 'bad' noun, as mentally ill, as evil…"

Is he following this?

"Do you see? The human mind functions according to these unconscious patterns. If you trace them back step-by-step to the very beginning and develop strong self-esteem, you are home free! Your mind and your actions are no longer controlled by unconscious esteem needs! The way to move forward is to go backward."

Bowen looked at his watch. "When did you first start having thoughts like this?"

Shit. He sees me as a mental case.

"Only recently. No one seems to be able to listen. They insist I need therapy."

"We can all benefit from therapy."

Hey! He is probably going through analysis.

"Are you in therapy?" I asked.

"Yes, and I don't always agree with what my therapist says."

He's growing thoughtful. Turning his attention inward. Pursue this. Sidetrack him.

"How do you feel about that?" I asked.

"It upsets me at times. Some of it is hard to accept, but..." He sat, thinking.

"How do you handle that?" I asked.

"I accept what he says...."

He suddenly caught what was happening and focused back on me. He looked at me sternly. "We *all* have to do that to get along," he insisted. "You have to submit to psychotherapy to find out about yourself."

"I don't agree. Just because *you* decided to believe what people tell you to think, doesn't mean I have to."

He looked at me intently. "Well, we always have other kinds of therapy."

Danger!

What in the hell! He is threatening me!

And these are the people out telling the public that mental hospitals are sanctuaries for people who need to get away from the stresses of the world, who need to be in a place where they can feel safe and be understood.

Bowen stood up. "I'm late for my meeting."

With faked sincerity I said, "It's too bad your schedule doesn't allow more time with patients."

Chapter Seventeen

The Great Escape

Tuesday morning Baum called me into his office. "I'm deciding what occupational therapy assignment to give you," he said.

"If I do anything," I said, "I'd like to be on the gardening crew. I need more fresh air and sunshine."

"I've been thinking of ceramics."

"Gardening would be best for me."

"No. Ceramics would be best."

Typical. Same old message. "I am in control of you, my child. I will decide what is good for you."

Wednesday afternoon I was sitting in the day room writing a letter. Miller had gathered four other patients together in the hall. He walked over to me. "Do you want to come with us to re-socialization therapy?"

I've never been unsocialized.

"No thanks."

"Come on with us. It's something different to do."

I looked into his eyes for a moment.

Go.

I stood up and followed him to where four other men stood. Miller led us to a part of the hospital I hadn't seen before. The room we entered was a former kitchen. It had stainless steel sinks and counters along one wall. In the center was a large steel table with a wooden top. The cement floor sloped toward a large drain. Large openings and high voltage electrical outlets between banks of cupboards outlined where stoves and refrigerators had once stood.

Re-socialization therapy was conducted by a thin lady about 60 years old who dyed her hair dark reddish-brown. She wore an old, dark maroon suit with a fluffy, high-necked blouse. She was a volunteer at the hospital.

"Good afternoon, boys!" she said. "I have lots of nice things planned for you. First we have a film on the 1936 Olympic games. Then we will talk about your projects. And later we will have cold watermelon!"

Another patient and I looked at each other with quiet sympathy. While Miller was busy setting up the projector, I wandered over to a pile of old magazines on a small table by the door.

Pick up the top magazine. Look at it.

I picked up the top magazine. It was an old copy of *Prevention* magazine. I opened it and looked at the first article. Something about body chemistry and health. I shrugged and put the magazine down. I walked over to a wooden chair and sat down. The lady fumbled with the projector while Miller walked over to the windows and started pulling shades down.

Go look at the magazine.

I did.

Go look at the magazine.

I'm not interested in body chemistry.

Go look at the magazine.

Maybe after the film.

Go look at the magazine.

Not now!

Go look at the magazine.

I will when I damn well please! I'm tired of having everyone telling me what to do!

Something lifted me out of my chair and moved me across the room.

All right! Don't get pushy. I'm going.

I picked up the magazine and looked through it.

Hmmm, an article by J.I. Rodale about psychiatry.

I took the magazine back to my chair and quickly read the article. Rodale talked about psychiatry not living up to its promises. He asked challenging questions. I stopped reading just as the film started.

What just happened?

Who cares? I need all the help I can get.

"What happened Al?"

"I don't know, Sam. It's still a mystery to me."

After we finished being re-socialized I walked back to the ward by myself, thinking about the article.

Rodale doesn't realize what psychiatric residents go through. They're poorly paid. They have to argue with patients about something they don't understand. They learn to believe in mental illness. They must or they don't make it into the elite group dedicated to eliminating sickness from others. They take years of personal therapy to rid themselves of doubts and reservations.

Hey!

Do you know what you are describing? Reduction of cognitive dissonance! Just like the communist indoctrination procedures! Just like cults do. There's the answer!

That's it!

The Schwartz testimony—"Paranoic self-deception is at the heart of communism."

It was gym time, so I went to my bunk to change clothes.

That's it! Paranoic self-deception is at the heart of psychiatry No wonder those poor saps couldn't see me. Their minds are controlled by a delusional paranoid belief system. It's a folie a deux...of thousands. It's like a massive cult!

I put on my brown shorts and yellow sweatshirt.

It all fits. The Festinger research on reduction of cognitive dissonance. Frank had to argue with patients that they were mentally ill. The residents who get accepted are the ones who start to believe what they are saying.

So the arguments are not for the patients, they are part of the indoctrination of psychiatrists! No wonder they never publish about this.

Then their white coats, the diplomas, their titles are cues that keep them in a hypnotic-like trance. Their perceptions of others, the special language they use, the labels they give to patients—all are programmed responses, just like with cult members.

I stood and looked out the window.

Seeing invisible diseases in others, trying to save people who don't want to be saved, are symptoms of paranoia. Believing their mission is to heal minds infected with sick ideas.

No wonder psychiatrists have been so silent about communism. They don't dare look too closely.

No wonder there is so little published about paranoia.

My mind was churning so hard I decided to stay on the ward. I paced around. Hundreds of tiny details started falling into place. Words unspoken, nervous laughter at conferences, the tenseness in so many therapists, the high suicide rate of psychiatrists, the looks on patient's faces, the lack of practical information in clinical courses, books and articles that didn't seem to say anything useful, explanations that didn't make sense, poorly answered questions, blaming patients when therapy failed. It all came welling up in my mind. I felt like all my life I'd been trying to understand the negative of a picture, and now the positive print was coming into focus.

Wait a minute. There's a problem here. If there is no such thing as schizophrenia or mental illness, how can paranoia exist?

I don't know. Christ, what a maze this is.

On Friday I asked Baum, "Can I have a pass this weekend?"

"Not yet."

Aha! Neither Kathleen nor Lerner told him about last weekend! That's a relief.

"When will the admissions conference on me be held?"

"Next week. You will be told."

"Good. Thank you."

I hope I can last that long.

The stress of having to endure this place is getting to me.

I went to the gym and worked out.

It became clear to me that my letters were having no effect on Baum and that he was controlled by his supervisor.

Friday afternoon Kathleen visited as usual. We had developed a routine. She parked in the circle outside the door of my building's lobby. When I saw her arrive I would stuff my dirty clothes in a shirt and walk out to see her. We would stay in the lobby and visit. When she left I would walk back to my bed with the clean clothes she had brought. The staff became used to seeing me walk down the hall and off the ward with my bundle of clothes.

Week four came. I spent Saturday morning reading more of James G. Miller's chapters on living systems. On one page I noticed a passage in an aside comment. He said, "...an abstracted system, in contrast to a hypothetical construct..."

Hey! That's the answer to your question!

Of course.

Paranoia is an abstracted system. Schizophrenia is a hypothetical construct. Mental illness, sin, evil are hypothetical constructs. Depression, automobile, pneumonia, tuberculosis, paranoia, and superego are abstracted systems.

Fantastic! Thank you, J.G. It's so clear. And this means there is nothing sick or ill about being paranoid. It is merely a describable pattern of words, thoughts, feelings, and actions.

Not like schizophrenia where there are over a dozen so-called types.

So the perception of mental illness is a paranoid perception. The metaphor has become a delusion.

Fantastic.

That's it.

The pattern is there.

Yes, and that's why you were so clear with Molly.

Right! My mind remained silent. My mind wasn't trying to label her to prepare for writing a report.

I spent the rest of the weekend walking, napping, and working out while this latest insight made hundreds of new connections.

Monday morning Baum came out on the ward to talk to me. "Your case conference will be held tomorrow," he said.

This guy is a lost cause. Might as well have some fun with him.

"Fine. By the way, I have everything figured out now."

"What do you mean?"

"Why none of you can hear what I'm trying to tell you. The psychiatric profession is controlled by a delusional system."

His eyes widened. He raised his eyebrows.

Nice. Present my perception of reality to him in a way that fits his notion of crazy talk.

"A person who believes that everyone around him is infected with invisible diseases is paranoid. The perception of mental illness is a delusion. The mental illness problem is in psychiatrists' minds."

An amused smile came over his face.

"Psychoanalysts are the primary source of the paranoid ideation in psychiatry."

He smiled. "Is that right?"

"Yes. But there's nothing sick about being paranoid. It is merely the perception of a frightened infant trying to act like the good mother. And that explains why so many psychiatrists unconsciously feel like the second Savior."

"Oh," he said, staring at me.

"Why do you think psychiatrists react as they do when someone says, 'I am Christ'?"

He squinted, puzzled. "What do you mean?"

"I can't explain it to you." With a serious voice I said, "Maybe you should talk to your therapist about that."

Baum shook his head, turned, and walked away.

Don't be such a smart ass.

Monday afternoon I wanted to get my mind away from my thoughts, so I decided to look through the copy of the *New Testament* Duane gave me. I arranged myself in a large, comfortable chair and examined the book.

It was a soft cover, red-letter edition. Inside on the first page Duane had written with a ball point pen:

Lord, Lord
God
I Jesus do it to
her sum total
is five and thirty
flirt agin will
Rogers & Hammerstein into crosey todae
Romeyn Cafe yesterday noon cruseytue
Jesus Christ

Now that is schizophrenic.

Why? It is just a string of words that has overwhelmed your mind. Why don't you swear at him instead? That would be more honest. Who says he must talk in a way that makes logical sense to you?

No one.

Who is supposed to be the strong, understanding person here, the one with the enlightened view?

Me.

So why must he talk in a way so that you are comfortable? Here you are, walking around believing you have achieved enlightenment, and then you let your mind do exactly what you criticize others for.

That's true.

You dumb shit.

I took a deep breath.

Oh boy…What can I do?

From now on when your mind labels someone, use that as a clue that you've been overwhelmed and have discovered an area for self-improvement.

Reading through the *New Testament* was enjoyable. I hadn't read the Bible since high school when I was in the Methodist Youth Fellowship. I fully appreciated the passage in Matthew in which Jesus said:

"And why beholdest thou the mote that is in thy brother's eye, but considerest not the beam that is in thine own eye? Or how will thou say to thy brother 'Let me pull out the mote out of thine eye,' and, behold, a beam is in thine own eye? Thou hypocrite, first cast out the beam out of thine own eye; and then shalt thou see clearly to cast out the mote out of thy brother's eye."

Amen. Jesus saw exactly what I see. He really saw it.

Wonderful. But how do you know you aren't the one who is paranoid and are projecting your unacceptable qualities onto psychiatrists?

Good question. I'll have to think about that. I'll have to find a way to monitor myself.

Tuesday morning an aide told me to remain on the ward after lunch. About 1:30 Baum walked onto the ward. He came over to me and said, "Please come with me. We will walk over together."

"I am to attend the conference?"

"Yes."

Well. This is interesting. It's a good idea. Too bad more places don't do it. Actually talk to the patients.

We didn't talk to each other as we walked through the corridors. He led me to a ward in a different building. He had me wait in a recreation room while he went into a small side room and shut the door.

A patient in the recreation room started to play the piano, then looked at me cautiously.

"Please play more," I said. "I would enjoy listening to you." For over half an hour I listened to one of the most beautiful piano recitals I've ever heard.

Baum came out of the room and called me over.

I said, "Thank you" to the pianist, walked over to Baum, and entered a small, plain conference room.

Nine people clustered around a rectangle table. All staring at me. The older man sitting at the end on my left would be the Senior psychiatrist—slender, hair thinning. The empty chair next to him is for me. Others look like residents and interns.

The senior psychiatrist said, "Hello, Doctor Siebert. Please sit down.

At last, a little respect.

I sat down and looked into his eyes.

Note jaw clenched, tension.

Engage eyes of person to his left and scan.

Eyes of next—scan.

Next—scan.

Next—scan.

Around end of table to the next—scan.

Next—Frenchy!

Dr. French and I grinned warmly at each other the moment we made eye contact.

Finally, someone with a warm response to me.

Next—scan

Next—Ugh. Baum.

The senior psychiatrist introduced himself to me and me to the group. He asked me, "How many psychoanalysts do you know?"

"Oh, several I guess."

"Who?"

"Dr. Farrell?"

"He's not an analyst."

"Oh."

"Anyone else?"

"Several at the University Hospital where I worked."

He sat silently looking at me. I sat silently looking at him. I was relaxed, my mind silent.

He clenched his jaw. Finally he said, "How do you feel about your stay in the hospital so far?"

"The aides and nurses are excellent. This is a first-rate facility. But I am signing myself out this afternoon."

His pupils contracted and his eyes narrowed.

"Why do you want to do that?"

"I only put up with staying here long enough for this admissions conference to be held. Now I am leaving."

"You waited for this conference?"

"Yes. I want to have it firmly established in the permanent written records of this hospital and the Veterans' Administration that when I came to the Menninger Foundation for my fellowship, they freaked out and forced me in here."

"Will you please step outside?"

"Certainly."

About five minutes later Baum came out.

"Mr. Siebert..."

"If you are going to be formal, call me Doctor Siebert."

His eyes blinked rapidly. "Doctor Siebert, please don't do this."

"I'm sorry, but I'm leaving."

"But this isn't fair!"

"Perhaps not, but I'm leaving."

"Will you please wait until tomorrow to leave?"

Yes or no?

Scan...

Yes, but watch out.

"Okay."

"Fine. We'll talk tomorrow. Please return to the ward now."

Walking back to the ward, I wondered,

Why did he ask if I know any psychoanalysts?

He must have had a reason.

Oh! Probably seeing if I could do any "reality testing." Seeing if I am aware of making gross generalizations about people I don't know.

Baum must not have communicated clearly. Hell. Why didn't he just ask about the source of my evidence? It's in the libraries. I've been through it all. Shelf after shelf of obsessive, paranoid psychoanalytic drivel. It's said that people are known by their works. All anyone has to do is look through their books and journals.

Besides, I never said to him analysts or psychiatrists are deluded. It is their thought system that is deluded.

Right. They're like the dyssocial delinquents. They are healthy, it is their profession that is deluded.

I sat by myself at dinner. I had some second thoughts about my new viewpoint.

This can't be true. Mental illness a paranoid delusion? All these nice, caring, intelligent people with their minds controlled by a paranoid system? It can't be. If it was true someone would have figured it out long before now.

Right. There must be another explanation.

The problem is all the facts and all my experiences confirm that my view of them is more accurate than their view of me.

The cafeteria was almost empty. I went over and took an extra dish of chocolate pudding.

Keep in mind that there is nothing sick about being paranoid, but be open to other explanations.

How about a hypnotic trance?

In whom? You or them?

Not me.

How do you know? How can a person find out if his thinking is delusional?

The next morning I signed out for "re-socialization therapy" but went instead to the office for Veterans' Assistance.

A man who looked like a veteran sat at one of the two desks in the office. "Hello," I said. "Could you help me, please? I need information about the Kansas commitment laws."

"I sure can," he said. He handed me several booklets and a duplicated copy of the Kansas statutes that cover commitments.

I sat in a chair and studied them for about half an hour.

Back at the ward I saw Bob, the young aide from upstairs. I said to him, "Getting an education is the best investment in the world. You can lose your job, your money, your reputation, but no one can ever take your education away. I hope you will go back to college."

"I am," he said. "I decided to return next year after I save some money for tuition."

"Great!" I said. We shook hands.

Baum came to the ward after lunch.

Attempting to be forceful he said, "You are severely mentally ill. You need to remain here for treatment for a long time."

"I'm leaving the hospital today."

"You should not leave because you might, in your condition, do something that will permanently hurt your career."

Like it hasn't been ruined already.

"I am leaving today."

"No, you aren't. I'm going to hold you here for three days while I decide if I'm going to permanently commit you."

He doesn't know the Kansas laws very well.

Use command voice. Reveal strength in eyes.

"The Kansas State laws *do not* allow you to do such a thing," I stated. "The three-day holding period provides time to *effect* commitment, not time to make a decision!"

Good impact. Add more authority. Strong stance.

"You are going to have to decide here and now what you are going to do."

I stared into his eyes with such force and intensity he became flustered. His mouth moved but no words came out. His eyes blinked rapidly. He fumbled for his pack of cigarettes as he turned and scurried down the hall to his office.

Probably to telephone his supervisor.

He went in and shut the door.

I walked back to the ward day room and waited for a few minutes. I looked out the window and saw our car.

Kathleen is here!

I walked down the hall to the lobby.

She's nowhere around. Where is she?

She must be in Baum's office! They are in there deciding what to do with my life!

I walked back to my bed.

They say possession is nine-tenths of the law, so let's change the variable in this situation.

I grabbed a shirt and put all my belongings in it. Then I walked back down the hall.

Alert! There's a new nurse.

I've never seen her before. She's never seen me. I don't have her conditioned.

Relax. Play it cool.

She's watching.

Out into the lobby.

Look around with puzzled look on face. Communicate: "Where is Kathleen?"

Turn completely around.

Damn. The nurse is still watching.

Peer toward the door.

Walk over. Look different directions.

Step outside and look around.

Okay. Walk over to the car.

Door unlocked?

Yes.

Good. Toss bundle in back seat.

Now around to the hood.

She's out in the lobby watching.

Open the hood.

There's the wire.

Loosen it.

Up comes the ignition key.

Down with the hood.

Into the car.

Start it up.

Now she's outside on the porch watching.

But she's not running in for help.

She seems amused.

Reverse gear.

I backed the left rear wheel over the curb.

Relax!

Take it easy!

You are now a visitor leaving the hospital.

Do not speed.

Don't attract attention.

Okay, out onto the street.

Left turn.

Easy does it.

Relax.

Be alert.

Now what? What would an escaped mental patient do if he had a car?

Drive like hell to get out of the state.

Right.

I drove the car to our apartment, put the car in our garage, and shut the doors.

Wilson and his wife took Kathleen out for horseback riding. I wonder how much she told them?

Take a chance.

I walked next door to Mr. Wilson's office, went inside, and asked his receptionist. "Is Mr. Wilson in?"

"Yes, he is. Go on back."

"Thank you."

Wilson was sitting at his desk doing paperwork.

"Mr. Wilson?"

"What? Oh. Hello, Al."

"Hi. Say, I locked myself out without a key. Could I trouble you to let me in?"

"You sure can."

He walked over to the house with me and unlocked the front door.

"Thanks a lot," I said, and went upstairs.

Now then, I need time to think.

If they put out a police alert, it will be for a man wearing an orange shirt, tan pants and white tennis shoes driving a metallic blue, four-door Rambler. Therefore...

I changed into my dark blue summer slacks and a white short-sleeved shirt. I put on a dark necktie, dark socks and my dress shoes. I went down the back stairs, past the garage, and around the back of the block so Mr. Wilson wouldn't see me leave. I walked downtown.

What do I know?

I know that police rarely look for escaped mental patients. And certainly not for someone who was a voluntary admission. The police have no legal authority with a voluntary patient until proceedings are started. There hasn't been time for that yet.

I know that these people have a big thing about wanting voluntary cooperation.

By now I may have convinced them I won't cooperate. There is a long waiting list to get into the hospital—people who won't cause trouble the way I would.

Just walk a while. What feeling do you pick up?

I walked at an easy pace for about 30 minutes.

Feelings okay. It's worth the risk to find out if possibly they have made a decision in your favor for a change.

I walked back to the apartment. As I got there, Kathleen was getting out of a taxi. She gave me a disgusted look. "Thanks a lot for leaving me out there with no way to get home," she said.

"What did you decide?"

"The doctor said he didn't think the hospital would help you very much. And I knew that if you were determined to get away, you'd walk across the country if you had to."

Very good! That she understands about me.

"So?"

"They aren't going to try to commit you."

"Fine. Do you have anything for lunch? I'm hungry."

I slept on the couch that night. The next morning I called Dr. Baum at the hospital.

"This is Doctor Siebert," I said. "I'll trade you an AMA signature for my wallet, keys, and watch."

"You are willing to come back out here?"

"Sure."

"All right. I'll have the papers at the nurses' station."

Kathleen rode along with me to the hospital.

Am I taking a risk walking back in there? Could they be tricking me? No.

"You drove back to the hospital the next day, Al? Without fearing they would grab you and lock you up?"

"Yes, I did. If there is one thing I wish I could get former mental patients to understand, it is that the mental illness fighters act in good faith, have good intentions, and truly believe they are helping sick people. The mental illness fighters don't know their profession is deluded. They can't. That is the way a delusion works."

"In other words the mental illness fighters suffer from the very kind of delusional thinking they attribute to others."

Al nods.

"And they don't recognize that they don't recognize that they are deluded."

"That's correct, Sam."

"Which is just what they say about their patients..."

"About being mentally ill without knowing they are mentally ill, yes. This explains the communication barrier between psychiatry and its critics."

"The barrier being?"

"Critics of psychiatry see what psychiatrists do to people and conclude that, since the harm is so obvious, the people running the mental hospitals are bad people with bad motives. The mental illness fighters, however, have intellectualized all their actions. They sincerely believe they are surrounded by people with invisible illnesses. They justify their habit of lying to trick people into treatment by their desire to help the sick. They truly mean well when they force people to submit to unwanted treatments. Then, like martyrs, they feel misunderstood when they are attacked or assaulted by angry ex-patients."

"The beliefs and actions of each side are understandable when you look through their eyes."

"Yes. Not only that, Sam, but imagine how much overwhelming guilt psychiatrists would feel if they were to fully experience what they've been doing to people."

The papers were at the desk as promised. I signed them. Then I said good-bye to the aides and nurses I knew. I thanked them for their support and concern. Baum came out of his office and made one last effort to save me. It was the same song, 97th verse.

"Please reconsider," he said. "You have a severe illness which will require many years of intense treatment. We don't want you to do anything that will ruin your career."

"I appreciate your concern," I said. "If it will make you feel any better, I am returning home and will talk to professionals there."

He seemed somewhat reassured by this. But he was responding to my manner, not my words. He didn't catch how I put him on.

We stood and looked at each other. We each felt deeply sorry for the other. Baum was truly sad to see a severely mentally ill person walking away from the excellent help being offered. I, in turn, felt sad for him. I saw his mind and his life controlled by a deluded system.

As I turned to leave, Baum said, "Wait." He went back into his office, reached into a drawer, and took out a stack of letters. He walked back and handed them to me. "Here," he said, "I didn't have these mailed."

What? He only allowed several of my letters to go out! Probably believes he was saving me from myself. Oh well.

I threw the letters into a waste basket in the lobby on my way out to the car. I drove around to the main building and went inside to the security office. The officer handed me a release form. I signed and dated it, "Al Siebert, 9/30/65." Then the officer handed me the sealed envelope with my watch, wallet, and keys.

Outside I noticed a piece of twine caught underneath the car. I yanked at it. It wouldn't come loose. I opened the car door and fished around under the driver's seat for my hunting knife. It wasn't there.

"Where is my knife?" I asked.

Kathleen lowered her head and came close to tears. "I took it out," she said. "I was afraid you would kill me."

Until that moment I hadn't fully realized how depressed she was.

And even here the ego speaks—believing I would trade my life for hers.

Back at the apartment Kathleen sat on the couch with her head down as I packed my clothing, personal items, and athletic gear getting ready to leave. She was acutely depressed.

She cried softly. "I can't go home now. I don't want to stay here. I have no place to go…I wish I could die."

Shit. This is something. Here I am supposed to be so severely mentally ill I need years of intensive treatment and yet I am the only one around to care for the real victim. Where are the wonderful Menninger people now?

"Will you do anything to yourself?"

"No. I can't. It's a sin."

I thought so. She obeys the Catholic laws.

"But if something happened, you wouldn't mind."

"No."

You can't walk off and leave her this way. She's a good person. She doesn't deserve this. What can be done? Acute depression, loss of hope, feeling helpless, worthless. Can I reverse that?

"You know something, you really disappoint me."

She looked up.

"My wife, Kathleen Siebert, giving up so easily. I married you because I saw a lot of strength in you. You can commit yourself to something difficult and really stick with it. I thought you had tremendous inner reserves and yet here you are. I say I have to go off by myself for a while and you're willing to just sit there and let me walk away. Giving up, just like that. Quitting."

She lifted her head. "You're going back home?"

"Right."

"Could I come too?"

"Do you have to ask?"

She sat up and asked, "If I move there, will you see me?"

"Of course. Right now I don't feel like living with you, but I like you and we'll see each other."

She straightened her back. "That's what I'll do," she declared. "I'll move there, too."

"That's more like the woman I married. Now I feel proud of you. Do you have enough money left to pay the movers?"

"I think so."

"Good. Now let's go to the bedroom for awhile."

Al lowers his head and holds his face with his hand.

"What's wrong, Al?"

"Re-experiencing what Kathleen went through. I didn't re-alize I still had such strong feelings. She paid a horrible price for acting and thinking the way a good person is supposed to. Her beliefs failed her. She did what she was told and it didn't work for her."

"That would be distressing."

"Smith and the others, that's different. They presented themselves as professionals. If they made mistakes—well, as Smith said to me, that's his problem. I like that attitude. I can identify with that."

"I wonder what he remembers about meeting you."

"Me, too. All the participants in this little drama will have their versions. Keep in mind also that the presentation of my ideas is more coherent now than it was then. At that time my mind was reaching for new combinations of perceptions. I was turning old ideas inside out and backward. I exposed Baum to some wild notions while I was brainstorming.

"One moment, however, stays with me most clearly. It is my memory of the feelings that came flooding up in me as I drove south out of Topeka that sunny afternoon late in September. It was the feeling that for the first time in my life my mind was totally free. It was glorious! It was a new feeling. Up until then my mind had been controlled by illusions and I hadn't known it."

I started yelling, "I'm free! I'm free! My mind is totally free! I can feel it!"

I shouted as loud as I could, "My mind is freeeeeee!"

Take it easy.

"My mind is freeeeeee!"

You're ruining your throat.

"That's tough! My mind is freeeee!"

Chapter Eighteen

Reflections

"The view from your living room is equally spectacular at night, Al. I like the way the lights from Vancouver reflect on the water."

"I know, Sam. I like sitting here in the dark late in the evenings. The reflections from hundreds of lights across the river fill the room with a soft light. And there is something fascinating about the way each light reaches in here.

"What is that?"

"My eyes receive a small amount of illumination from each light over there no matter where I stand. Try walking back and forth."

"I see what you mean. The streaks of light reflecting off the water seem to follow the observer."

"It's interesting. And this tells me that the lamp in my window is sending a small amount of illumination to anyone who looks this way. But no matter, while we were eating you said you have more questions."

"I have dozens of questions, Al. Where did you go when you left Topeka?"

"I drove to New Orleans. I stayed there several days. Went to bars in the French Quarter. Listened to jazz. Reassessed my situation."

"What was your assessment?"

"I knew I had made a major discovery, but I also knew I risked getting locked up, drugged, and brain damaged if I prodded psychiatry too hard. I decided I needed time to record all my experiences and think things through. With that as my immediate goal, I drove to New Mexico to the home of one of my fraternity brothers."

"You just showed up?"

"Yes, after stopping in Santa Fe to call him for directions. Tom, his wife, and two young sons lived in an adobe home in the Pueblo San Ildefanso. They let me stay in a spare bedroom.

"Where is that pueblo?"

"Close to Los Alamos where Tom worked as a laser research physicist. He and his wife made me feel like part of the family. I was free to take naps, run, and write when I wished. I spent a lot of time making notes about all the conversations and events I'd been through. I was still emotionally high. I knew I had discovered a treasure of insights. I felt immersed in the core of the life force of the human race. Except for a sore throat, I felt terrific."

"Did you tell Tom about your experiences?"

"A brief version. He listened with good humor. He, in turn, talked to me about coherent light—the laser research he was doing.

"Speaking of light, Sam, I was delighted to learn that light can affect other light. I told him my reasons for rejecting the 'big bang' theory so dominant in astronomy. He said my reasoning was valid."

"I thought the big bang was solidly proven, Al. That is the impression I've gotten from the popular press. Why do you disagree?"

"My thought experiment led me to discover that being a photon of light traveling across the universe toward earth felt like trying to enter a large office building at quitting time."

"Or trying to walk down a university hallway between classes?"

"Exactly, Sam. To arrive at earth a light photon has had to punch its way through zillions of photons coming at it from the opposite direction for millions of years. Hubble's instruments measured 'tired light.' His interpretation that the sources of the light, the stars at the outer edges of the universe, are exploding away from us is inaccurate."

"Interesting. Do you have any evidence to confirm your view?"

"No hard evidence. The definitive test won't occur until we contact life outside our solar system. I believe that astronomers on every planet in the universe detect the very same phenomenon. We could go to any planet in the universe and hear their astronomers talking about a 'big bang' theory."

"What's funny is I can hear it now. Your first question to people from another world—'Do your astronomers believe the universe is exploding?'"

"That's right, Sam! Actually, though, I'm bringing this up because I see the 'big bang' theory as yet another example of how people's minds can be locked into a group's belief system. A group belief can exert a powerful control over the thinking of its individual members."

"I think I'm beginning to see your point, Al. When someone's mind is free, that person can adopt or remain free from beliefs held by a group. When you described how psychiatrists and their ex-patients view each other, you showed an ability to go back and forth from one group's beliefs to the other."

"Exactly. It's like being able to put on the distinctive clothing of any group and then take it off when one wants to leave. The members of many groups, however, especially those wanting to change other people, believe their mental garb is their identity."

"Their belief system feels completely valid to them."

"Absolutely. The difference is that a person with strong personal identity can step into each different world, understand how a group's beliefs, feelings, and actions appear totally correct, and leave when one wants. It is empathy at the highest level."

"Something not possible for a person who depends on group acceptance for esteem and identity."

"Yes. That's it exactly, Sam. Speaking of stepping into a different world, I enjoyed an interesting historical coincidence while I was staying with Tom."

"What was that?"

"One afternoon he and his wife took me several miles up the road to visit the adobe home where Robert Oppenheimer, Enricho Fermi, and other atomic scientists met to create the plan for the first atomic bomb. The owner showed us the kitchen and living room and where the atomic scientists spent many days."

"Neat."

"I thought so. There was no sign or plaque or anything on the house. It was a private home. I remember the couple had a big, black, retarded dog named Clod."

Sam laughs. "I can picture that. How long did you stay with Tom and his family?"

"About three weeks."

"And then where did you go?"

"I found The Ranger in San Jose. He was working for the telephone company selling yellow pages advertising. I stayed with him in his apartment in a large complex for singles. I stayed two weeks before returning to Portland. I got home just before Thanksgiving..."

"Wait a minute. What did The Ranger say about your being in the VA hospital? If you had asked him to rescue you, what would he have done?"

"I asked him that one evening. We were sitting near the swimming pool drinking beer and watching the action. He said, 'My plan was to fly to Kansas, look in the classifieds, and purchase an old car from a private party for cash. I'd come to the hospital during visiting hours, reconnoiter the place, and locate your ward. The next day I'd look for an aide about my size. I'd catch him in a secluded area, take his uniform and keys, tie him up, gag him, and stash him out of sight. I'd let myself into your ward, tell the aide or nurse on duty you were wanted for an interview in another part of the hospital, and take you out. Not a difficult mission.'"

"That would have been impressive to see happen. Do you believe he would have succeeded?"

"No doubt about it. It was easily in his skill range. I told him how much it meant to know he was there for me as deep back-up."

"What a friend."

"I'd have done the same for him. I enjoyed my two weeks with him. We partied in the evenings. I slept and wrote during the days. When I left I drove north up US highway 101. My memory of driving up the coast is still very strong. Fabulous ocean vistas. Waves breaking on the sandy beaches interspersed between rugged cliffs. Unbroken forests flowed like a soft, dark green blanket across endless rows of mountains. A few miles after I crossed into Oregon a huge double rainbow arched ahead of me with one end in the ocean. I took it as a cosmic welcome home."

"Was Kathleen waiting for you in Portland?"

"Yes. She had stayed at my mother's apartment until the furniture arrived. Then she rented a small apartment for herself near a bus line. I told her I didn't want to live with her, at least not right away. She found work right away as a temporary legal secretary. My sister set up a bed for me in the basement of her home. I stayed there, to the delight of my nieces and nephew. They'd come and jump on me almost every morning to get me up."

"How did your family react to Kathleen when they found out what happened?"

"They treated her kindly. She was the one in distress and struggling. She was warmly welcomed at our Thanksgiving and Christmas gatherings."

"You weren't angry at her?"

"Not at all. I felt sorry for her. I felt very angry at the Menninger people."

"How did you handle that?"

"I wrote letters to them."

"To Smith and the others?"

"No, to the psychology department faculty. I composed letters while I was working as a gardener, had them printed..."

"Tell me about working as a gardener. You didn't get a job teaching or start a private practice?"

"I was tired of having my head filled with ideas, so I got a job as a private gardener for a couple with a large home in the heights. He owned a trucking company. I regarded my gardening job as a sabbatical."

"Were you qualified?"

"Close enough. I'd worked as a gardener for the electric company the summer before I went to graduate school. Working outdoors at the Youell's home and going home tired was just what I needed. Earning a living by talking and writing about ideas always seemed suspect to me. Getting paid for mowing grass, weeding, raking, pruning trees, and hauling clippings felt more legitimate.

"I felt like one of my favorite cartoons. It shows a college graduate standing with his proud parents after commencement. He's saying to them, '*Now* can I be a fireman?' I felt like that. 'Okay, I got a Ph.D. *Now* can I be a gardener?'"

Sam smiles. "How long did you do that, Al?"

"About a year. Until I decided what to do with myself."

"Which was..."

"To become a self-employed professor. Jim McConnell was very supportive. He identified with my experience because of the way he was being denounced by scientists insisting that chromosomes cannot be altered by learning. He had me purchase a cassette recorder. We exchanged cassette tape letters frequently. It was from talking with him that I decided to earn a living using my best strength, my ability to teach. The other options were undesirable."

"Such as?"

"Like I told McConnell, I didn't want to become a faculty member at a university. I didn't want to go into a private practice because I don't like listening to people talk about their problems. I didn't want to work in a mental hospital because I didn't want to associate with so many incompetent people."

"I see. What about the Menninger letters?"

"While I was working as a gardener my mind kept thinking about all the things I wanted to say to them. I decided to go ahead and do it. I would take a few days to compose a letter, have it typed and duplicated. Then I mailed it to about half of the psychology faculty at the Menninger Foundation. I really blasted them. It felt great! I sent ten letters and a page of poems."

"You weren't concerned they would think..."

"That I was crazy? I wanted them to think I had gone absolutely bonkers, was a wacky psycho-ceramic. I wanted..."

"Psycho-ceramic?"

"Crack pot. I wanted to take control of their perception of me. I subjected their minds to system input overload with words and thoughts they would experience as schizophrenic."

"But why?"

"To expand the belief that I was psychotic out from Smith and Farrell to the entire Menninger staff. I wanted them to laugh and joke about me. I wanted to anchor my being there in the memory of many people. I wanted to get them to invest self-esteem in the accuracy of their diagnosis of me."

"I've never heard of such a thing, Al. You weren't concerned about what they would think about you?"

"Keep in mind, Sam, I had nothing to lose. I wrote the letters so I would feel better and I was challenging them. Like I did with that psychologist in the VA hospital. But whatever they thought about me has never concerned me. Like my mother taught me, 'Sticks and stones...'"

"Did any of them respond?"

"No. I didn't care. Losing me was their loss."

"I'd like to read the letters and the poems."

"I'll give you a set. I'll also give you a copy of what I titled 'My Personal Guidelines for Avoiding Paranoia Using the Mental Illness Fighters as an Anti-Model.'"

"So you followed up on your question, how do you know that you're not the one who is deluded?"

"I sure did. I spent weeks on it."

"I'm very curious about what you came up with."

Al opens a folder. "Here it is. It's four pages long, single-spaced. Oh! And look at this."

"What is it?"

"It is a letter Dr. Harry Levinson wrote to me. It arrived at our apartment in Topeka after I left. Kathleen brought it with her when she moved to Oregon."

"Levinson is the Menninger psychologist who had written the *Reader's Digest* article about mental health. You wrote to him from the back ward."

Al nods. "Here, go ahead and read it."

"It's on Menninger Foundation stationary dated September 29, 1965. He says, 'Thank you very much for your very thoughtful comment on my article. I wished I could have said it as well and as completely as you have said in your letter.'"

"Al, that is amusing. He had no idea where you were when you wrote to him?"

"Evidently not. I always chuckle when I run across it."

"What happened between you and Kathleen?"

"I'd visit her or take her for a drive about once a week. She wanted us to get back together, but my emotional connection with her was totally gone. The real capper occurred several weeks before our loan from the Menninger credit union was due to be paid off. I was at her apartment. I asked her to give me the loan agreement I signed with the credit union because I wanted to send them the money I owed."

"She told me she already paid it off. I got angry. I said I wanted to make Smith sweat until the last minute before paying off the loan.

"She said she assumed I was so angry at him I wasn't going to pay it. She said she'd made payments every month.

"I said, 'Damn it. You still haven't learned to stop taking actions that interfere with my plans without asking me.' I walked out. I was pissed. Once again she'd put me in a bad light and then acted like a martyr."

"But you never told her about your plan for making Smith sweat until the last moment."

"Good point. You're right." Al laughs. "One of my flaws is to set myself up to feel victimized by women's martyr habits. Anyway, Kathleen moved back home to live with her parents a few months later. She eventually filed for a divorce."

"What happened with you and Laura?"

"I wrote to her but she never answered my letters. I didn't pursue her. I'm very easy to get rid of if someone doesn't want me around."

"Did you try to do anything about psychiatric practices?"

"Yes, I did. I made an appointment to see a medical school psychiatrist known for using ECT. I told him about the unilateral ECT research I'd done for Waggoner and gave him a written summary of the findings."

"Was he receptive?"

"Not at all. He dismissed the unilateral method as unproven. He told me that his technique of giving rapid, small dosage shocks was better than one big jolt. I found out later he was co-owner of the company that made and marketed the ECT machines designed for his unusual technique."

"Was the unilateral research data ever published?"

"Yes, it was. Stanley Cannicott and R. W. Waggoner published their article in the February, 1967, issue of *The Archives of General Psychiatry.*

"Were you listed as a coauthor?"

"No. They didn't even credit me in the footnotes."

"But it was your research design. You conducted the testing and analyzed the data."

"That's okay. I'm sure Waggoner was unhappy with me about having only 24 subjects. The important thing is that the research got published."

"What else did you do?"

"I read every story about survivors and whistleblowers I could find. I interviewed every survivor I heard about. I needed to learn how to be a survivor in deadly situations. I saturated myself with survivor stories."

"So your interest in survivors was more than just curiosity about combat survivors."

"You bet. Sam, my mind had awakened to consciousness in a culture that can be deadly for a person who speaks out about how things could be working better."

"Survival was your first priority."

"Absolutely. And to my great surprise I developed a strong interest in ESP."

"The way J.B. Rhine had predicted you would!"

"I know. I felt chagrined. But that is where my path took me. I started teaching an adult education course in parapsychology to learn more about it."

"Because teaching a subject is one of the best ways to learn it."

"That's true. The teacher learns more than the student. And I did learn a lot. I also started teaching intro psych and developmental psych in the local nursing schools. I enjoyed that. The student nurses liked me and I didn't have to be on a university faculty."

"But what about your psychiatric history? Didn't that concern anyone?"

"I didn't tell them. I just showed the administrators my transcript from Michigan and my article on teaching. They were delighted to have an instructor of my caliber teaching for them, and I got better student evaluations than they were used to seeing."

"You didn't make the Menninger incident an issue, so people accepted you as an effective psychology instructor."

"Right. I didn't make it an *open* issue, but I didn't drop the matter entirely. In September, 1967, I sent a certified letter to the Education Director at the Menninger Foundation demanding a payment of $15,000 for my fellowship."

Sam laughs. "You're outrageous!"

"Well, they never officially notified me that my fellowship was cancelled, and I went through the educational experience they arranged for me. I figured they owed me."

"Did they respond?"

"They never did!"

"Okay, so you were teaching psychology to student nurses..."

"And in the evenings at the college. That is where I got the idea for a short workshop titled 'Practical Psychology for Business People.' It was very successful—119 people showed up the first night. That is how my workshop career got started."

"And led to your television series by that name on public television."

"Right. It all started when I saw business people taking an entire semester of psychology just to get a few useful ideas."

"You decided to save them time—lots of time—by condensing the most important information into one evening."

"It worked, Sam. I let business people tell me what psychology they wanted to know instead of me telling them what they should know."

"You made psychology 'user friendly.'"

"Yes, although that term didn't exist when I was doing it. Meanwhile, another source of income opened up for me. In 1970 McConnell was hired to edit the first psychology textbook published by *Psychology Today*. He had me write the student manual and the instructor's manual that went with the textbook."

"Did they sell well?"

"Yes, my student manual sold about 50,000 copies. And I was especially pleased to have an opportunity to alert students to flaws and incompetencies in psychiatry."

"How did you do that?"

"By adding challenging questions and issues at the ends of the chapters on mental disorders and psychotherapies. I wasn't preachy, I just gave them alternative perspectives."

"That's a plan a teacher would think up."

"I did the same thing several years later when I coauthored the student manual for McConnell's textbook, *Understanding Human Behavior*."

"How many students have you reached this way?"

"Counting all editions, several million at least if you figure resales and borrowing."

"That is a subtle way to plant seeds for change."

"It is. But in 1970 I began to make direct efforts as well. I wrote a 'Bill of Rights for Mental Patients' that was published in the Sunday Magazine of *The Oregonian*."

"How did people react?"

"It caused a big stir. My television producer from the Practical Psychology series had me interviewed in a special program about deficiencies in psychiatry. After the program was aired the producer told me a group of local psychiatrists had tried to stop the broadcast. They showed the station manager a letter from Menninger's saying I was a paranoid schizophrenic signed out against medical advice."

"But how could the VA hospital or Menninger's release that sort of confidential medical information?"

"Like I said..."

"Psychiatrists could do whatever they wanted back then. How did you feel about that?"

"I felt both pleased and nervous. It verified that my letters to the Menninger staff had succeeded. It confirmed that psychiatrists are like a gang of neighborhood children who yell bad names at a person who upsets them and go around trying to get others to think bad things about the person.

"I felt a little nervous, but I had my bases covered. My family would have fought commitment efforts, and I knew that if any action was taken against me, I'd have my attorney demand an open court hearing. Psychiatrists hate that. They will do almost anything to keep commitment hearings private in a judge's chambers. In open hearings they are unable to prove that the treatment they have in mind for the committed person is effective, safe, and appropriate."

"Like a drug approved by the Food and Drug Administration?"

"Exactly. In fact, if the FDA criteria for effectiveness, safety, and appropriateness were applied to psychiatric treatments, most of them would be banned."

"In my psychology courses effectiveness issues were rarely addressed."

"Right. That's because most psychiatric treatments get a cure rate below the level of a placebo."

"A placebo—such as giving a patient a sugar pill instead of medicine—is more effective than most psychotherapies?"

"Yes, and psychoanalysis has the lowest rate of all."

"Al, how could you have such a successful career if psychiatrists were telling people you are psychotic and signed out against medical advice?"

"They weren't 'telling people,' only media executives when they were threatened. A similar thing happened again in 1977. What I knew is that if I kept making myself useful, my life would go quite well. Real people, the people who show up and make the world work, would not see me the way a few psychiatrists did if I didn't tell them. It was my hidden secret. In 1974, for example, I passed the written and oral examinations to become licensed as a psychologist in Oregon. There was no problem. By then I had also become a member of the American, Western, and Oregon Psychology Associations. I was president of my Toastmasters club. I was married to a fabulous woman."

"I remember. What happened in 1977?"

"The Mental Health Association of Oregon received a small grant to fund the writing of five articles scrutinizing psychiatric treatments and practices. The series was pre-approved for publication in *The Oregonian*. I was selected to write one of the articles. Mine, the first in the series, was titled, 'Mental Illness Concept Stems From Faulty Paradigm.'"

"The newspaper published an article with that headline?"

"Yes. Here it is. See? I started the article asking, 'What would you do if you discovered that thousands of respected people believe in something that is a delusion?' In the article I described my encounter with Rod, the resident who wanted the patient to believe he was acting for her own good. I described my interview with Molly and how quickly she recovered. I concluded the article asking readers, 'what do you think?'"

"What reaction did your article get?"

"A group of prominent psychiatrists demanded a meeting with the publisher the same day my article came out. They succeeded in persuading him to kill the rest of the series."

"Do you know what they told him?"

"Secondhand. The project coordinator told me the psychiatrists emphasized how harmful it would be for patients to have doubts about their therapists."

"That's like Nixon trying to stop the Watergate investigation by insisting that people need to believe in the president of the United States."

"Much like that, only the argument succeeded in this case. Meanwhile, dozens of letters came into the Mental Health Association praising my article."

"Al, I can't say I'm delighted to learn what you went through, but it's important to me to understand. It would have been harrowing for me."

"I warned you."

"You did. What is your explanation of what is going on with psychiatry in particular and the mental health industry in general?"

"Do you want a macro, micro, or sociological answer?"

"All three. What do you see at the macro level?"

"Big picture...After a large land area becomes populated and develops a culture, it give rise to an 'ism.' Hinduism emerged in India. Buddhism, Confucianism, and Taoism developed in Asiatic regions; Judaism in the Mediterranean. Shintoism emerged in Japan. Mohammadism spread across Asia Minor, southern Asia, and populated areas in Africa. Catholicism blossomed in southern Europe. In northern Europe Communism sprang into existence in the remnants of the old Mongol empire."

"That's a brief history of the human race I've never heard before."

"It's simplified but accurate. My point is that North America is no exception to the historical pattern. I call ours 'psychoanalism.'"

"More like a religion than a medical specialty?"

"Some critics call psychiatry a religion, but it is more like a government sponsored cult. Look at the signs. The members must go through special training to learn a language that has meaning only for them. To become insiders they must confess their private thoughts and purge themselves of critical thinking. The ones accepted as insiders believe they are specially enlightened and feel surrounded by hostile, destructive people. They strive to convert and save unenlightened outsiders. One of the most devastating things that can happen to a member is to be declared one of the defective outsiders."

"That does sound like a cult. You said it is government sponsored?"

"Look at it, Sam. Psychiatry receives billions of dollars from state, federal, and local governments. Its beliefs are taught in state run schools. It can use the police powers of cities and states to incarcerate people designated as needing curing. And psychiatrists have been given legal immunity from liability for harm they do."

"What accounts for that?"

"Now we're getting to sociological factors. All states have laws exempting psychiatrists from liability if they conform to their established practices. I discovered in the law library that there has never been a judgment in the history of American psychiatry where a psychiatrist had to pay damages for harm caused by mistakenly diagnosing a person as mentally ill."

"That is a startling fact."

"It is. Especially when you realize that for decades more people were in hospitals for mental illness than for all other illnesses combined. Did you know that psychiatrists qualify for the lowest malpractice insurance rates of all medical specialties?"

"The ramifications of what you are saying are very troubling, Al."

Al nods. "Thousands of former mental patients agree. Did you know that there are several dozen anti-psychiatry groups in the US? Did you know that psychiatry is the only medical specialty that must arrange for police protection against street demonstrations by its former patients at its national conventions?"

"I didn't know that."

"That's because the news media is part of a social collusion."

Sam squints his eyes and looks at Al. "You're not saying there is a secret plot afoot, are you?"

Al smiles. "It isn't a *conscious* plot. The media indirectly sustains a collusion of sorts between our society and psychiatrists by brushing aside efforts by former mental patients attempting to get their stories published."

"Explain how the collusion works."

"It's an unverbalized collusion that goes like this: Families and communities are relieved to have a place to send people who act, think, and talk in upsetting ways but who haven't broken any laws. They keep their selfish motives hidden by rationalizing, like Kathleen did with me, that they aren't imprisoning a disturbing person, they are sending him to a hospital and doing it for his own good. The collusion includes a sort of big social wink to psychiatry.

"A social wink?"

"Yes. The wink says: 'In exchange for taking these disturbing people out of our communities we will give you social status, job security, praise and esteem for your dedication to a noble cause, more control over patients than other physicians, your own buildings, public employees to work for you, prestige, and lots of money. We will convert you into aggrandized nouns and treat you like the most powerful, knowing, loving members of our society. We will support this pretense by not holding you accountable for lack of success. Further, we will also exempt you from liability for any harm you do to your patients.'"

"Like a child's game of 'Let's Pretend,' it's a pretense that benefits both sides."

"Exactly."

"Al, explain what you mean by 'aggrandized noun.'"

"This brings us to the micro level, to the roots of the social collusion. Remember Melanie Klein's description of how each infant experiences two different beings in its life? A good, powerful, nurturing, comforting, all-knowing being and a bad, hurting, dangerous one?"

"Yes. She called it the good-mother/bad-mother split."

"Right. This experience predisposes adult humans to perceive some people as good nouns and other people as bad nouns. The act of swearing often includes declaring that someone is a bad noun."

"Like 'bastard,' 'son-of-a bitch'..."

"Right. An aggrandized noun is a person legally converted from being an ordinary human into a 'doctor,' a 'minister'..."

"A 'professor,' a 'senator'..."

"Right, Sam. But the problem is that any socially desirable noun can be perceived in aggrandized ways only to the extent that other humans are turned into pejorative nouns."

"Such as..."

"A 'criminal,' a 'pervert,' a 'sinner'..."

"You're talking about labeling," Sam says.

"Right. And my point is that people with pejorative or bad labels are essential to people whose esteem and identity are based on being a good noun."

"Let me see if I understand, Al. You are saying that in our society 'doctors' called 'psychiatrists' are reenacting an infant's memory of the powerful, loving, good mother. To maintain the perceptual contrast that supports their identity, they *must* surround themselves with 'schizophrenics' and other humans they label as mentally disordered."

"Yes!"

"You're saying the heart of the problem lies in the human unconscious, not out in the world."

"Right! The primary source of the problem psychiatrists want to eliminate lies deep in their own brains. Aggrandized nouns are inseparably linked to pejorative nouns. You can't have one without the other. Good nouns and bad nouns are like islands connected together under the surface of the ocean. That is why psychiatry can never succeed at reaching it's avowed purpose, the curing of mental illnesses. It has itself trapped in a 'no win' situation."

"So anyone who shows how to eliminate the mental illness problem threatens their..."

"Throws them into an extreme identity crisis. The person is attacked, ignored, as with Dr. Thomas Szasz, or declared mentally ill. Anything but listened to."

"Which is not what you would expect from a mental health professional."

"True, but they aren't professional in the true sense of that term. The group norms of the mental illness fighters discourage professionalism."

"What do you mean by that?"

"In my business workshops I emphasize that people with professionalism judge themselves by the results of their actions. They seek critical feedback from their customers and learn from experience. For example, a man I know told me he wrote a letter to a software company criticizing one of its programs. The company contacted him and paid him a fee to help them eliminate the problem.

"Psychiatrists, in contrast, have a closed system of thinking. They reject feedback from their patients and outside sources. They judge themselves by their intentions, not by results. They blame their patients when their prescribed treatments don't work. They avoid learning from experience. In today's world no business could survive acting the way psychiatry does."

"Can you give me an example of them avoiding learning?"

"Sure. No psychiatrist or psychologist has ever shown an interest in my interview with Molly. The Menninger people ignored it. No one in the mental health field contacted me after my article in *The Oregonian* in 1977. In the 1980s I presented her story in papers I presented at Western Psychology Association conferences. I got no interest afterwards. When I submitted articles to psychology journals the editors rejected them."

"Al, what do you think it will take to get psychiatry to listen?"

"There is no reason for it to listen, Sam. It receives too many social, emotional, and monetary benefits for not listening to bothersome feedback. Psychiatry is like a huge, emotionally retarded animal."

"Ha!"

"It is not an intelligent living system."

"How do you avoid feeling distressed by what you know? You seem at peace with all this. How do you stay calm?"

"By seeing that psychoanalism is a creation of our society, not of some deluded doctors. It is an indicator of where we are at this time in history. Our society will outgrow this condition when it is ready. I'm focused on witnessing and recording what went on here. That's why Ken Donaldson and I created the Archives for the Autobiographies of Psychiatric Survivors. The Archives preserves their unpublished stories for the future."

"Ken Donaldson is..."

"He just died, unfortunately. He was the first mental patient to win a Supreme Court case against a mental hospital. The Supreme Court ruled he should collect damages for being involuntarily held in a locked ward of a Florida State Mental Hospital for twelve years without any treatment."

"I remember reading about that."

"He was quite a man. He developed support for his predicament by getting aides to sneak his letters out of the hospital. His book is titled *Insanity Inside Out*. We have his records and several hundred others in the Archives now."

"Yours too?"

"You bet. Along with my admissions conference report from the VA hospital and the discharge summary."

"You have copies?"

"Oh yes, right here. See? Signed by Baum, his supervisor, and the Associate Chief of Staff. This eight-page report verifies that their reaction to my transformational experience was to diagnose me as 'schizophrenic, paranoid type.' This is the documentation I stayed in the hospital to get."

"You don't mind if I read this?"

"Not at all."

"How did you react when you first read this report?"

"If I didn't know it was me, I'd think it was describing a deeply disturbed person. Baum distorted what I told him and manipulated my personal history to make me look very sick."

"What would be an example?"

"I'll show you. Here, Baum begins his report saying I claimed to be 'the greatest person on earth.' Here he says the major factor in my so called illness was from not mourning when my father died."

"You were eleven then."

"Yes. Evidently Baum didn't think I expressed enough feeling of loss when I told him about my father's death. Here he says he suspected 'profound depression and guilt' under my 'elation and congeniality.' And back here, he reports me as fearful and angry about having to take psychological tests."

"That is a much different picture than what you have described."

"That's true, but his report is an excellent example of what psychiatric residents learn to do in their training."

"What did he say about your letters?"

"Very little. On page five he says, 'His letters to his good friends have been as impersonal as were those that he wrote to such people as Billy Graham....He shows no interest or consideration for the other person.' That is all he said."

"He didn't respond to the content of your letters?"

"Not in any way, Sam. Everything I wrote went right by him."

"What did he say about your emotional strength and coping skills?"

"Nothing. See, at the end of the report he says that without hospitalization and therapy my prognosis is poor and that I'm signed out against medical advice."

"Al, you said earlier that a psychiatric report is a projective test for the doctor who makes it. What did the report reveal about Baum?"

"A lot, but the one thing that jumped out at me was his statement, 'The patient's infantile longing for omnipotence is to be realized through his intellect.' In that statement Baum reveals what it is about psychiatry that attracts so many highly intelligent people. That sentence summarizes what it took me months to figure out about them."

"Al, I am personally glad you didn't agree with the psychiatric perception of you and stay in the hospital for their 'treatment.'"

"I shudder, Sam, when I think of what might have happened to me if I'd been less of a rebel. Actually, I see the whole thing as a clash between two very different ways of being, and I'm very glad I'm me no matter what names they call me."

"What is your prognosis about the future?"

"I'm very optimistic. Centuries from now this period of history will be seen as still in the dark ages of the human mind."

"You think so?"

"Absolutely, Sam."

"What do you see ahead?"

"The human race transforming to its next level of development."

"What would be some signs?"

"Look at the response to Jean Auel's book, *The Clan of the Cave Bear.* Thousands of people identified with the quandary of Ayla, the little Cro-Magnon girl found and raised by a clan of Neanderthals. Her dilemma is engrossing. What do you do when you have a Cro-Magnon brain and everyone is trying to train you to be a good Neanderthal? I believe people felt a sympathetic response to Ayla because now, thousands of years later, there is a new breed of human emerging on the planet, a person whose nature is as different from Cro-Magnon as Cro-Magnon was from Neanderthal."

"I see your point. Do you have a name for this new breed?"

"The synergistic human. The signs are everywhere. Titles and labels don't count much any more. Many people now work without job titles and are learning how to thrive in non-stop change. Tens of thousands of people have started home-based businesses. Many thousands of people support themselves working several part-time jobs. All these circumstances require people to be increasingly adaptable, self-confident, empathic, multi-faceted, creative, intuitive, self-reliant, and synergistic."

"The survivor personality traits?"

"Survivor personality, serendipity personality, successful schizophrenia, synergistic personality—they are all the same. The synergistic person has a talent for serendipity, and that is what gives such a person a major survival advantage. I've seen the transformation unfolding for many years. It is exciting to watch."

"You are genuinely happy about everything, aren't you, Al."

"I am! What I went through was one of the two best things that ever happened to me. This is the best time in the history of the human race to be alive and actively participating in the action. The old Cro-Magnon organizations are decaying. People are freeing themselves from fears about what others might think. They are learning to not wait to be told what to do. People are learning how to learn from everyday experiences. They are getting healthier and living longer. They are interacting with each other and the planet in ways better for everyone. In the future even psychiatrists will be very effective."

"You see hope for them too."

"Eventually. After the older ones have died off."

"Why do you say that?"

"I agree with Sigmund Freud's observation that a paranoid person cannot give up a delusional belief any more easily than giving up an arm or a leg. I feel sorry for the older ones. They're like Captain Queeg."

"The old navy captain in *The Caine Mutiny*. Humphrey Bogart played him in the movie."

"Playing with his steel balls. It's sad. They fought the good fight, they won the important victories, but now they are the dead hand of the past barring the way to progress. The progress will occur, however, once a newer generation takes over."

"And you're sure that will happen?"

"Absolutely. Keep in mind that as individuals most psychiatrists are mentally healthy. It is their belief system that is deluded. Healthy people keep striving to be better. The new version of the Diagnostic and Statistical Manual of Mental Disorders, DSM IV, has a substantially increased section on emotional conditions that are not mental illness. This is a major shift. The wall has a crack in it."

"Like the Berlin wall?"

"Yes. When our society breaks out of the delusion of mental illness, it will make a huge leap forward. Many people now labeled as schizophrenics, for example, will be seen as an asset. They will be interviewed, listened to, and understood better."

"You admit that schizophrenia exists, then."

"Of course. As do delusions, depression, and so forth. It is the perception of these conditions as sickness that handicaps well-intentioned therapists. The perception of mental illness is a stress reaction in the beholder. The problem is in the viewer, not the viewee."

"But you aren't wanting to rescue psychiatrists or mental patients."

"Or society, no."

"Whatever happened to your thought about being the most valuable person who will ever exist?"

"That was just an experimental emotional tool. It led me to the source of the magic you asked about."

"The magic!" Sam straightens up and leans toward Al. "Yes! The magic. Tell me more."

"I learned from my interviews with survivors of extreme tortures about the life force within all of us. It is subtle but far more powerful than anyone's individual being. It is in every cell, in every molecule in our bodies. What you view as my magic isn't mine. It is life itself."

"This helps explain how you are so successful without working hard. How do you tap into the life force?"

"My way is with a question that penetrates deeper than personal intentions, self-esteem, selfishness, or unselfishness. I ask myself: How can I interact with what is happening so that things work well for all of us?"

"Not just for yourself alone but for yourself and others?"

"Right, but you may have to modify it to fit your nature. Let me know what happens."

"I don't understand this qualification, Al."

"You must link your emotions and actions to the words you use. My words won't work as well for you as they do for me. Play with it. Try different phrasings. I'll be curious about what you come up with."

Index

Acknowledgements

I want to express thanks and appreciation to the many people who have given me friendship, encouragement, and feedback. I especially wish to acknowledge the following:

Kenneth Donaldson for his unwavering determination to gain his freedom, his persistence in pressing his case in the courts, and his advocacy for psychiatric reform.

Jim McConnell for his friendship during a difficult period in my life and for believing in me.

Wilbert J. McKeachie for seeing abilities in me I didn't know I had, for his mentoring, and for creating extraordinary learning opportunities at the University of Michigan.

Sam Kimball for years of friendship and his talent for broad-minded inquiry.

My mother for leaving my mind alone and always believing in me no matter what I did.

My sister and her family for their constant love and support

All psychiatric survivors who have endured emotional brutality and managed to create good lives for themselves.

Archives for the Autobiographies of Psychiatric Survivors

The Kenneth Donaldson Archives exists to preserve the autobiographical stories of psychiatric survivors. The archives was founded in 1980 when Ken Donaldson and Al Siebert discovered that many psychiatric survivors were not successful getting their book manuscripts published.

The archives is a place for psychiatric survivors to send their *unpublished book manuscripts*. The archives does not publish stories, nor will it release the names of persons submitting stories without written permission. Any person submitting a manuscript retains all rights to their story and controls the time of release of the information.

There is no fee.

For guidelines about submitting material to the Kenneth Donaldson Archives see the THRIVEnet World Wide Web sibling page, Psychiatric Survivors, on the internet (access the THRIVEnet home page, URL: http://www.webcom.com/~odyssey1/thrive/net.html), or write to:

P.O. Box 535, Portland, OR 97207

About the Authors

Sam Kimball received his B.A. from Linfield College and his M.A. in English from the University of Washington. He took extensive training in clinical psychology at Portland State University and went on to earn a Ph.D. in American Literature from the University of Florida. A member of Phi Beta Kappa, he is Associate Professor of English at the University of North Florida where he has received awards for teaching excellence. Currently he is completing a book on "Literature, Infanticide, and Culture."

Al Siebert received his B.A. in psychology from Willamette University and his M.A. and Ph.D. in clinical psychology from the University of Michigan. He has conducted management psychology workshops for over 25 years, served as a voluntary rap group facilitator with Vietnam veterans for over three years, and has been interviewed many times on television including the *NBC Today Show*. His description of the survivor personality is quoted in many books and articles. He has worked with many organizations undergoing downsizing and reorganization. He is recipient of the Governor's Award for being the State of Oregon's "External Trainer of the Year." Currently he gives keynotes at professional conferences on "Surviving and Thriving in a World of Non-Stop Change."

Al Siebert runs the THRIVEnet domain on the World Wide Web. THRIVEnet is dedicated to "Facilitating the emerging new breed of human."

THRIVEnet's URL: http://www.webcom.com/~odyssey1/thrive/net.html

His E-Mail address is: A Siebert@aol.com

Also Availiable:

Books:

The Survivor Personality ISBN: 0-944227-06-6
   Al Siebert, Ph.D. $14.95

The Adult Student's Guide to Survival and Success: Time
   For College (2nd ed.) ISBN: 0-944227-03-1
   Al Siebert & Bernadine Gilpin $12.95

Schizophrenia is Not a Disease or Illness—Psychiatry is Deluded
   Al Siebert, Ph.D. ISBN: 0-944227-11-2
   $9.95

Booklet:

Thriving During Disruptive Change: Practical Guidelines
During Downsizing and Reorganization
   Al Siebert, Ph.D. ISBN 0-994227-09-0
   $4.95
   (Volume prices available)

Send orders and requests for information to:
   Practical Psychology Press
   P.O. Box 535
   Portland, OR 97207
   800/504-3295

Please add $2.00 postage & handling for books, $1.00 for
the booklet.
   Satisfaction guaranteed.